DRUGS AND THE CRIMINAL JUSTICE SYSTEM

Other books in this series:

Volume II. Sage Criminal Justice System Annuals

DRUGS AND THE CRIMINAL JUSTICE SYSTEM

JAMES A. INCIARDI
and
CARL D. CHAMBERS
Editors

 SAGE Publications *Beverly Hills · London*

HV
6791
.I55

For information address:

SAGE PUBLICATIONS, INC.
275 South Beverly Drive
Beverly Hills, California 90212

SAGE PUBLICATIONS LTD
St George's House / 44 Hatton Garden
London E C 1

Printed in the United States of America

International Standard Book Number 0-8039-0200-x

Library of Congress Catalog Card No. 72-98036

FIRST PRINTING

CONTENTS

DRUGS AND THE CRIMINAL JUSTICE SYSTEM

PREFACE

Our efforts at understanding the problem of drug abuse in contemporary society have been hampered by a lack of comprehensive data pertaining to the relationship of drug use to various patterns of deviant behavior and to social institutions generally. We have tended to view the issue of drug use in a restricted legal, medical, or moralistic framework, while the reality of the behavior under study is complex and entwined in the very fabric of society.

The present volume constitutes an important advance in our knowledge of drug use and its relationship to criminal behavior. Significant material is presented pertaining to the effect of legal controls upon drug use, the probable efficacy of diverse modes of treatment and their cost, the changing characteristics of the drug consuming population and the specific substances selected for use.

Beyond these particular issues and others—public policy, funding, experimentation, methodology, and myths—the authors have provided us with an articulated appraisal of a complex problem. They have managed to contrast and compare the salient problems involved in unraveling the association between drug use and criminal behavior. Their arguments, for the most part, are considered and substantiated. They discuss the central issues cogently. While it is unlikely that the reader will agree with all of the arguments advanced, he will find in the present work sufficient facts and discussion upon which to base an intelligent view of this social problem.

—John C. Ball, Ph.D.
Department of Psychiatry
Temple University
April, 1973

FOREWORD

We are all too familiar with the devastating impact of drug dependence and addiction on the individual, the family, and society as a whole. The costs in human and economic terms are enormous. Whether the number of people whose lives are lost to the destructive endless cycle of drug addiction and the criminal justice system will continue to grow is closely related to our response as a nation to the critical issues discussed by the authors of *Drugs and the Criminal Justice System.*

James A. Inciardi and Carl D. Chambers have thoughtfully assembled a selection of articles, including several of their own, which raise fundamental questions regarding the response of the criminal justice system to the problems of drug dependence. At a point in time when the proliferation of literature in this field boggles the minds of legislators, officials administering our criminal justice system, parents and other concerned citizens, this volume provides a wide range of thought-provoking perspectives.

The failure of this nation's approach to drug addiction and dependence can be largely attributed to a strategy which has ignored the medical and social aspects of the problem and has focused instead almost exclusively on law enforcement solutions. Of course, we all recognize that law enforcement must play an essential role in a comprehensive attack on drug abuse. Our failure to develop a workable strategy for combating street crime contributes to a daily escalation of fear which is leading many Americans to significantly change their life styles. It has engendered an epidemic of silent terror which in turn paradoxically, but understandably, has led many of our citizens to support even more illogical drug control policies.

Before we can effectively take up the challenge of reform we need thorough scientific research which will support sound alternatives. We must be aware that in spite of the fact that at any one time 25 percent of the individuals involved in the criminal justice system are drug dependent, nothing really effective has been done to provide these individuals with productive, alternative drug-free life styles. We must develop these rational alternatives.

The authors of these articles provide hard facts, careful analyses, and many constructive suggestions for those seeking new directions for the criminal justice system. Messrs. King, Glaser, and Greenberg attempt to put drug abuse and crime in a historical perspective and suggest that drug-related crime is often a function of irrational and unenforceable drug laws. Messrs. Petersen, Meiselas, and Brill provide a review and discussion of treatment available for drug-dependent persons within the criminal justice system, including commentaries on the appropriateness and success of incarceration in the treatment of drug dependence. While "common sense" supports the hypothesis that drug dependence per se is a major contribution to the crime problem, Drs. Chambers and Gould report that little empirical evidence supports this alleged nexus. In fact, heroin addicts are frequently enmeshed in a criminal life style prior to their drug dependence. Dr. McGlothlin provides hard facts on the relative economic and social costs of various proposals to control opiate dependence. Dr. Inciardi reviews the extensive mythology of drug dependence, how these myths emerged, and how they affect our current policies and programing.

I recommend a careful review of the concerns expressed by these authors. The ramifications of ill-founded policy can be profound. For example, I have been alarmed that methadone maintenance for heroin addicts could be used to "smoke-screen" the impact of drug dependence on our society and the social and economic conditions that spawn dependence. While it is true that maintenance permits a few to move from drug dependence to a drug-free existence, a philosophy which accepts the substitution of a legal narcotic (methadone) for an illegal narcotic (heroin) is not without its problems. If, however, maintenance is not even an effective deterrent to crime, as several of the authors suggest, perhaps it is time that we reassess the usefulness of this modality.

My experience as Chairman of the U.S. Senate Subcommittee to Investigate Juvenile Delinquency lends support to a theme expressed throughout the book, namely, that one of our basic theoretical "problems" is that we have been wedded to a monotheistic concept of drug use as being solely heroin street addiction. In fact, today, we are confronted with growing legions of polydrug abusers who use heroin, amphetamines, PCP, LSD, barbiturates, cocaine, methaqualone, methadone, and many other drugs. An important first step in our effort to develop a criminal justice system that responds rationally to drug-dependent persons is to isolate such misconceptions, and then see to it that they are no longer afforded credence.

This book succeeds in focusing attention on the mythology of drug dependence. It provides a valuable assessment of where we are currently, as well as helpful advice as to what we must do to extricate those already involved in the tragic cycle of drug dependence and to prevent even greater numbers of our people from establishing destructive patterns of drug use, while simultaneously protecting the citizens of our nation.

>   *—Birch Bayh*
>   United States Senate
>   April, 1973

INTRODUCTION

It is difficult to imagine a more controversial interrelationship than that pursued in this volume—the interrelationship of those systems which must address the reduction of drug supply and drug demand. And nowhere is the controversy more emotional or potent than in the specific relationship between drug taking and criminal behavior. The professional literature, regrettably, offers little assistance to the serious student who attempts to grasp some understanding of the phenomena at large: all conceivable positions have been shrouded by a pseudo-empiricism, or they suffer from a fragmented scientific effort.

As the authors began to conceptualize the format for this volume, a number of issues came to the fore which demanded consideration:

- What do we really *know* about the relationship between the use of drugs and crime?
- What are the "costs" to society if we do not treat drug users?
- Should drug use and/or addiction be considered within the arena of "victimless" crime?
- Do our drug laws and their enforcement produce more casualties than they prevent or eliminate?
- Can law and the criminal justice system increase the efficacy of treatment?
- Should "law" focus on apprehending violators of the drug use/possession statutes, on reducing the number of income-producing crimes by addicts, on curtailing the availability of drugs?

The initial contemplation of these issues, in turn, offered primacy to an alternative selection of critical questions:

- Within how many contexts are drugs used and misused?
- How dangerous is a given drug? Should we legalize or prohibit it? Should we jail the user? What kind of legislation, if any, should society create to manage the supply of and demand for the drug?

- Do all drugs possess the potential for "social toxicity?"
- On which set of norms should social policy be based?

Given the salient nature of the issues at hand, investigators and other workers in the drug field were located to share their thoughts and experiences. And while contributors were given the task of examining the interlocking phenomena relative to drug-taking, drug-seeking, and the criminal justice superstructure, no attempt was made to restrict or overly focus their writings. As such, the collection of papers emerged as a multidisciplinary investigation. And in providing the reader with a comprehensive portrait of our present state of knowledge concerning the drugs/criminal justice nexus, this volume is part historical narrative, part personal essay, part theoretical and speculative analysis, and part systematic empirical inquiry.

—James A. Inciardi
Coral Gables, Florida

—Carl D. Chambers
Miami, Florida
April, 1973

Chapter 1

"THE AMERICAN SYSTEM":
LEGAL SANCTIONS TO REPRESS DRUG ABUSE

RUFUS KING

Though drug misuse seems self-evidently a problem which ought to belong in the individual and personal category, and though drug addiction ought to lie deep in the domain of medical authorities, no understanding of the contemporary drug scene in the United States can be achieved without focusing principally on the history of the legal role over the past hundred years.

It would have been very hard, a century ago, to find any basis in our great national charter for *federal* interference with the drug-taking habits of citizens of this republic. If limitations of the First Amendment (self-expression), the Fifth (due process), or the Eighth (inappropriate punishment) had not sufficed to keep Uncle Sam from arrogating to himself the role of drug-cop, there yet remained the Ninth (preserving rights "retained by the people") and Tenth (reserving all powers not expressly "delegated to the United States" for the states or the people). Furthermore, when militant anti-alcohol forces triumphed in their campaign to use federal authority to enforce National Prohibition against intoxicating beverages, it was accepted by all concerned that only a specific constitutional amendment could authorize this.

Yet simultaneously the nation was saddled with a prohibition commitment against opiates and coca products that has been fanatically pursued by federal enforcers ever since. In this instance, at least, ambitious lawmakers and empire-building policemen appear to have created social attitudes instead of, as the system is supposed to work, merely reflecting and responding to them.

BACKGROUND

Opium-smoking and opium-eating never took much hold in America in colonial days or during the eighteenth and nineteenth centuries, though the drug was a popular medicine of many uses and universally available at low cost (Terry and Pellens, 1928). The pipe habit was well known from the accounts of missionaries and flourished among Chinese laborers brought to the Far West in the railroad-building era (1840-60), but the "opium den" emerged mainly as a feature of dime-novel fantasies. San Francisco led off with the first anti-smoking ordinance in 1875.

Opium had been known through most of the Eastern Hemisphere from antiquity, and indeed even since the appearance of wonder-drugs in this century it (morphine) has remained among the medical profession's most general and effective analgesic prescriptions. Morphine was isolated around 1806, codeine in 1832, and the first effective hypodermic was developed in 1845. During the Civil War opium and morphine were in such demand to control dysentery and ease the suffering of wounded soldiers that addiction among veterans was tolerantly known as "the Army disease."

Heroin was refined from morphine base in 1898. As with other innovations in this field, some medical men hailed it as the long-awaited panacea, a non-addicting substance and therefore suitable as a "cure" for morphinism and alcoholism. Cocaine was first produced in 1883, found limited acceptance as an anesthetic and analgesic, and commenced to be abused on a small scale. Cocaine sniffing was an exotic practice largely associated in the public mind with prostitutes and denizens of the underworld. Principal American familiarity with the coca plant came from its use as an ingredient in the nation's most popular soft drink.

By the turn of the twentieth century drug abuse, principally addiction to opiates, had become widespread enough to cause mild concern. (But let us note here, once and for all, that coffee, tea, alcohol, and nicotine are drugs too, by every definition, and that at least the latter two are now sickening and killing Americans on a scale not even significantly relatable to the alleged ravages of heroin [Brecher, 1972].) Patent medicines, popular tonics, and even soothing potions for children were loaded with opium (and alcohol). Though estimates of the addict population in the early 1900s varied as widely as they do today, the most respected observers (Kolb and DuMez, 1924) set the figure for this period in the range of 200,000. Victims were believed to be preponderantly female, middle-aged, white, Southern, rural, and from privileged or middle classes.

No one then dreamed of associating drug abuse with criminality.

A vigorous campaign led by the American Medical Association resulted in the first federal Food and Drug Act (Act of June 30, 1906, P.L. 59-384, 34 Stat. 768), which required drug manufacturers who made use of interstate commerce to disclose the ingredients in their products by appropriate labeling. Many states paralleled this with laws imposing modest controls, including prescriptions, registration, and record-keeping in connection with the sale of opiates and cocaine (Kremers and Urdang, 1963). But the ubiquitous intent was merely to draw the traffic in these substances into observable channels, to make it easier for the medical professions and public health authorities to cope with problems of abuse as they arose.

The first federal *control* enactment, the Harrison Narcotics Act of 1914 (Act of December 17, 1914, P.L. 63-223, 38 Stat. 785), relied upon a then extraordinary extension of the federal tax power to require manufacturers, distributors, and dispensers of opiates and coca products to register with the Treasury Department and to keep records of transactions involving these substances. But besides this purpose, likewise merely to help bring the traffic into manageable channels, the Harrison Act was Congress' response to pressures that had been generated from quite another direction.

The United States stumbled into its role as drug-abuse repressor at home largely because of its somewhat wobbly first steps as colonialist and emerging Great Power abroad.

Responsibility for having deliberately addicted the Chinese to opium falls most heavily on the British East India Company, which took over a monopoly of Indian opium production (the main source for the China trade) from the Great Mogul in 1757. Chinese emperors resisted futilely with anti-smoking and anti-opium edicts, but as the demand for tea, silks, spices, and Chinese artifacts soared in the clipper era, Western traders, including some of our Yankee ancestors, pressed relentlessly to expand and exploit the counterbalancing opium market in the Flower Kingdom (Collis, 1946).

The Chinese fought two Opium Wars, in intermittent episodes between 1840 and 1860, against this exploitation, but the end was total capitulation to the Western forces, with humiliating concessions and indemnities, and full legal-ization of inbound shipments of the drug (though smoking remained a capital offense for Chinese subjects). In 1894 opium comprised 14 percent of China's total imports, supplemented by large-scale domestic production under the protection of autonomous warlords all over China. By 1900, according to one estimate, 27 percent of the adult male population of the country was addicted in some degree.

When Admiral Dewey pounced on the Spanish Fleet in Manila Bay and seized the Philippines as partial revenge for the sinking of the Maine (1898), the United States suddenly found itself embroiled in all the toughest problems of colonial administration in a remote, alien, and hostile territory (Taylor, 1969). Unlike the Cubans, who welcomed their American liberators, the Filipinos resisted bitterly and were not effectively subdued until 1901. Thereupon Civil Governor W. H. Taft found himself facing, among other things, a runaway opium problem, inherited from the Spaniards who had auctioned out contracts to provide opium for the local populace.

Governor Taft commissioned a study of alternative ways to deal with the situation; his Opium Investigating Committee recommended licensing and gradual restriction of opium supplies, coupled with efforts to wean users away from the drug (U.S. War Dept., 1906). But on the other side of the world in Washington, Yankee lawmakers were being swept away by missionary and moralistic zeal. Secretary Hay was pushing his "open door" policy to break up exploitative monopolies in China. In 1902 Congress prohibited trafficking in guns, liquor, and opium by U.S. traders with natives on Pacific islands (Act of February 14, 1902, P.L. 57-10, 32 Stat. 33). And in 1905, taking matters out of Taft's hands, the U.S. lawmakers decreed total prohibition of all non-medical uses of opium in the Philippines on and after March 1, 1908 (Act of March 3, 1905, P.L. 58-141, 33 Stat. 928, 944). When that date came, the Philippine traffic quickly went underground, and the Americans had their first direct taste of large-scale clandestine drug operations.

Simultaneously (1908) President Theodore Roosevelt proposed that all powers concerned with the international opium traffic should meet to consider cooperative measures to put an end to it (Renborg, 1947; 1957). Out of this came the Shanghai Conference (1909) and the Hague Opium Convention, signed in 1912 by delegates from thirteen governments. Under this Convention (38 Stat. 1912, 1930, T.S. No. 612) each High Contracting Party proposed to bind itself to restrain its nationals from trafficking in opium and coca products, and to impose domestic controls on its citizens to curb non-medicinal uses.

But other nations shared little of America's enthusiasm for the Hague project. By 1915 only three, the United States, China, and the Netherlands, had ratified, and the Convention might never have amounted to anything had not the United States used its dominant position at the Paris Peace Conference to sponsor a provision that ratification of the 1919 Peace Treaties should be deemed automatic ratification of the Hague pact.

Harrison Act of 1914

Meanwhile, however, Congress had already moved to fulfill the U.S. obligation by enacting the Harrison Act (Act of December 17, 1914, P.L.

63-223, 38 Stat. 785). And it bears stressing again that in that day federal intervention into matters of local choice and personal concern was virtually unprecedented. Even in traditional law enforcement categories, Congress had theretofore ventured into local provinces in only a handful of pioneering acts: lotteries, 1895 (Act of March 2, 1895, P.L. 53-191, 28 Stat. 963); poaching, 1900 (Act of May 25, 1900, P.L. 55-553, 31 Stat. 188); train robbery, 1902 (Act of July 1, 1902, P.L. 57-243, 32 Stat. 727); and white slaving, 1910 (Act of June 25, 1910, P.L. 61-277, 36 Stat. 825).

Under the Harrison Act persons required to register with the Treasury Department were obliged to obtain occupational licenses at nominal cost.

In 1919 a small stamp tax—one cent per ounce—was added (Revenue Act of 1918, Act of February 24, 1919, P.L. 65-254, 40 Stat. 1057, 1130), and to facilitate collection of this tax it was made unlawful for anyone to purchase, sell, dispense, or distribute drugs except from an original stamped package. But there was an important exception to the Harrison Act requirements: no records needed to be kept, nor dispensing requirements observed, by any licensed physician, dentist, or veterinary surgeon so long as the drugs were given "in the course of his professional practice only" (Harrison Act, Sec. 2 [a]).[1]

Had the latter exemption been interpreted broadly, as Congress seemed to intend, the Act would have left ultimate control, and ultimate decisions as to distribution and administration, in the hands of medical authorities and local health officials. What happened, however, was something else.

Just at this time the nation was plunging into its disastrous experiment with National Prohibition. The Eighteenth Amendment, ratified in January 1919 and implemented by the Volstead Act (National Prohibition Act, Act of October 28, 1919, P.L. 66-66, 41 Stat. 305), was assigned to Treasury for enforcement; the new Prohibition Unit set up in Treasury to carry out this assignment was also charged with enforcing the tax provisions of the Harrison Act; and the T-men who thereupon set out with fanatical zeal to stamp out liquor-drinking simultaneously stretched the modest sanctions of the Harrison Act into a comparable mandate for all-out war on drugs. In 1919 Treasury spokesmen shook the nation with alarmed reports of one-and-a-half million dangerous addicts at large in the streets, an epidemic of heavy addiction among youths, and the appearance of smuggling and peddling rings of unprecedented cunning and power.

Coupled with the momentum thus derived from Prohibition, other factors also played a part in making this bureaucratic usurpation of power possible. Wartime propaganda had linked the sinister German spy with "dope," and mothers had been led to fear that their babies might be turned into fearsome heroin maniacs by secret agents of the Hun handing out poisoned candy in schoolyards. In New York, a local campaign led by Mrs. William K. Vanderbilt and other society leaders, partly to keep up with rival ladies who had become famous as suffragettes, had resulted in the repressive Town-Boylan law, enacted by that state in 1914. New Yorkers were warned of armies of dangerous fiends roaming Harlem and the Bronx. Spectacular raids on Chinatown "dens" raised the specter of helpless America seduced and betrayed by inscrutable Orientals organized into "tongs" and fronting for the Yellow Peril. Prominent figures within the medical profession itself disowned responsibility for ministering to the needs of addicts, and joined the chorus demanding total repression of drug trafficking and drug abuse (King, 1972).

In this same era, nonetheless, other medical spokesmen and public authorities, realizing that Treasury's sudden prohibition campaign would strand respectable addicts who had never been in any conflict with the law before (even conservative contemporary estimates put their number around 200,000) opened so-called clinics to provide relief (Musto, 1972). These clinics, appearing in 1919-20 in some forty cities throughout the country, were immediately caught up in controversy. Some were poorly administered and amounted to no more than "feeding stations," as was alleged; others drew congregations of "undesirables" to protesting neighborhoods; still others served their purpose well and dealt more or less adequately with addicts who applied to them. But by early 1923 all had been closed, thanks to warnings, threats, and where necessary actual prosecutions initiated by the federal agents (Terry and Pellens, 1928; Lindesmith, 1965).

At this juncture, the United States Supreme Court played an important part in shaping the pattern. The Harrison Act itself barely survived a constitutional challenge, by a 5 to 4 decision in *United States v. Doremus* (249 U.S. 86 [1919]). But in a series of three interpretative opinions which followed, *Webb v. United States* (249 U.S. 96 [1919]), *Jin Fuey Moy v. United States* (254 U.S. 189 [1920]), and *United States v. Behrman* (258 U.S. 280 [1922]), the High Court let itself be persuaded, in the inflamed climate of those years, to accept the government's extreme contention that "in the course of . . . professional practice" meant doctors could only administer controlled drugs *to patients for conditions other than mere symptoms of addiction,* and could not administer or prescribe for addicts as such under any circumstances. The effect of this, almost certainly at variance with Congress' initial intent, was to cut addicts off entirely from all sources of relief except smugglers, pushers, and dope rings. Exit the addict-patient; enter the addict-criminal.[2]

And from the law enforcement viewpoint, what would have been a minor regulatory and tax-collection assignment thus emerged as a major prohibition "war," glorified ever since in yeasty hyperboles about national survival and metaphors of the battlefield. [3]

Prohibition Era

In the mid-1920s there were more federal prisoners serving time for drug-law violations than for liquor offenses, though this was in the very heyday of Prohibition (Schmeckebier, 1929). The number of doctors actually prosecuted all the way to conviction and sentencing were few, but this was only because formal indictments and prosecution proved unnecessary; the Narcotics Division reported thousands of cases in which it had dropped charges against, i.e., warned and threatened, persons registered under the Act (U.S. Treasury, 1920). And even in prosecutions of non-registered offenders, the arrest-conviction ratio was notably low. For 1925, for example, 10,297 federal arrests produced only 5,600 convictions, suggesting, again, use of the arrest and indictment processes to oppress and harass in doubtful cases (Schmeckebier, 1929).

As federal prisons became choked with addict-inmates, the Department of Justice sought help from Congress, and in 1929 the so-called Porter Act of January 19, 1929 (P.L. 70-672, 45 Stat. 1085) was passed (over bitter opposition from the Surgeon General, who wanted no part of the problem) to authorize the U.S. Public Health Service to establish two special facilities, first called "narcotic farms" and later renamed "hospitals." The first of these was opened—six years later, in 1935—at Lexington, Kentucky, and the second at Ft. Worth, Texas, in 1938. Under the Porter Act, addicted persons convicted in federal courts could be sent to the Public Health Service hospitals to serve their terms there in lieu of being committed to ordinary imprisonment. The hospitals thus soon came to be run like medium-security penal institutions. They were also authorized to accept voluntary patients, but this never worked well because of the prison-like atmosphere and because once physical withdrawal had been accomplished most voluntary inmates insisted upon leaving in short order.[4]

Bureau of Narcotics

In 1930, following a scandal in the Prohibition Bureau, Congress created a separate Bureau of Narcotics, and President Hoover appointed Harry J. Anslinger, who had commenced his career in the Foreign Service and had been serving as an Assistant Prohibition Commissioner in charge of foreign controls, to head it. Thereafter, for the next three decades, Anslinger dominated U.S. attitudes and policies towards drug abuse both at home and (as perennial U.S. delegate to all international drug conferences) throughout the rest of the world. He was an indefatigable proponent of the notion that drug addiction poses a fearful threat to mankind, calling for heroic efforts (by his Bureau) to combat it by all means, in all directions, and at all levels (see Anslinger and Tompkins, 1953, Anslinger and Oursler, 1961).

Whereas in the 1920s the federal agency had tended to preempt local drug-law enforcement, once Anslinger consolidated his position he launched a drive to bring the states into line with repressive laws of their own. In 1932 the prestigious National Conference of Commissioners on Uniform State Laws promulgated a Uniform Narcotic Drug Act, freely acknowledging that its work followed the federal pattern and had been aimed at parallelling federal controls as closely as possible (9B Uniform Laws Annotated 415; Eldridge, 1967). State legislators rushed to adopt this measure, so that by the end of the decade virtually every jurisdiction in the United States had either the Uniform Act or some parallel repressive law of its own.

Because the basis of the federal enactment was technically only tax collection, these state laws provided overlapping offenses, punishing possession, transportation, sale, possessing hypodermics, etc., as offenses violating the states' police powers. But far from conflicting with the federal campaign, this proliferation simply gave the federal men a bouquet of options; where the state courts were notably severe, or rules of evidence more lax, or conviction otherwise more likely, the T-men would simply hand their cases over to local authorities for prosecution. In some instances defendants were even convicted and sentenced in federal and state courts for the same transaction. And of course the system worked in reverse, so state authorities could turn *their* victims over to the local U.S. Attorney if it appeared that harsher treatment could be expected in the federal forum.

On his home ground, no empire-builder in Washington cultivated relations with Congress more assiduously than the Commissioner of Narcotics. Any expression of interest from Capitol Hill would produce floods of material and personal attention from the Bureau in response, and it was even possible for addicted persons of sufficient prominence and good connections to be "treated" with tacit Bureau protection. The payoff for this was what Commissioner Anslinger wanted in the way of appropriations for his forces, and new federal legislation he usually got virtually for the asking.

Marijuana, the smoking preparation made by drying and shredding the tops and leaves of cannabis sativa, the common help plant, and hashish, the must stronger extracted resin, were known for millenia throughout the ancient world as both medicine and intoxicant. But in modern times, though tincture of cannabis continued to be widely used by physicians, the drug had little recreational impact on Europe outside avant-garde circles, and was virtually unknown in the United States until the 1930s (see, generally, Grinspoon, 1971; Kaplan, 1970; Solomon, 1966). Cannabis is supposed to have been brought to Latin America by the Spaniards, and pot-smoking came to the American Southwest with Mexican laborers imported across the Rio Grande and to Gulf Coast ports with sailors and traders from the Caribbean. Sensational local exposes of alleged debauchery with marijuana induced Louisiana and Colorado to lead off with repressive state laws (in 1927 and 1929).

A few cranks around the country had been waging crusades against the "weed of madness," with little effect (see King, 1972; Lindesmith, 1965), but in the mid-thirties the Federal Bureau of Narcotics began warning of a threatened marijuana epidemic and urging a vigorous campaign against it (Anslinger and Cooper, 1937). In 1937 Congress responded with the Marijuana Tax Act (Act of August 2, 1937, P.L. 75-238, 50 Stat. 551), bringing the drug squarely within the repressive pattern previously applied to opium and cocaine by the Harrison Act.

Under this measure physicians and others desiring to prescribe cannabis were required to obtain a Treasury license (for $1.00 annually), and similar licenses were provided for other dispensers ($3.00), researchers ($1.00), and importers, manufacturers and compounders ($24.00). But the Narcotics Bureau, as issuing authority, restricted licenses to approved research projects, and the number thus issued was never more than a negligible handful. So the result was merely another nationwide enforcement empire and new categories of federal crime.[5]

By 1937, when the Marijuana Tax Act was pushed through Congress, the T-men had begun to sound another note that would become their major theme for the ensuing decade: the charge that American drug problems were caused by too-light penalties and by too much leniency on the part of sentencing judges. This campaign bore its first fruit in the 1937 Act, in the form of increased penalties for second and subsequent drug offenses.[6]

Through this entire period the federal authorities insisted that the U.S. addict population remained stabilized at between 50,000 and 60,000. No one challenged the figure, and non-official persons had no access to any data from which the estimate could have been checked. Even during World War II, when for several years ordinary travel and communication between drug-producing countries and the United States were cut off, the Bureau never tolerated a reduction to below 30,000, and the war affected its enforcement activities very little (U.S. Treasury, 1945). While other Geneva-based international organizations vanished, Anslinger contrived to bring drug officials of the League Secretariat, the Drug Supervisory Body, and the Permanent Central Opium Board to Washington where, though they had little to do, they survived intact until their work was picked up by new agencies within the United Nations framework (Anslinger and Tompkins, 1953).

Except for the appearance of amphetamines (widely prescribed for military personnel to combat fatigue and prolong wakefulness, and hence popularized among returning veterans) and a notable increase in barbiturate abuse, including significant numbers of overdose deaths,[7] there were few changes in the

American drug scene in the immediate post-war years. It was suggested that opiate addiction might be concentrating more in urban centers and involving larger numbers of blacks, but the estimated total purportedly held steady (see Lindesmith, 1965: Ch. 4).[8] On the international front, Anslinger began to make headway with his grand design to pull all drug treaties and protocols into a new Single Convention (Single Convention on Narcotic Drugs, December 13, 1964, ratified by U.S. June 24, 1967, T.S. No. 1407; see Taylor, 1969).

But another surge of near-hysteria gripped the country in 1950, starting with a short-lived furor about juvenile delinquency ("dangerous young hoodlums"), and fueled by the Senate Crime (Kefauver) Committee disclosures about the menace of organized crime. The Narcotics Bureau exploited the Kefauver hearings to accomplish two things—building the myth of a sinister and omnipotent Mafia as the T-men's worldwide challenger (U.S. Senate Special Committee, 1951a/b; King, 1971), and persuading Congress to increase the penalties for drug offenses, with a revival of mandatory minimums. Enlightened penologists had long been fighting to discourage mandatory minimums—by which lawmakers tie the hands of judges so that *at least* a prescribed minimum sentence must be given to all persons convicted of particular offenses—because they wipe out humane discretion in the sentencing function and play havoc with modern probation and parole systems. But in the inflamed atmosphere of the day, Congress rushed through the so-called Boggs Act (Act of November 2, 1951, P.L. 82-255, 65 Stat. 767) fixing mandatory sentence ranges, with increases for repeated offenses (2 to 5 years, 5 to 10 years, etc.) for all federal drug violations. Many state legislatures followed with "little Boggs Acts," some specifying terms as long as 10 to 40 years for offenses in the trafficking categories (Eldridge, 1967: Appendix B).

Hearings were also held at this time (1951) on the alleged need for federal sanctions to curb abuse of barbiturates and amphetamines (U.S. House Ways and Means Committee, 1951), but the Narcotics Bureau opposed all such proposals and they got nowhere.

QUESTIONS AND CONTROVERSIES

In 1955 the American Bar Association requested Congress to make a complete review and re-evaluation of federal drug policies and laws. Simultaneously a joint committee, representing the ABA and the American Medical Association, was established to study the role of these two sister professions vis-a-vis drug problems. The Congressional response was the creation of a committee chaired by Senator Price Daniel of Texas, which launched a sweeping investigation over all the United States.

But those who hoped the Congressional review might modify the harshness of federal policies were disappointed; the committee's chief investigator was a career Bureau agent, and from the outset its hearings merely featured the evils of drug abuse, the criminality of addicts, and the importance of expanded enforcement efforts and still harsher penalties. At the end, after accumulating some 8,000 pages of testimony (U.S. Senate Judiciary Committee, 1955), the committee produced two reports, one a nine-page document on law enforcement recommending stiffer penalties, additional powers for T-men, and larger appropriations for the Bureau (Sen. Rep. 84-1440), and the other, running to twenty-one pages, dealing with treatment but consisting principally of a diatribe against the clinic experiments of 1920. The Committee recommended that addicts be first incarcerated in "civil-type commitment," then released under tightly supervised probation, with incurable backsliders being committed to "an indeterminate quarantine-type of confinement at a suitable narcotics farm" (Sen. Rep. 84-1850).

Simultaneously (1956) a House committee again held hearings on the new perils of barbiturates and amphetamines, but once more the Bureau registered opposition to inclusion of these substances in the federal prohibition pattern and nothing came of it (U.S. House Ways and Mean Committee, 1955-6).

The result of the Daniel recommendations was the Narcotic Control Act of 1956 (Act of July 18, 1956, P.L. 84-728, 70 Stat. 567). It raised minimum and maximum penalties for *all* drug offenses to 2 to 10 years, 5 to 20 years, and 10 to 40 years for succeeding convictions, with 5 to 20 years and 10 to 40 years for any offense involving smuggling or sale. A special penalty was set for selling heroin to a minor—from a minimum of 10 years to life, or death if a jury so recommended.[9] Discretion to suspend sentences, grant probation, or provide parole eligibility was denied sentencing judges, except for first offenders convicted of possession only.

Narcotic agents and customs officers were authorized to carry weapons, serve warrants, and arrest without warrants. A new compounding offense—using any interstate communication facility in connection with a drug violation—was added, with a separate 2 to 5 year penalty. And all persons who had ever been convicted of a drug offense or who were currently addicts or users were required to register and obtain special certificates when leaving the United States, surrendering their certificates upon reentry (minimum sentence one year, and up to three, for violating this requirement).

The ABA-AMA study concluded in November 1957 with five recommendations: an experiment with an outpatient facility or "clinic"; a study of causative and relapse factors; an evaluation of educational campaigns and other preventative techniques; a comparative study of federal and state laws; and an evaluation of the effectiveness of current enforcement policies (Lindesmith, 1961). But this evoked a furious attack from the Narcotics Bureau, including a widely-circulated Treasury document containing alleged "comments" on the report (U.S. Treasury, 1958), and intervention with the project's sponsoring foundation to cut off its funds.[10]

But while Mr. Anslinger remained invulnerable to attacks from Capitol Hill and impervious to private criticism, his empire was soon rocked by political forces generated in the White House; and since the early 1960s U.S. drug policies have been kept almost continuously in turmoil by manipulations directed from the Oval Room.

One of President Kennedy's most stalwart supporters in winning the 1960 nomination and election was Governor Edmund (Pat) Brown of California. Brown had won two years earlier in a gubernatorial campaign involving drug issues (his opponent, former Senator William Knowland, had attacked him as being "soft" on drug offenders during Brown's eight-year tenure as California Attorney General). Californians had remained stirred up on account of this, and the issue was raised again in local elections there in 1960, whereupon Governor Brown began pressuring the Kennedy forces to sponsor a White House Conference on Drugs. The suggestion met with a cool reception because of Anslinger's strong opposition and because the subject was not then of much national interest.

At home in Sacramento, Brown designated 1961 as "Fight Narcotics Year," simultaneously launching a statewide campaign to focus public attention on the newly discovered menace of amphetamines and other "dangerous" drugs outside the traditional federal categories.

Nevertheless, only Californians might have been reached by all this—and the ensuing story might, consequently, have been quite different—had not Kennedy's arch-rival, Mr. Nixon, decided to run for governor against Brown in 1962 and to renew the attacks on Brown as a "coddler" of dope peddlers and dope fiends. The response from Washington was all-out; the President himself appeared in California on Brown's behalf; in May 1962 he personally announced that the idea of a White House Conference was now under study; and early in September, on the eve of the California contest, the Conference was formally announced.

But even so, the President simultaneously released a study sharply minimizing the problem: the total number of drug *users* in the whole nation was set at 45,000; heroin was declared to have no effects significantly different from morphine; doctors should be permitted to treat addicts and had a clear right to do so under existing laws; the hazards of marijuana were "exaggerated"; and as for increasing drug abuse among juveniles, "the available statistics do not indicate such an incidence now" (Ad Hoc Panel on Drug Abuse, 1962).

White House Conference

The two themes stressed at the Conference (hastily convened on September 27, 1962) were somewhat tangential: that the new menace about which the nation should be most concerned was so-called dangerous drugs, amphetamines and barbiturates; and that the most effective approach was treatment and rehabilitation, patterned after civil commitment programs already initiated by Governor Brown in California and being urged by Mayor Wagner (another Kennedy ally) in New York (White House Conference on Narcotic and Drug Abuse, 1962).

The Conference accomplished its main purpose; Brown won again and Nixon announced his withdrawal from public life.[11] But the attending publicity had stirred enough interest so that when nothing more happened there was muttering criticism of the President's apparent lack of concern about drug problems. The upshot was the appointment, early in 1963, of a brand-new Advisory Commission to make another study. This commission rushed out a hasty Interim Report, issued on April Fool's Day, but its final work only reached the White House in November 1963, just before the tragedy at Dallas. And its recommendations were again somewhat out of line with earlier thrusts (President's Advisory Commission on Narcotic and Drug Abuse, 1963a/b).

This Final Report proposed disbanding the Narcotics Bureau and removing all drug matters from Treasury, turning enforcement over to the Department of Justice, international aspects to a Special Assistant in the White House, and educational and health functions to the Department of Health, Education, and Welfare. It bore down on the need for controlling drugs in the new categories—now not only barbiturates and amphetamines but also LSD-25, ether, and airplane glue. It recommended that the federal Narcotics hospitals stop taking any patients except those convicted of crimes or involuntarily committed by civil procedures, and that the Bureau of Prisons establish a special program for addicts in federal institutions.

Partially offsetting the harshness of these recommendations, the Final Report urged dropping all mandatory minimum sentences from the federal statutes and called for a revision of federal regulations to allow doctors to set up their own standards of good medical practice for the treatment of addicts.[12]

The first of these White House themes to bear fruit was the extension of the federal prohibition to barbiturates and amphetamines. One of President Johnson's first messages to the 89th Congress, in January 1965, called for legislation forthwith to control newly-revealed abuses of depressants and stimulants (III Congressional Record 368, January 7, 1965). The result was the Drug Abuse Control Amendments of 1965 (Act of July 15, 1965, P.L. 89-74, 79 Stat. 226), differing from the Harrison Act in that they relied on Congress' interstate commerce powers and were to be enforced by a new Bureau of Drug Abuse Control in the Food and Drug Administration, but requiring Harrison-type registration by everyone handling the controlled substances, and imposing comparable if slightly milder criminal penalties for violations.[13]

A remarkable innovation in this law—added as a concession to placate the powerful drug lobbies and also, allegedly, to pay the debt incurred when drug manufacturers had earlier contributed millions of dollars' worth of medical supplies to save face for the Administration by bailing out Bay of Pigs hostages—was a provision imposing severe criminal sanctions for *counterfeiting* (i.e., merely appropriating the proprietary name of) any trade-marked drug product, even though the counterfeit substance was itself perfectly pure and accurately compounded.[14]

1966 Narcotic Addiction Rehabilitation Act

The next year, Congress passed the Narcotic Addict Rehabilitation Act (Act of November 8, 1966, P.L. 89-793, 80 Stat. 1438), a measure which had been pushed on Capitol Hill for several years by Republican leaders without success.[15] In theory, this measure was to provide alternatives to arrest and criminal prosecution for addicts. In practice, it was so severely limited that it has never had much effect. Under it, addicts[16] are divided into three categories. The first permits persons *accused* of crimes—but only if the crime involved no violence and no trafficking in drugs and the person was not on probation and not more than a second offender—to opt for civil commitment in lieu of prosecution, if a court approves and the Surgeon General certifies there is room for him in some treatment program. In the second category, persons found *guilty* of crimes other than those excluded above (plus addict-traffickers if their offenses are shown to have been primarily to obtain drugs for their own personal use) may, if the sentencing court so elects and the Attorney General certifies that there are adequate treatment facilities and personnel available, be committed for an indeterminate period of up to ten years (or the maximum sentence for the offense itself, if that is less) for treatment in confinement or, after a maximum of six months, treatment in parole-like conditional release. And finally in the third category, persons not involved in any crime may commit themselves, or may be involuntarily committed on petition of a relative, for three-and-a-half years of confinement and post-confinement conditional release —again provided the Surgeon General certifies that facilities are available to carry out this program in his case.[17]

The Drug Abuse Control Amendments had not specifically included hallucinogens, but they gave the Secretary of Health, Education, and Welfare authority to add such substances if he found them to have a dangerous potential for abuse, and the Secretary brought LSD into the control pattern in 1966. The popular media continued to portray horrors allegedly associated with "acid" and "bad trips," however, and this pushed the President into action again. When the 90th Congress convened in 1968, the White House warned that this newest category of drugs "threaten(s) our Nation's health, vitality and self-respect," and declared that law enforcement efforts were hampered because penalties for LSD transactions were too low. Congress responded with a new LSD penalty bill in October 1968 (Act of October 24, 1968, P.L. 90-639, 82 Stat. 1361).[18]

During this period the Food and Drug Administration was headed by Dr. James L. Goddard, a career Public Health Service physician who appeared to be organizing FDA's newly-established Bureau of Drug Abuse control along lines emphasizing medical orientation and public education rather than exclusively hard-fisted law enforcement. He and his Bureau director, John Finlator, collided repeatedly with Capitol Hill exponents of tougher laws, and this played a part, at least, in provoking another drastic move from the White House. Though President Johnson's Commission on Law Enforcement and Administration of Justice had recently completed an elaborate study of the whole federal drug-enforcement effort without recommending any organizational changes (President's Commission, 1967a/b), early in 1968 he used his powers under the Reorganization Act to wipe out both the old Bureau of Narcotics in the Treasury Department and the new Bureau in the Food and Drug Administration, transferring *everything*, including educational and scientific responsibilities as well as law enforcement, to a new Bureau of Narcotics and Dangerous Drugs in the Department of Justice (U.S. House Committee on Government Operations, 1968).

When this shift was made, the Attorney General who would have shaped the new Bureau and set its policies was Ramsey Clark. But before he fairly made a start, Mr. Nixon and Mr. Mitchell arrived on the scene, calling for toughly enforced law and order. And no Administration in this whole narrative has been more vigorous in promoting repressive drug abuse policies, nor has any President ever *personally* played the drug theme so relentlessly.

Federal Organization

In 1968 the official figure for the nation's entire addict population was 63,000; by July 1969 President Nixon was warning a frightened public that drugs had become "a serious national threat," that the number of addicts had grown to hundreds of thousands, and that the problem now involved several million college students as well as youngsters in high schools and junior high schools. To deal with the situation—"this rising sickness in our land"—the President called for complete revision of all federal drug laws, ordering the

Department of Justice simultaneously to initiate a new model law for the fifty states which would coordinate their activities more closely with the federal effort.

The federal revision which resulted was entitled "Comprehensive Drug Abuse Prevention and Control Act of 1970" (Act of October 27, 1970, P.L. 91-513, 84 Stat. 1236), and was indeed an omnibus measure, running to some sixty pages and consolidating all existing repressive measures in the Federal Code. The basis of federal power was shifted at last from tax collection to the full sweep of Congress' power over interstate commerce. All abusable substances were reclassified into five schedules, with restrictions and penalties graded downward from the classification most dangerous and most likely to be abused (with marijuana illogically locked into the severest). The Administration asked for increased mandatory minimums, but Congress balked at this and set up stiff maximums (5-10-15 years, $10,000-$50,000 in fines), which double automatically for repeated offenses. Two new penal categories, promoting a "continuing criminal enterprise" or being a "dangerous Special Drug Offender," are punished by 10 years to life (20 years to life for a repetition) and a straight 25 years, respectively.[19]

The Department of Justice also carried out the President's other directive, preparing and promulgating a new Uniform Controlled Dangerous Substances Act, through the National Conference of Commissioners on Uniform State Laws. This act, already adopted by more than forty state legislatures, parallels the federal categories and enforcement provisions so closely that it practically reduces local forces to auxiliaries working within the federal framework.[20]

In June 1971 President Nixon, now terming drug abuse America's Public Enemy No. 1, created a "Special Action Office for Drug Abuse Prevention" in the White House (Executive Order No. 11599, 36 Federal Register 11793 [June 19, 1971]), and asked Congress for an unparalleled concentration of power, with lavish funds to be doled out for approved treatment and rehabilitation functions. Congress responded with the Special Action Office for Drug Abuse Prevention Act (Act of March 21, 1972, P.L. 92-255, 86 Stat. 65), committing almost a billion dollars to the President's virtually unrestricted discretion.[21] In January 1972 the White House also created a new Office of Drug Abuse Law Enforcement (Executive Order No. 11641, 37 Federal Register 2421 [February 1, 1972]), located in Justice but headed by a White House "consultant," to concentrate enforcement activities in a special unit of several hundred agents and attorneys operating right on top of the Justice Department's regular Bureau.

CURRENT DILEMMAS

Obviously, this spectacular explosion in the federal bureaucracy and federal funding—at a time when the Administration has cut deeply into expenditures for bona fide welfare items like health, housing, and education—could not be easily justified on the basis of the addict population of 60,000 with which America has been familiar for so many decades. By the end of 1972 the figure officially promulgated as the number of persons addicted to drugs in the United States had reached 600,000.

Finally, the federal establishment appears to be executing a series of maneuvers aimed at throttling the one development that could threaten its enforcement empire, the spread of methadone treatment and maintenance programs. Methadone, developed by the Germans during World War II when access to natural opium crops was cut off, is an almost-exact equivalent of morphine and heroin (which are themselves so nearly alike that they metabolize indistinguishably). It soon came to be widely administered in the United States as the drug of choice in easing addicts' discomfort during withdrawal. But from the outset, when Dole and Nyswander began *maintaining* addict-patients with saturation dosages in New York in the middle 1960s, law-enforcers resisted. When programs started up in New York, Baltimore, Washington, Chicago, and other high-addiction spots, they were usually harassed by the police, infiltrated, and often their patients were intimidated and their sources of funds attacked. Doctors who prescribed methadone were threatened and sometimes prosecuted.

Nevertheless, these pioneering programs made headway, helped in some communities by demonstrably beneficial effects on street crime as addicts' compulsion to raise money for the black market was reduced, and helped by the myth that methadone is really a "good" drug which "blocks" the effects of evil heroin.

So in June 1970 the new Justice Department Bureau and the Food and Drug Administration made a determination to the effect that using methadone for maintenance programs, as opposed to a withdrawal aid, was "experimental," with the technical result that all methadone maintenance programs were required to file applications for special authorization and qualify under the severely restrictive regulations developed to curb reckless experimenting with damaging substances like thalidomide (Proposed, Regulation and "Guidelines," 35 Federal Register 9014 [June 11, 1970], 36 Federal Register 6075 [April 2, 1971]). Most programs were thereafter actually allowed to go on operating, at sufferance of the two Bureaus, but expansions have been discouraged—with the piteous result that in many parts of the country there are long waiting lists of addict-candidates for whom no place can be found in existing programs and facilities.

An even worse situation is now in prospect, for new regulations *will withdraw methadone absolutely from discretionary use by private practitioners and dispensing by pharmacists,* and restrict it solely to administration in "approved" programs. (Methadone: Proposed Special Requirements for Use, 37 Federal Register 6940 [April 6, 1972], 37 Federal Register 26790 [December 15, 1972]). The result of this restriction, coupled with the power vested in the Special Action Office (SAODAP), will be that federal enforcement officials are going to have a monopoly over methadone as cruel and strict as the monopoly over heroin which law enforcement efforts now preserve for the wicked peddler.

And the end of America's fifty-year self-torment is not remotely in sight.

NOTES

1. This exemption was eliminated, in effect, by the Comprehensive Drug Abuse Prevention and Control Act of 1970, P.L. 91-513, 84 Stat. 1236, which provides that the Secretary of Health, Education, and Welfare and the Attorney General shall determine "appropriate methods of medical practice" and advise Congress. See 42 U.S.C. 257a.

2. The Court emphatically reversed itself in 1925, in *Linder v. United States,* 268 U.S. 5, disavowing the *Behrman* opinion and holding that addicts were entitled to medical care like other patients. But the reversal had practically no effect. See 62 Yale Law Journal 736, 751 (1953).

3. "I consider keeping dangerous drugs out of the United States just as important as keeping armed enemy forces from landing in the United States . . . Our goal is the unconditional surrender of the merchants of death who traffic in heroin. Our goal is the total banishment of drug abuse from the American life. Our children's lives are what we are fighting for." Richard M. Nixon, September 18, 1972.

4. This was sometimes countered at Lexington by "blue-grassing," requiring voluntary patients to plead guilty to a one-year misdemeanor in local Kentucky courts, the sentence suspended on condition the patient stayed in the hospital.

5. The Uniform State Act (9B Uniform Laws Annotated 415) was also amended to include marijuana in 1942.

6. For smuggling and trafficking, the progression was from 5 to 10 to 20 years (all maximums, i.e., "up to").

7. Barbiturate deaths, honestly attributed, exceeded 1,000 per year in the postwar decade; Marilyn Monroe was the best-known victim. There is, incidentally, no such thing as an honestly-attributed *heroin* o.d. death. Heroin is simply *not* the killer it is so often officially claimed to be. See Brecher (1972: Ch. 12).

8. Beginning in 1953 the Bureau reported "active" addicts in last-digit figures, e.g., for 1958, 51,636. See also Maurer and Vogel (1967).

9. For an illuminating case history under this provision, see Kobler (1962).

10. So successfully (private foundations are understandably nervous about *any* pressure emanating from a U.S. Treasury agency) that the ABA-AMA venture could not even publish its own reports. See Lindesmith (1961), Eldridge (1967); another critical study completed early in 1958 *by a sister federal agency* was similarly blocked for five years (see Livingston, 1963).

11. Commissioner Anslinger's resignation was also accepted, though he continued as U.S. delegate to the U.N. Commission on Narcotic Drugs for eight more years, until 1970.

12. This is the basic difference in the so-called British "system" and experience; the doctors there set their own standards long ago and still largely control the situation, despite U.S. official propaganda to the contrary. See Schur (1956).

13. One year for unauthorized possession (other than for personal use); 3 years for possession with intent to defraud, etc.; 3 years for any repeated offenses; 2 years for any sale to persons under 21, increasing to 6 years for repeating this offense.

14. Nowhere else in American jurisprudence has mere trade infringement per se been made a felony, as in this instance. But the value to drug manufacturers is also unique because nowhere else are proprietary items, costing pennies to produce, priced in dollars.

15. The rehabilitation approach had given Governor Rockefeller and the New York Congressional delegation a means of counteracting the Kennedy-Brown-Wagner exploitation of "dangerous" drugs and broader enforcement; but this balance shifted when Robert Kennedy took Senator Keating's New York seat in January 1965.

16. Defined sweepingly as anyone who has "lost the power of self-control with reference to his addiction."

17. The Surgeon General and the Attorney General have only certified applicants to federal facilities by the handful. The bulk of the program has depended on small federally funded local projects, scattered by patronage considerations instead of concentrated in the few urban centers where drug problems are acute. Between ten and fifteen thousand persons have gone through *some* NARA processing to date.

18. The new penalties avoided mandatory minimums, however, merely providing 1 year for *all* possession (with special consideration for first offenders), and 5 years for trafficking (increasing to 10 and 15 years for sales to minors).

19. The Act even centers control of many education and research functions in the Attorney General, and entrusts the classifying and reclassifying of drug substances to him. It also confers civil enforcement powers (administrative investigation, immunity, injunction, etc.) on him and permits his agents to make warrantless arrests and "no knock" entries.

20. The federal act also set up a National Commission on Marijuana and Drug Abuse which has filed a moderate report (1972) urging partial decriminalization of marijuana use.

21. The Act also creates a new National Drug Abuse Training Center, a National Institute on Drug Abuse (to take over functions of the Department of Health, Education, and Welfare in 1975), and a new National Advisory Council on Drug Abuse.

REFERENCES

ANSLINGER, H. J. and C. R. COOPER (1937) "Marijuana: assassin of youth." American Magazine CXXIV (July): 19, 150.

ANSLINGER, H. J. and W. OURSLER (1961) The Murderers: The Story of the Narcotic Gangs. New York: Farrar, Straus, Cudahy.

ANSLINGER, H. J. and W. F. TOMPKINS (1953) The Traffic in Narcotics. New York: Funk, Wagnalls.

Ad Hoc Panel on Drug Abuse (1962) Progress Report. Washington: The White House.

BRECHER, E. M. (1972) Licit and Illicit Drugs: The Consumers Union Report. Boston: Little, Brown.

COLLIS, M. (1946) Foreign Mud. New York: Knopf.

ELDRIDGE, W. B. (1967) Narcotics and the Law. Chicago: American Bar Foundation.

GRINSPOON, L. (1971) Marijuana Reconsidered. Cambridge: Harvard Univ. Press.

KAPLAN, J. (1970) Marijuana–The New Prohibition. New York: World.

KING, R. (1971) "Wild shots in the war on crime." Journal of Public Law, Emory Univ. Law School, 1, 85.

——— (1972) The Drug Hang-Up. New York: Norton. (Available in 1973 in paper, Springfield, Ill.: Charles C Thomas.)

KOLB, L. and A. G. DUMEZ (1924) The Prevalence and Trend of Drug Addiction in the United States and Factors Influencing It. Washington: Government Printing Office.

KOBLER, J. (1962) "The narcotics dilemma: crime or disease?" Saturday Evening Post (Sept. 8).

KREMERS, E. and G. URDANG (1963) History of Pharmacy. Philadelphia: Lippincott.

LINDESMITH, A. R. [ed.] (1961) Drug Addiction: Crime or Disease? Bloomington: Indiana Univ. Press.

——— (1965) The Addict and the Law. Bloomington: Indiana Univ. Press.

LIVINGSTON, R. B. [ed.] (1963) Narcotic Drug Addiction Problems, Public Health Service Pub. No. 1050. Washington: Government Printing Office.

MAURER, D. W. and V. H. VOGEL (1967) Narcotics and Narcotic Addiction. Springfield, Ill.: Charles C Thomas.

MUSTO, D. (1972) Narcotics and America. New Haven: Yale Univ. Press.

National Commission on Marijuana and Drug Abuse (1972) Marijuana: A Signal of Misunderstanding. Washington: Government Printing Office.

President's Advisory Commission on Narcotic and Drug Abuse (1963a) Interim Report (April 1). Washington: The White House.

——— (1963b) Final Report. Washington: Government Printing Office.

President's Commission on Law Enforcement and Administration of Justice (1967a) The Challenge of Crime in a Free Society. Washington: Government Printing Office.

——— (1967b) Task Force Report: Narcotics and Drug Abuse. Washington: Government Printing Office.

RENBORG, B. A. (1947) International Drug Control. Washington: Carnegie Endowment.

——— (1957) "International control of narcotics," Law and Contemporary Problems, Duke University School of Law, 22, 86.

SCHMECKEBIER, L. F. (1929) The Bureau of Prohibition. Washington: Brookings Institution.

SCHUR, E. M. (1956) Narcotic Addiction in Britain and America. Bloomington: Indiana Univ. Press.

SOLOMON, D. [ed.] (1966) The Marijuana Papers. Indianapolis: Bobbs-Merrill.

TAYLOR, A. H. (1969) American Diplomacy and the Narcotics Traffic 1900-39. Durham: Duke Univ. Press.

TERRY, C. E. and M. PELLENS (1928) The Opium Problem. New York: Bureau of Social Hygiene.

U.S. House Committee on Government Operations (1968) "Reorganization plan no. 1 of 1968." Hearings, March 19-21. Washington: Government Printing Office.

U.S. House Ways and Means Committee (1951) "Control of narcotics, marijuana, and barbiturates." Hearings, April 7, 14, 17. Washington: Government Printing Office.

——— (1955-6) "Traffic in, and control of, narcotics, barbiturates, and amphetamines." Hearings, October 13, 1955, through January 30, 1956. Washington: Government Printing Office.

U.S. Senate Judiciary Committee, Subcommittee on Improvements in the Federal Criminal Code (1955) "Illicit narcotics traffic." Hearings, Parts 1-10, June 2-November 25. Washington: Government Printing Office.

U.S. Senate Special Committee to Investigate Organized Crime in Interstate Commerce (1951a) Third Interim Report, Sen. Rep. 82-307. Washington: Government Printing Office.

——— (1951b) Final Report, Sen. Rep. 82-725. Washington: Government Printing Office.

U.S. Treasury, Advisory Committee to the Federal Bureau of Narcotics (1958) Comments on Narcotic Drugs—Interim Report of the American Bar Association and the American Medical Association on Narcotic Drugs. Washington: Government Printing Office.

U.S. Treasury, Bureau of Internal Revenue (1920) Annual Reports. Washington: Government Printing Office.

U.S. Treasury, Bureau of Narcotics (1945) Traffic in Opium and Other Dangerous Drugs. Washington: Government Printing Office.

U.S. War Department, Bureau of Insular Affairs (1906). Report of the Philippine Opium Commission. Washington: Government Printing Office.

White House Conference on Narcotic and Drug Abuse (1962) Proceedings. Washington: Government Printing Office.

Chapter 2

INTERLOCKING DUALITIES IN DRUG USE, DRUG CONTROL, AND CRIME

DANIEL GLASER

Two patterns of narcotic addiction may be distinguished as consequences, in large part, of two policies of drug control, and two types of crime. It will be argued that (1) these interlocking dualities reflect a complex interaction among legal, economic, physiological, psychological, and cultural variables, and (2) these interrelationships explain the association of much drug use with crime, and the failure of many large-scale efforts to control drug use.

THE TWO PATTERNS OF DRUG USE

The two patterns of narcotics use in the United States reported by Ball (1965) are illustrative of a pervasive contrast in all drug-taking which we may differentiate as *instrumental* and *appreciative*. These sometimes blend into each other so that it is difficult to distinguish them, but quite often their contrast is clear.

Instrumental drug use is intended for a specific physiological effect. The long-distance driver who takes caffein or benzedrine to stay awake, the insomniac who takes barbiturates to fall asleep, the person who takes LSD in a deliberate effort to experience hallucinations ("to take a trip"), the opiate addict who takes more opiates primarily because his body has adjusted to the presence of these drugs (developed opiate tolerance) and he suffers cramps, chills, and nausea (withdrawal effects) whenever most of the opiates previously injected are metabolized—all such use of drugs is instrumental, to create a specific effect by purely chemical reactions.

Appreciative drug use is done to conform to socio-cultural expectations in particular situations where shared norms and values encourage it. The patron at a tavern or the guest at a dinner or a party who in that situation takes the beer, wine, highballs, champagne, marijuana, or pills that are provided, if he does it mainly because he assumes it is the thing that is expected by the others there, is using drugs appreciatively. There is much diversity in norms on what one offers persons and on their obligation to accept it. Appreciative drug use is most distinctly a group phenomenon, always somewhat linked to a type of group situation—and to a particular era in the history and a particular locale in the geographic variability of cultures and subcultures.

Instrumental drug use is readily done alone. It may also be undertaken collaboratively, as when addicts share one set of "works" (cooker, tourniquet, and needle) or when an experienced LSD user stands by to protect an initiate against panic reactions when first encountering hallucinatory effects. Indeed, instrumental drug use—to seek definite physiological effects deliberately— acquires additional attractions when done in a group. These attractions are the appreciative aspects, such as sense of fellowship or intimacy with other users, sophisticated commentary on drug effects, and one's reputation as an expert or connoisseur of drugs. Only groups can provide such attractions, and they may be available from a group independently of a drug's physiological effects, or even when there are no clear physiological effects.

Some types of appreciative drug use start as collective pursuits, or are done alone while imagining how a reference group would react, or are initially motivated only by private ideas about the drug but eventually become lone activities through processes of operant or respondent conditioning. Thus tobacco smoking typically is begun in adolescent peer group situations where conformity in smoking is necessary if one is not to be mocked by the others, or it is initiated alone by an adolescent who perceives it as symbolizing adulthood. Ultimately, most smoking is habitual, however, with little conscious thought about it, and no deliberate effort to induce a particular physiological effect or an altered self-conception.

Returning to the two patterns of narcotic use in the United States (Ball, 1965), we note that the older pattern—predominant before World War II—was instrumental. Opiate use in this period usually was initiated for medical purposes: (1) to relieve the pains of arthritis and other ailments of middle and old age; (2) by women, to alleviate menstrual or menopause discomfort; (3) by many persons of diverse age under medical care, who were given morphine or other opiates to relieve discomfort from a specific injury or ailment. This instrumental pattern was especially frequent in the rural South. Continued heavy use of opiates will almost always acquire an instrumental aspect when physiological dependence occurs and the users discover that opiates relieve withdrawal symptoms; this instrumental aspect is superimposed on any appreciative basis for its use.

The newer pattern of opiate use predominant in the United States since World War II is initially more appreciative than instrumental. It occurs mainly among youth in urban areas who have a background of delinquency, of other drug taking, and of failure or dissatisfaction in conventional educational and occupational pursuits. Minority group youth from poor families are over-represented in this newer pattern of opiate use. The percentage of minority group members began to decline slowly in the late 1960s when this appreciative pattern grew more rapidly among alienated youth of higher economic class background. These alienated youth from the higher socio-economic classes have never predominated, however, in the known opiate addict population. The appreciative users within this newer pattern consume opiates in small groups, the opiate they use is almost always heroin, they often mix opiate injection with use of other types of drug, and there prevails among them much cultivation of expertise and exclusiveness in drug experiences.

Among many opiate takers today the dosage used is often so low that physiological dependence is mild or non-existent. Those who become heavy users, however, often cope with their physiological dependence by voluntarily committing themselves to detoxification centers not in order to terminate appreciative drug use, but to reduce their opiate tolerance and their consequent need to take large and regular doses instrumentally to combat withdrawal effects (Finestone, 1957; Chein, 1966; Chein et al., 1964; Glaser, Lander, and Abbot, 1971).

It will be contended that growth of the appreciative pattern of narcotic use in the United States is in large part a consequence of change in the policy and practice of drug use control by American police agencies.

THE TWO PATTERNS OF DRUG USE CONTROL

The many efforts of government agencies to control drug use can be conceptually divided into two policy extremes, *prohibition* and *regulation.* Prohibition is directed at suppressing all use of a drug, while regulation is concerned only with restricting the circumstances, procedures, and subjects of drug use. Regulation is illustrated by efforts to limit the hours and places where drugs may be distributed, the age or condition of persons to whom drugs may be sold, the personal character of drug sellers, or the methods of advertising drugs for sale. Violations of regulations are usually misdemeanors, punished most often by fines or by suspension or revocation of license. Prohibition laws usually forbid all drug use, with penalties for violation severe, although there may still be a small amount of licensing drug usage for medical or research purposes. Contrasts between an orientation geared primarily to prohibition as against a concern limited to regulation are easily cited. Most of the United States shifted from fairly complete permissiveness or only limited regulation to prohibition of alcohol use following passage of the Eighteenth Amendment to the U.S. Constitution in 1919. Prohibition was then repealed in 1933 by the Twenty-first Amendment. By many objective criteria alcohol is one of the most disabling of the drugs that man uses, but its control since repeal is limited to regulation.

The most conclusive evidence of a contrast between crucial aspects of the American and the British systems for control of opiates, indicating that the British practice regulation and the Americans prohibition, is provided by Frederick B. Glaser and John C. Ball (1971) (although they concentrate on showing that some alleged features of the British procedure are mythological). They point out that the 1914 Harrison Act of the United States and the 1920 Dangerous Drug Act of Great Britain are very similar, both being based on a 1912 International Conference at the Hague to promote opiate regulation. What they stress far less, but indicate has marked consequences for policy guidance, is that the American system gradually became one of prohibition (especially after World War II), while the British system remained more limited to regulation. Since the post-World War II legislation, opiate use has become a far costlier problem for American society than it was prior to World War II.

In Britain until the late 1960s an opiate addict could obtain a prescription for opiates, including heroin, from any physician who was convinced that his patient was physiologically dependent on opiates. In 1968 the British restricted authority to prescribe opiates for maintenance of physiological dependence to a limited number of medical facilities, and placed greater emphasis on persuading addicts to shift from heroin to the less disabling methadone or to complete abstinence.

In the United States the Harrison Act was at first interpreted diversely; the Supreme Court both upheld and reversed—in different cases—lower court actions which convicted physicians for providing opiates to addicts for relief of withdrawal symptoms (Lindesmith, 1965: 5-11). The Federal Bureau of Narcotics, established in 1930, consistently warned members of the medical profession that they risked prosecution if they prescribed opiates for addicts, and successfully prosecuted some who did. This American policy, under police rather than medical direction, changed the law's original regulatory emphasis to one of prohibition. More significantly, the Bureau and other police agencies, especially after World War II, persuaded almost all state legislatures and the federal Congress to supplement the Harrison Act by more clearly prohibitionary and punitive legislation. This legislation applied not just to opiates but also to marijuana and to a variety of other drugs, although some abused substances, such as alcohol and inhalant glue, are still only regulated rather than forbidden for most of the population.

Regulation rather than prohibition prevails in most of Europe and many other parts of the world. A salient advantage of regulation is that it permits files of police and health authorities to be much more complete and current on the number and characteristics of drug users than files where prohibition prevails and drug users are motivated to keep their drug use hidden from authorities. Further consequences of a prohibition rather than a regulation approach to drug control become evident when one examines how problems of policing depend upon the behavior to be policed.

TWO TYPES OF CRIME

Crime is any act lawfully punishable by the state. The variety of behavior which governments have declared criminal is great, and there are many ways to classify offenses, but the distinction most relevant to drug phenomena is between crimes which are *complainant-generating* and those which are not. The significance of complainant-generating crimes for public policy is that these are the offenses which the police most readily know about; they include acts such as burglarly and robbery in which people consider themselves victims and report the crime to the police, and acts which are crimes only if they occur in public, such as indecent exposure, disorderly conduct, and until quite recently, drunkenness. Offenses which are not complainant-generating are those done in private by persons who are collaborating and hence have no interest in notifying the police of their activity; these crimes include the illegal use and sale of drugs, as well as such diverse activities as prostitution, illegal gambling, and homosexual acts, e.g., victimless crimes.

Drugs and crime are most directly related when the use of drugs is defined by law as a crime. Actually, statutes rarely specify drug *usage* as an offense, even when punishment of users is their obvious intent. This intent became evident in the 1950s and 1960s when American federal and state legislators and judges not only escalated penalties for drug *possession* but stipulated that felonious possession could be proven by medical tests showing the presence of drugs in urine or blood.

It is only because of legal technicalities that lawmakers and prosecutors prefer drug possession to drug use as a criminal charge when seeking state punishment for users. Possession is more easily proven than use and has wider applicability as a charge. Penalties for possession permit prosecution not only of users but also of those who supply users, and sometimes even of those who knowingly harbor users who possess drugs. In combating sellers the laws against possession are supplemented by separate penalties for illegal sale, and by stipulation that illegal possession of large amounts of a drug is presumptive evidene of intent to sell.

These laws do much more than relate drug use to crime by definition. Their main impact lies in their social and economic consequences. When drugs can be procured only through criminal channels their price usually increases considerably, but more important, users must then obtain drugs by contacting criminals. Furthermore, if demand for drugs is relatively inelastic and the amount wanted is great, illicit manufacture and distribution become a profitable area of investment for organized crime. If the illegal drugs can be procured only at distant locations and must be extensively processed, the demand for them generates a complex network of relationships among criminals of different types and statuses of widely scattered places. It also promotes corruption of public officials at some supply or transfer points (Cressey, 1969). All of this adds to the already-mentioned criminalization of users in the retail distribution areas.

Trafficking in illegal drugs for which there is great and persistent demand is especially profitable because it is inherently impossible for the police to intercept more than a small percentage of such transactions. In complainant-generating crimes the police receive reports on a large proportion of the offenses—probably over 90 percent of certain types, such as murder and auto theft. Contrastingly, in almost all drug sales and usage no one complains to the police since sellers, buyers, and users all want secrecy and they are handling an easily hidden commodity. Furthermore, the channels of sale and resale are so extended and diverse in the transfer of the product from the raw material producer to the final consumer, and the profits so high, that police interception of people at any single point in the network of distribution does not cut off supplies for long; it simply expands the flow through other channels or promotes the creation of new sources. This opening of new routes when old ones are closed follows police action of all types, from the arrest of a street pusher to a diplomatic agreement for the suppression of opium or marijuana growth by a supplier nation. *Prohibition of drugs in great demand is feasible only in a tightly regulated society or in an isolated community; it has never closed more than a minute percentage of the actual or potential channels of supply for any profitable illegal drug market in America.*

The foregoing conclusion is well supported by recent United States history.

Interviews with college students in the 1960s revealed that their marijuana supply came via a large variety of direct and indirect routes from growing areas (mainly in Mexico), with large and small entrepreneurs—fulltime and parttime—in competition with each other (Carey, 1968). In 1969 and 1970 the U.S. Department of Justice organized "Operation Intercept," an intensive check of vehicles entering the United States from Mexico. The Department also promoted and assisted allegedly intensive Mexican police action against growing and selling marijuana in Mexico. These efforts clearly did not long affect the supply of marijuana in the United States. The extra vehicle checking soon diminished because the border crossing delay it created aroused too much protest from travelers and because it did not intercept enough marijuana to justify its cost.

Reports circulating among California students in 1971 were that it had become unsafe to purchase much marijuana as a tourist in Mexico because organized American and Mexican criminals in federation had taken over export to the United States by bribing Mexican officials. It is alleged that agents of the criminal traffic organization still sold to American tourists but urged Mexican police to arrest any tourist who purchased enough to sell in the United States. Police report, however, that students and other users now grow large amounts of marijuana in closets and other rooms with sunlamps following widespread publication of instructions in the underground press.

While authoritative statistics on these changes in supply channel are unavailable, failure of the suppression campaign is conclusively demonstrated by public surveys. The Gallup Poll, for example, reported that the percentage of American students who had used marijuana increased from 5 percent in 1967 to 22 percent in 1969 to 42 percent in December 1970. Most surveys now yield higher figures and indicate that marijuana use is increasing everywhere at a rapid rate. Most importantly, recent surveys within the general population have provided empirical data to substantiate what we have "known" for some time—the regular use of marijuana is not restricted to high school and college students nor to any specific socio-economic class (Chambers, 1971; Chambers and Inciardi, 1971). Of the regular users of marijuana identified in these comprehensive 1971 surveys, slightly over one-half (52 percent) were not students. At least 13 percent of all *white collar workers* have some marijuana experience and 5 percent currently smoke the drug at least six times per month. At least 15 percent of all *blue collar workers* have some marijuana experience and 4 percent smoke marijuana at least six times per month.

In light of this experience with marijuana it is difficult to believe that American efforts to pay Turkey for suppressing opium growth and to assist the French in barring manufacture of heroin from morphine will long affect the heroin supply wherever it is in great demand in the United States. As long as a lucrative heroin market exists and many alternative channels of supply are feasible, diverse sources will be developed to pursue the profits in sale of heroin. Increasing arrests of South Americans and Southeast Asians for heroin smuggling suggest that alternative routes already are established and functioning. A more effective control policy might well be to try to alter the demand and the sources of supply to meet it. This policy implication is supported by examination of further ramifications of American experience in control and treatment of drug use.

OTHER IMPLICATIONS OF THE INTERLOCKING DUALITIES

The prohibition approach to drug control in the United States before World War II apparently was not effective enough to prevent the instrumental narcotics users of that period from obtaining morphine, codeine, or other opiates through medical supply channels. Most had begun drug use under medical auspices, and they maintained contacts and developed strategies (e.g., feigning illness, going to several physicians, forging prescriptions) to obtain opiates later when their drug appetite was due purely to addiction.

An acute shortage of opiates for addicts developed in the United States during World War II because shipments from opium-producing countries were cut off or impaired by enemy military actions. The armed forces often preempted the medical opiate supply, and addict contacts with physicians or pharmacists were frequently interrupted by geographic movement of much of the American population. Since money was plentiful and addicts were desperate, the price they would pay for illegal opiates increased, and the tremendous profits in narcotics selling attracted professional criminals. They had to be internationally organized to procure opiates independently of medical channels. Also, since heroin was used in medical practice in the rest of the world, especially in treating addicts—although banned to medical practice by the United States government—the opiates imported by criminal organizations increasingly consisted of heroin rather than morphine or other opiates. Because heroin is speedily metabolized, it relieves withdrawal symptoms more rapidly than do most other opiates, and its presence is more apt to be associated with distinct sensations which some may regard as euphoric. Likewise, its effects wear off more rapidly than do other opiates, and this quality results in its users having more urgent needs for more drugs to relieve withdrawal symptoms.

The entrance of organized crime into large-scale narcotic trafficking after World War II more than met the demand of the older instrumental addict; these organizations also developed a new and greater market of appreciative users in the drug peddlers' home neighborhoods, the slums. As indicated earlier, when compared to the instrumental addicts the new users were younger, much more often members of minority groups, more frequently used other illegal drugs before opiates or with opiates, and more often had prior records of crime and delinquency (Ball, 1965; O'Donnell, 1966). Whenever their use of heroin was sufficient to make them aware of withdrawal symptoms and the relief of these symptoms by more opiates, these appreciative users also became instrumental users.

The causal processes leading to initial opiate use seem to be distinctly different in the newer than in the older of the two patterns of use in the United States. The instrumental users generally start taking narcotics for medical purposes, but the appreciative users do it—as they would put it—"for kicks." Drug use is often called an escape. Indeed, for the instrumental user the narcotics provide an escape from pain and stress, but for the appreciative user the drugs are perhaps not so much an escape as an opportunity. In the appreciative user's social circle and with his view of the world, opiate use represents a chance to feel superior to the "squares," to seem more sophisticated and more daring. This is an especially attractive opportunity for youths who obtain an early sense of manliness and leadership as juvenile delinquents but thereafter are handicapped as young adults by having poor school records and no salable work skills. Being slum residents and belonging to minority groups add to their handicaps in legitimate employment, and thus augment the comparative appeal of the more accessible opportunities to be connoisseurs of drugs. Even the various types of crime pursued professionally to support drug use, the "hustles" of addicts, become a source of pride in accomplishment that provide much prestige in drug-using social circles. The interpretation in this paragraph has been called the "relative deprivation-differential anticipation" theory of opiate use (Glaser, Lander, and Abbot, 1971). It is applicable primarily to the post-World War II American slum youth user, but not to instrumental users.

Two direct and four indirect actual or alleged relationships between crime and drug use are relevant to the interlocking dualities. The first direct relationship has already been mentioned, the fact that prohibition laws make drug use or possession a crime in itself. It is significant to note that laws against public drunkenness—the most frequent basis for arrest in the United States— might almost be thought of as making heavy use of alcohol a crime, but these laws make drunkenness criminal only when manifested in a public place, and most states have abolished even these drunkenness laws.

Drunkenness offenses might also be interpreted as instances of the second direct relationship between drugs and crime, one more often alleged than actual, that the chemical action of a drug on the human body causes a person to commit crimes. This is the "dope fiend" mythology widely promulgated by proponents of prohibition laws, notably those against alcohol, opiate, and marijuana. They allege that many assaults, robberies, and rapes result from users being "crazed" by these drugs. Two distinct considerations must be taken into account to replace this simplistic interpretation by a more adequate understanding.

First of all, it should be kept in mind that several of the most widely abused of the illegal drugs have physiological effects that impede both criminal and non-criminal activity; at least for that period of time when the physiological effects are the most pronounced, they evoke drowsiness and indifference to one's surroundings, needs, or desires. This statement applies most strongly to the opiates and barbiturates, less to marijuana and to LSD and other hallucinogens, and probably least of all to the stimulants. The most frequently used drugs that are appropriately labeled stimulants are the amphetamines and cocaine. They arouse hypersensitivity for a limited period, often followed later by heightened irritability, evocation of latent paranoid tendencies, and ultimately, heightened fatigue.

A second consideration to be noted in assessing "dope fiend" theories is that the purely psychological effects of drugs upon behavior are primarily through effects on mood and physical or mental capacity; they cannot alone cause specific types of complex activity, such as a premeditated offense, any more than they can directly and alone cause a person to solve a mathematical problem or speak a foreign language. Complex social behavior requires a learning experience, not a chemical intake, so drugs affect crime only through physiological processes indirectly related to behavior rather than determining conduct. Such an indirect effect is the reduction of inhibitions by alcohol or the heightening or irritability by stimulants. These effects are least characteristic of the opiates and marijuana, the drugs against which the "dope fiend" mythology has most often been promulgated in recent years.

Alcohol has been found in the blood of a majority of persons tested when accused of assaults, rapes, and murders. Alcohol has also been found in most victims of assault and murder (Glaser and O'Leary, 1966). Subcultures of violence happen to value both drinking and an assaultive response to insult as symbolizing manliness, but not all subcultures valuing drinking are also subcultures emphasizing violence. Indeed, not all who drink commit crimes when drunk. They may have attitudes conducive to crime which they normally inhibit but which are aroused when the physiological effect of alcohol on the brain reduces critical thinking and inhibitory processes. Yet even reduction of inhibition is not purely physiological; how one behaves when drunk is very much a function of one's perception of group expectations or tolerance in the situation where one is drunk, just as behavior when sober reflects one's view of what is expected if sober. That is why a given amount of alcohol consumed is more likely to be followed by deviant behavior in some groups or situations than in others (MacAndrew and Edgerton, 1969).

The physiological effects from large dosage of stimulants, such as the amphetamines, may make an assaultively inclined person more easily aroused than he otherwise would be, but the frequency of such drug-induced offenses probably is negligible compared to other drug-linked crime. *The reduction of seriously assaultive crime is much more likely to be fostered by gun control, and by upgrading the public's education and reducing its poverty, than by any control policy for any type of drug, including alcohol.*

The remaining three indirect relationships of drug use to crime are all, in fact, effects of prohibition policies much more than of drug use itself. One such effect, of course, is the fact that persons who are addicted but cannot afford the price of drugs will commit crimes to get money to pay for drugs. This effect is most pronounced in the drugs which are both most addictive and most prohibitied, which in the United States means primarily the opiates. Heavy dosage heroin addicts spend from $20 to $100 or more per day on drugs, and since they are disproportionately from poor backgrounds they cannot pay for this from legitimate income. Some speculators have suggested that a majority of the prostitution and a large percentage of theft and burglary in New York City are committed to support opiate addiction. It should also be noted, however, that the involvement of addicts in the totality of these crimes is certainly far less than generally believed or publicized. Such addiction-supporting crimes are also extensive everywhere else in the United States where the "new" pattern of appreciative heroin use has resulted in physiological dependence and hence instrumental use.

Drugs which are regulated are generally not as expensive as drugs which are prohibited. Because addictive regulated drugs, such as alcohol and barbiturates, are not as costly as addictive prohibitied drugs, those addicted to regulated drugs generally support their habit by legitimate earnings, or commit only petty and infrequent property crimes for funds to purchase drugs. Thus petty theft and forgery are associated with chronic alcoholism, but this association is not as consistent as that between serious property crime and addiction to heroin. *The first of the distinctly prohibition-engendered types of crime is addiction-supporting professional property crime.*

The involvement of large-scale criminal organizations in the sale of illegal drugs is a second effect of prohibition, already indicated. Because these criminal entrepreneurs operate outside the law in their drug transactions, they are not bound by business etiquette in their competition with each other, in their collection of debts, or in their non-drug investments. Terror, violence, extortion, bribery, or any other expedient strategy is relied upon by these criminals not only in the sale of illegal goods or services, but also in their investments in legitimate businesses of all types, from taverns to savings and loan associations (Cressey, 1969).

The most serious impact of prohibition of drug use on crime probably is that which is most indirect—its consequences for the total administration of justice in a society. This effect occurs only when the prohibited drug is widely used, as was alcohol when the Eighteenth Amendment was in force, and as marijuana is today. While police efforts to enforce prohibition lead to the arrest of only a minute percentage of users and distributors, the number of arrestees for a prohibited drug that is very popular is usually sufficient to overload the police and the courts; such overloads evoke grossly irregular procedures to cope with work pressures. Indeed, difficulties of enforcing a law against offenses that are not complainant-generating frequently cause police to rely mainly on informers, to entrap, to use wiretaps or hidden microphones ("bugs"), to arrest or search before they have either a warrant or probable cause, and to violate the law by offering drugs to physiologically dependent addicts if they inform. Under these conditions, hasty and inconsistent bargaining occurs in the courts in order to clear the dockets, so that penalties bear little consistent relationship to offense or to the character of the offender, but are highly related to the social status of the accused and to his retention of an astute lawyer. The result of these conditions may be a heightened disrespect for the police and the courts in large sections of the public, which thereby acquire attitudes conducive to other types of law violation and to non-cooperation in law enforcement situations, such as testifying in complainant-generating offenses.

The many types of interaction among diverse variables that have been described as functions of the interlocking dualities in drug use, drug control, and crime may affect each other in a dialectical manner. As has already been suggested in part, this may account for a repetitive historical cycle in drug control policies.

TRENDS IN DRUG CONTROL POLICY

Somewhat parallel sequences seem to have occurred in the social control of several types of drugs, suggesting that similar causal events were responsible for changes in social policies for them, and that the same type of progression can be anticipated in the control of other drugs. Three stages can be distinguished in this sequence: *permissiveness, prohibition, regulation.* The shift from one stage to the next is not always abrupt, however, so the coexistence of the two stages is possible, and none may ever completely prevail.

Permissiveness exists towards the use of any drug as long as its effects are not seen as threatening, especially if the drug is smoked or taken in some other fashion which does not suggest that it is a medication. If the drug is perceived as a medication, standard pharmaceutical regulations may be imposed on its distribution, but these will be only minimally restrictive as long as the drug is not viewed as dangerous.

Social movements to enact *prohibition* laws have been promoted by "moral entrepreneurs" when they regarded a drug as dangerous and promulgated an interpretation of its use as morally reprehensible (Becker, 1963). When that which is to be prohibited is used only by small or low-status segments of the population—as was the case with opiates and marijuana in 1914 and 1937 respectively, and again in the 1950s when legislation was enacted prohibiting them—passage of the legislation reflects a combination of the prohibitionists' exaggerated accounts of the harmful effects of these substances and the ignorance or indifference on this matter of the rest of the population. Under these circumstances legislators have a highly vocal group against them if they oppose prohibition, but there is little objection if they support it, so they vote for drug prohibition as though they were voting for Motherhood, even when they have no direct awareness as a problem. When a drug is used by large and influential segments of the population, however, prohibition movements polarize the electorate. Such polarization in recent years has usually occurred only after failure of prohibition to be effective rather than before it was enacted.

The decline and fall of a prohibition policy appears to have several stages. The first stage is an increased popularity of the prohibited substance in an influential segment of the population. Sometimes the prohibition of a drug makes its appreciative use more attractive to youth, as drug use then symbolizes independence from adult authority. College students in the 1920s apparently played a major role in the growth of opposition to the Eighteenth Amendment; as youth away from home they were inclined to experiment with deviant conduct, and after graduation they eventually became a new elite which had experienced the prohibited activity as not dangerous. The use of marijuana is now reported by a majority of college students, and especially among those at private colleges and universities and among fraternity members, who are the students most likely to be influential in the future. An additional source of opposition to prohibition is the fact that prosecution of students, especially those in expensive schools and fraternities, gives a criminal record to children of the most respected and influential segments of the population. Such events enlist opposition to prohibition even among parents who do not use the drug.

When influential opposition to prohibition grows, the law tends to be enforced very selectively, so that only those of low status or in large-scale violations are likely to be prosecuted. This differential law enforcement occurred under the Eighteenth Amendment and is presently occurring under marijuana prohibition. Only a minute proportion of middle class youth arrested for marijuana possession are now convicted for this offense, and few of those convicted are imprisoned. This inequity, however, increases disrespect for the law and thereby accelerates repeal of prohibition. Opposition to severe punishment for heroin use is also likely to increase due to the growing proportion of youthful heroin addicts who are not of minority group or lower-class background, and the large proportion who are veterans of the war in Vietnam.

When moderate use of a prohibited drug is clearly not dangerous to health or to self-control, the repeal of prohibition is preceded by a reduction or elimination of penalties for moderate use. This occurred shortly before repeal of the Eighteenth Amendment, when beer with 3.2 percent or less alcohol was legally defined as not an intoxicating beverage, hence not subject to prohibition. Currently, penalties for the possession of small amounts of marijuana are being reduced in many states that have changed this offense from a felony to a misdemeanor. Rigorous research—rather than clinical impressions from atypical samples—is demonstrating that marijuana is not as disabling as is alcohol after each occasion of extensive use. The many mental and general-hospital patients committed for the effects of chronic alcoholism suggest that in long-term heavy usage marijuana is also probably no more dangerous psychologically or physically than alcohol. Pressure for repeal of marijuana prohibition is likely to be augmented as such evidence accumulates.

When addiction to a prohibited drug is very clearly dangerous to health, as is addiction to alcohol or to opiates, prior to repeal of the prohibition there is a growth in the perception of the addiction as a health problem rather than a moral issue. This changed perspective leads to what Pitts (1968) calls "the medicalization of deviance"; the deviant is committed to a hospital instead of to a prison and the objective becomes to cure him rather than to punish him. This reaction to various types of drug addict accelerated rapidly after 1962, when the Supreme Court—in Robinson v. California—ruled that laws which made it a crime to be an addict were unconstitutional, but suggested in this ruling that it would be legitimate to declare addiction a disease justifying civil commitment for treatment in a state hospital.

In the 1960s California and New York developed large-scale civil commitment institutions in which addicts are confined until deemed ready for conditional release. Most of these commitments are, for the addicts, an alternative to prison sentences for complainant-generating crimes in which they engaged to support their habit. The period of civil control, in or out of the institution, is normally three years in New York and seven in California, with earlier discharge possible if there is no relapse to drug use during a prolonged release to "aftercare" supervision. Addicts cooperate in being committed if they think that they will get their freedom earlier in this way than if sentenced to prison. A few even voluntarily commit themselves for treatment, but for most it is still an involuntary participation in treatment with their major motivation for cooperation the prospect of earlier release if staff write favorable reports on them.

Civil commitment agencies have not been markedly successful in curing addicts. Indeed, imperfect available follow-up data suggest that relapse to drug use is probably more frequent among addicts civilly committed to state addiction treatment centers than among addicts sentenced to state prisons. The reason for this failure may well be the appreciative aspect of the post-World War II pattern of narcotics use. Confining addicts exclusively and involuntarily with other addicts for treatment they do not really desire means placing them in a social environment consisting almost entirely of persons sharing the drug subculture and longing to return to it. With the extensive time for intimate talks that characterizes institutional life, the hospitalized addicts spend a greater part of their time exclusively in groups discussing and endorsing procurement and enjoyment of drugs than they would on the outside or in a prison. In these settings prestige comes from sophistication in drug talk, and much suggestion and support is heard there for the justification of drug use and for the avoidance of a sense of degradation by it. This intensity of socialization in the appreciative drug use subculture is the greatest defect of treatment in civil commitment facilities; it is a much more serious defect than the other features for which these institutions have been frequently criticized, such as their location in what previously were prison buildings rather than hospitals, the prior employment of much of their staff in prisons, and the few differences between their programs and those of prisons.

Regulation as a means of drug control usually consists of licensing the distribution of a drug under conditions that minimize some of the social costs of its unrestricted use. Thus most states or cities have "good character" tests in the licensing of alcoholic beverage purveyors, they penalize sales to persons already intoxicated, they restrict the hours and location of sales places, and they prohibit sales to children. The United States government bans advertisement of liquor on television, and many communities restrict the size or location of alcoholic beverage advertising signs.

Great Britain and most other Western European countries regulate opiate sales to addicts instead of prohibiting them. They require authorization from designated physicians for sale of a drug. These physicians determine the amount and frequency of opiate provision for each addict. In the United States methadone maintenance programs may be considered a form of licensed distribution of opiates, since methadone is a synthetic opiate. It is much less disabling than heroin or morphine because it metabolizes more slowly, and it can be taken orally instead of by injection. The British are also increasingly switching addicts to methadone. With both British distribution of opiates and American methadone maintenance programs there is much less crime by the addicts than were opiates are prohibited, because addicts get drugs free or for a nominal fee, and drug-taking under medical supervision is less likely to be disabling than unregulated drug-taking. The exorbitant prices now paid for prohibited opiates by addicts is due primarily to the charges levied by organized criminals; opiates, and especially methadone, are relatively cheap drugs when regulated instead of prohibited. Thus the linkage of opiate use both to addiction-supporting and to organized crime under prohibition policies has been almost completely eliminated under regulation. This feature, plus the higher failure rate and higher cost of civil commitment programs, has resulted in a rapid growth of methadone maintenance.

When a drug is widely used in legitimate medicine and has no satisfactory substitutes in such use, but is also dangerously misused outside of medical practice, regulation through pharmaceutical distribution control procedures prevails and prohibition is not probable. Such regulation apparently was the purpose of the Harrison Act in the United States and of similar opiate control legislation in Britain and other countries after the Hague Conference of 1912; these laws differed in effect only because that of the United States was interpreted as forbidding physicians to prescribe opiates to addicts, and was augmented after World War II by more clearly prohibitive and punitive state and federal laws. Regulation is still the primary control for barbiturates and amphetamines, two groups of drugs in widespread medical use which are also frequently abused and can be extremely dangerous. Public concern over abuses and dangers in this circumstance of widespread medical use leads mainly to tightening of manufacturing and distribution controls, but does not approach complete prohibition because of the many interests of patients, physicians, and pharmaceutical firms in maintaining ready access to the drugs for medical purposes.

Projecting the trends now evident, in the light of the consequences noted for alternative policies it seems safe to predict that the ultimate form of control for all non-medical drugs in the United States will greatly resemble the present controls for alcohol. People will seldom be confined involuntarily just because they use a drug; all drugs will be regulated, but rigorous and punitive prohibition will be abandoned. Those who use drugs to the point of impairing their health or their work performance, but commit no crimes against anyone, will be recruited for diverse forms of voluntary treatment. These forms will include: (1) mutual aid groups of ex-addicts in the Alcholics Anonymous and Synanon tradition; (2) drug antagonists, such as antabuse for alcohol and naloxone or cyclazocine for opiates; (3) drug substitution programs, such as methadone; (4) psychotherapy or sociotherapy; (5) mixtures and variations of the foregoing. Involuntary treatment will occur only if the person commits a crime against someone else's person or property, in which case the treatment will be part of a total correctional program in an institution or in the community.

Probably in the future drugs will be available to those who crave them sufficiently, with no risk of criminal prosecution if they use authorized procurement procedures and only fines or other lesser penalties for illegal use. The legitimate procurement procedures may be fairly simple for the less dangerous drug like marijuana, but the dispensation of more dangerous drugs will doubtless be under medical supervision. There will continue to be much interest in discouraging drug use, but this will be attempted primarily by public education, by restrictions on drug advertising, and by setting limits to the places and conditions where drugs are sold.

These trends will not completely eliminate all association between drug use and crime, but they should result in marked reduction of property crimes committed to pay for drug purchases, and they should eliminate the role of organized crime in drug distribution. Perhaps most important, these trends should reduce the differential association of drug users with traditional criminals, their being labeled as criminals, and hence their development of identifications and attitudes favorable to all types of law violation.

REFERENCES

BALL, J. C. (1965) "Two patterns of narcotic drug addiction in the United States." Journal of Criminal Law, Criminology and Police Science 56 (June): 203-211.

BECKER, H. S. (1963) Outsiders. New York: Free Press.

CAREY, J. T. (1968) The College Drug Scene. Englewood Cliffs, N.J.: Prentice-Hall.

CHAMBERS, C. D. (1971) Differential Drug Use Within the New York State Labor Force. New York: Narcotic Addiction Control Commission.

CHAMBERS, C. D. and J. A. INCIARDI (1971) An Assessment of Drug Use Within the General Population (Special Report No. 2). New York: Narcotic Addiction Control Commission.

CHEIN, I. (1966) "Psychological, social and epidemiological factors in drug addiction," in Rehabilitating the Narcotic Addict. Washington: Government Printing Office.

CHEIN, I., D. L. GERARD, R. S. LEE, and E. ROSENFELD (1964) The Road to H. New York: Basic Books.

CRESSEY, D. R. (1969) Theft of a Nation. New York: Harper and Row.

FINESTONE, H. (1957) "Cats, kicks and color." Social Problems 5 (July): 3-13.

GLASER, D. (1971) "Criminology and public policy." American Sociologist 6 (June): 30-37.

GLASER, D., B. LANDER and W. ABBOTT (1971) "Opiate addicted and non-addicted siblings in a slum area." Social Problems 18 (Spring): 510-521.

GLASER, D. and V. O'LEARY (1966) The Alcoholic Offender. Washington: Government Printing Office.

GLASER, F. B. and J. C. BALL (1971) "The British narcotic 'register' in 1970: a factual review." Journal of the Amer. Medical Association 216 (May 17): 1177-1182.

LINDESMITH, A. R. (1965) The Addict and the Law. Bloomington: Indiana Univ. Press.

MacANDREW, C. and R. B. EDGERTON (1969) Drunken Compartment. Chicago: Aldine.

O'DONNELL, J. A. (1966) "Narcotic addiction and crime." Social Problems 13 (Spring): 374-385.

PITTS, J. R. (1968) "Social control: (1) the concept," in International Encyclopedia of the Social Sciences. New York: Macmillan.

Chapter 3

CRIME AND THE ADDICT:
BEYOND COMMON SENSE

LEROY C. GOULD

Drug addiction is a major contributor to our nation's crime problem. Most Americans, including many social scientists and drug control policymakers, accept this hypothesis as true without serious question. Street crime has been on the increase, addiction has been on the increase, addicts steal to support their drug habits; surely it follows that addiction contributes to our overall increase in crime.

In one sense, of course, the hypothesis is true by definition. Since possessing illegal drugs is itself a crime, and since addicts have to possess drugs in order to be addicts, addiction increases the total amount of crime. It is not possession, however, or for that matter the illegal sale of drugs which is at issue. Instead, most people are concerned with the impact of drug addiction on "street crime": robbery, assault, larceny, burglary, etc. Whether or not drug addiction increases the rate of these crimes, although it may seem very likely on common-sense grounds, is an empirical matter which, surprisingly, has little direct evidence in its support.

But calculations based on indirect evidence are compelling. On the issue of addict theft, consider the following:

There are 100,000 addicts in New York City with an average habit of $30.00 per day. This means addicts must have some $1.1 billion a year to pay for their heroin (100,000 x 365 x $30.00). Because the addict must sell the property he steals to a fence for only about a quarter of its value, or less, addicts must steal some $4 to $5 billion a year to pay for their heroin [Singer, 1971: 3].

Other calculations, however, indicate that these computations must be incorrect since there is nowhere near $4 to $5 billion worth of theft a year in New York City, in total:

If we credit addicts with *all* of the shoplifting, *all* of the theft from homes, and *all* of the theft from persons, total property stolen by addicts in a year in New York City amounts to some $330 million. You can throw in all the "fudge factors" you want, add all the other miscellaneous crimes that addicts commit, but no matter what you do, it is difficult to find a basis for estimating that addicts steal over a half billion dollars a year, and a quarter billion looks like a better estimate, although perhaps on the high side. After all, there must be some thieves who are not addicts [Singer, 1971: 5-6].

Singer concludes that there must be fewer than 100,000 addicts in New York City. One could also conclude that addicts commit far less crime than most people think. Either conclusion would have to be based, however, on very meager evidence concerning either how many addicts there are, or how much the "typical" addict steals.

Estimating the number of addicts in the population is an extremely dubious activity. The use of drugs is illegal and people are not inclined to divulge information willingly about their illegal affairs. Information about a person's addiction status does not usually become known to outsiders until that person has come into contact with a medical or law enforcement agency. An addict registry, which begins with the names of those who have come into contact with these agencies, will underestimate the number of people who are using drugs unless it includes a correction factor to overcome this obvious bias. Since these correction factors themselves can be based on little more than hunch or political necessity, however, final estimates may be grossly incorrect. One careful analysis of an addict registry in New York (Chein, 1964: 17-22) concluded that it probably overestimated the number of addicts.

Are Addicts Responsible for Crimes of Violence?

Of the seven "serious" crimes included in the FBI Index of Crimes (manslaughter, rape, assault, robbery,[1] burglary, larceny, and auto theft) Americans are most fearful of the first four, crimes against the person

(President's Crime Commission, 1967a: 87-89). But, with the exception of robbery, these are not the crimes that drug addicts are most likely to commit.

A recent study contracted by the U.S. Bureau of Narcotics and Dangerous Drugs (BNDD) (1971) provides some of the most comprehensive data on this point. Beginning with 1,722 persons arrested for serious crimes other than violation of narcotic laws[2] in Chicago, New Orleans, San Antonio, New York City,[3] Los Angeles, and St. Louis, this study team conducted lengthy interviews pertaining to present and past drug use, analyzed urine specimins for the presence of illegal drugs (heroin, cocaine, methadone, amphetemines, and barbiturates), and checked all names against the BNDD registry of drug users and the FBI Registry of Criminal Offenders. Table 1 summarizes some of the findings of this study.

Twenty-three percent of the arrestees in this study were, as determined by their own admission or by urine analysis, heroin users. Another 7 percent, by their own admission, had previously used heroin but were currently non-users. Thirty-two percent said that they had used other illegal drugs. Drug users,

Table 1.   ARRESTEES IN SIX AMERICAN CITIES WHO WERE DRUG USERS AND NON-DRUG USERS

	Current Heroin Users[1]		Past Heroin Users[2]		Other Drug Users[3]		Non-Drug Users		Total	
	N	%	N	%	N	%	N	%	N	%
Serious crimes Against the person[4]	30	7	14	12	93	17	163	25	300	17
Less serious crimes against the person[5]	14	3	5	4	46	8	77	12	142	8
Robbery	94	23	20	17	94	17	79	12	287	17
Other property crimes[6]	237	61	75	64	253	47	265	40	830	49
All other crimes[7]	26	6	3	3	60	11	74	11	163	9
Total	401	100	117	100	546	100	658	100	1722	100
Percent of grand total	23		7		32		38		100	

1. Determined by urine analysis or positive interview response.
2. Determined by interview.
3. Marijuana, barbiturates, and amphetamines—use determined by urine analysis and interview.
4. Criminal homicide, forcible rape, aggravated assault, and kidnapping.
5. Other assault and sex offenses (except forcible rape and commercialized vice).
6. Larceny, burglary, theft, auto theft, arson, forgery, counterfeiting, fraud, embezzlement, stolen property, and vandalism.
7. Weapons, prostitution, and commercialized vice.

especially heroin users, were most heavily represented among those arrested for crimes against property (61 percent for current heroin users), and least represented among those arrested for crimes against the person (7 percent for current heroin users in the serious crimes against the person category and 3 percent in the less serious crimes category).

How Much Do Addicts Steal?

It is clear from this study that very large percentages of those arrested for theft are drug users. This does not, however, tell us how many drug users are thieves or how much addict-thieves steal. Until recently, these were mostly matters of guess, based on interviews with known "hard-core" addicts. Some very recent studies have changed this picture somewhat.

The best of these studies was conducted by Patrick Hughes and his colleagues (1971) in Chicago. Beginning with a "natural" heroin-using community which was defined as those who regularly frequented one drug-selling "copping" center,[4] the researchers, through interviews and observations, found out the major occupations of 104 heroin addicts.[5] The occupational breakdown of this heroin-using community was as follows:

	%
Big Dealers	4
Street Dealers	6
Parttime Dealers	15
Bag Followers	3
Touts	5
Hustlers	38
Workers	29

Dealers, bag followers, and touts are all involved in one way or another with the sale of drugs; big dealers wholesale drugs, street dealers and parttime dealers retail them, touts carry out liaison work between dealers and buyers, and bag followers promote sales for a particular dealer. Hustlers engage in illegal, but not directly drug-related, economic pursuits. Workers, although they may engage in illegal economic pursuits from time to time, receive the bulk of their income from legitimate sources: work, welfare, or family. In all, 33 percent of the population received their primary income through the sale of drugs, 29 percent depended primarily upon legitimate sources of income to support themselves and their drug use, and 38 percent were involved in non-drug crime as a primary source of income. How many of this last group were thieves, or how much of their total criminal activity was theft, is not reported (indeed, the authors did not know for sure), but shoplifting is mentioned as the single most frequently used hustle. Prostitution, pimping, gambling, and various con-games have often been cited by addicts in other studies as commonly employed hustles, so it is fair to say that not all of the hustling was theft. Even a generous estimate would not place the proportion higher than one third, and a lower figure is quite likely.

The most readily available source of income for addicts in the United States is drug sales or activities closely related to drug sales. Even after excluding drug importing and wholesaling, which are reportedly closed to addicts, there are still huge profits in street dealing. In New York City and surrounding communities, according to the report of current dealers, profit margins for retail drug sales range between 100 and 200 percent. From this it follows that half or more of the money spent on heroin could be obtained through the sale of heroin. If all heroin users used the same amount, then hypothetically half the drug users could finance their drug use by selling to the other half. In practice, this does not follow directly, however, since some of those who sell drugs support themselves as well as their drug habit through income from drug sales. Dealing is their occupation. Hughes found that 33 percent of his study population made their living through the sale of drugs. This is very understandable in light of the high profit margins in this line of work.

Although not as representative of heroin-using populations in the community as the Chicago study, those coming into various treatment centers for heroin addiction offer another estimate of how many heroin users are engaged in theft. In the Haight-Ashbury Free Medical Clinic in San Francisco (Newmeyer, 1972), the percentage of thieves was found to be 39, and another 10 percent claimed to pursue thievery, burglary, or "hustling" stolen goods as a secondary source of support. Table 2 gives a complete breakdown of response to the question: "By what means do you support your habit?"

Table 2. PRIMARY AND SECONDARY MEANS OF SUPPORT OF 259 DRUG PATIENTS AT THE HAIGHT-ASHBURY MEDICAL CENTERS

	Primary Support	*Secondary Support*
Job	15%	3%
Spouse	4	1
Welfare	4	1
Other legal	13	18
Thievery, burglary, or "hustling" of stolen goods	39	10
Dealing	21	7
Pimping or prostituting	5	2
Total	100%	
Number	259	
Non-respondents	44	

SOURCE: Newmeyer, 1972.

Since those people who have turned to theft to support their heroin use are probably more likely to come to the attention of treatment programs than the occasional heroin "chippers" who support their heroin use out of legitimate sources of income, studies based on populations of addict-patients probably overestimate the proportion of all heroin users who are involved in theft. Even among this population, however, less than half were involved in theft on a regular or parttime basis. But whatever the proportion involved in theft, a half, a third, or a quarter, addicts could account for a lot of theft.

Do Addicts Steal Because They Are Addicted?

That some addicts steal, however, does not necessarily mean that addiction per se increases theft. For this to follow, it would have to be true that addicts steal *because* they are addicted, or at least that they steal *more* than they would have otherwise in order to support their drug habits. Such a conclusion would appear to be quite reasonable: black-market drugs are extremely expensive in the United States; addicts will pay any price to obtain the drugs they need; theft is one way of obtaining the money to afford these high prices. Surely addiction causes addicts, at least some of them, to steal. Perhaps they might have stolen some anyway had they not been addicts, but addiction must increase the amount that they steal.

If drugs were not expensive, if addicts did not have to steal to support their cost, and if addicts were still found to steal more than non-addicts, then this conclusion would not seem so obvious. Indeed, one might, under these conditions, conclude that people who are inclined to be addicts, for whatever reason, might also be inclined to be thieves and that although the two seem to go together, the one does not necessarily cause the other. This is exactly the conclusion reached by many researchers in Great Britain, where drugs are available at low cost to addicts in state-run clinics but where addicts have been found to have a relatively high theft rate (James and D'Orban, 1970). In England, where addicts do not have to steal in order to buy their drugs but steal anyway, people conclude that addict-thieves are thieves first and addicts second; in America where addicts steal and drugs are expensive, people conclude that addict-thieves are addicts first and thieves second.

Americans and the British may, of course, both be correct for their respective countries. There are less than 5,000 registered addicts in Britain (May, 1972) which gives a per-capita addiction rate which is surely several orders of magnitude lower than that in this country. Perhaps those inclined to get involved with drugs in Britain are different from those who get involved with drugs in the United States. Perhaps American addicts do steal because they are addicted while their British counterparts do not. More likely, however, American and

British addicts have more in common than their respective narcotics control systems and British addicts, like some American addicts, would steal to support their drug use, too, if they had to pay American prices for heroin. It is probably not addiction per se which causes theft, but addiction coupled with high prices for drugs.

Although the data are of dubious validity, those data which do exist suggest that American addicts by and large do steal more when they are using drugs than they did before becoming addicted. The most commonly cited data on this point comes from interviews with applicants to drug treatment programs and from those who have been enrolled in such programs for a period of time. Those entering treatment typically report far more involvement with theft than those who have been in treatment for awhile (Gearing, 1970).

There are two biases immediately apparent in these data, however. First of all, addicts trying to get into treatment programs, many of which have long waiting lists, are probably inclined at the time of their first interview to exaggerate the seriousness of their circumstances, including their involvement in crime; the more pathetic and desperate their situation, the greater their chances for early program acceptance. Once in treatment, however, the pressures on drug users would seem to be just the opposite. That is, they would be inclined to put forth the best image possible, including a de-emphasis on their involvement in crime. Despite the professed anonymity of interviews in drug treatment clinics, it is doubtful that drug patients take these assurances very seriously. A second bias in these studies concerns the fact that drug users more likely than not apply for treatment *when* they have been arrested. Not only does applying for treatment look good to the sentencing judge, but treatment is sometimes a court stipulation or condition of probation. Therefore, drug users are most likely to find their way to a treatment program at that point in their drug use career when they are also involved with crime. A year or two earlier, they might not have been thieves. Program applicants, therefore, are not a valid comparison group for drug treatment patients. Nevertheless, the BNDD study of arrestees (1971: 333-369) described earlier also found higher arrest rates for those who used drugs than for non-drug users, and this study, since it did not involve addict-patients, was not vulnerable to the two biases cited above. The study was based on interviews and law enforcement agency records, however, which surely are not free from their own forms of bias.

Does Addiction Increase Theft?

Nevertheless, it still seems reasonable to conclude that American addicts, at least some of them, probably do steal to support the cost of drugs. But this in itself does not mean necessarily that addiction increases the total amount of theft in America.

Most people seem to take for granted that the total amount of theft is determined simply by how many people there are who are inclined to steal. As more people, such as drug addicts, become so inclined, the amount of theft increases.

This view is too simple. There are factors other than the willingness of people to steal which also affect the total amount of theft. One of these factors is the risk involved in theft. Another is the blackmarket for stolen goods.

Any property (other than cash) which is stolen for profit must be sold on a blackmarket before a monetary profit can be realized. A blackmarket, though, just like a legitimate market, is not limitless. Surely it must be subject to the classical economic factors of supply and demand.[6]

Demand in the blackmarket, at least in part, should depend on how many people there are who are willing to buy goods which have been discounted through the mechanism of theft. Some people would not pay anything for such goods. Others would be willing to buy them at only a slight discount over prevailing prices in the legal market. Just how many people there are in the market for stolen goods, then, should vary with the discount prevailing at the time.

Supply in the blackmarket should depend upon such factors as the availability of goods for theft, the risk involved in stealing them, how much time and energy it takes to market the goods, and how many people there are who are available to assume these "costs" of doing business. Presumably, some people would not steal no matter how great the potential earnings or how small the risks, while others will take great risks for only small returns. Just how many people are involved in theft at any one time, though, should be influenced by these risk-gains criteria which should in turn be dependent, at least in part, upon the prevailing prices for stolen goods in the blackmarket.

Theft of cash, quite obviously, would not depend upon a blackmarket. It should depend, however, upon the risks involved versus the potential gains. Not only is cash highly liquid and thus among the most heavily guarded properties in our society, but there is very little of it anymore left in a position where the average thief can get at it. Few people keep much cash in their homes—they use banks instead; and few people carry much cash on their person—they use credit cards or checks. Even businesses have come to rely more and more upon checks and credit cards which reduce the supply of cash available for theft from those sources.

As addicts enter the labor force of thieves, they will probably drive down prices for stolen goods. This in turn should do two things: make theft less profitable and expand the blackmarket. As profitability in theft declines, however, individual thieves will be faced with two options: work harder—that is steal more—or get a new hustle. One might suspect that some thieves would choose one option and other thieves the other. Since addicts are probably more motivated than non-addicts to steal and since they probably have fewer opportunities for other sources of income (particularly legitimate opportunities), it might be expected that non-addicts will leave the criminal labor force more quickly and in greater numbers than addicts as theft becomes a less profitable enterprise. Addiction, then, would not increase theft in direct proportion to the number of addicts who steal, but would change the composition of the labor force of thieves. To the extent, however, that a labor market with a high percentage of addicts in it lowers the prevailing prices for stolen goods and keeps these prices depressed, there should be more theft because the lower prices should expand the total stolen goods market. This expansion, however, would surely not be limitless. There must be a profit margin below which even addicts cannot afford to operate and that margin may not be too much lower than it is for non-addicts. For one thing, drug addicts have to spend a considerable amount of their time "chasing the bag" and thus have less time to devote to theft than non-addicts; and for another thing, they are usually subject to considerable police surveilance which makes theft riskier for them than for the average thief. In balance, drug addicts may out-hustle non-addicts in the marketplace of theft and by so doing drive prices down and expand total amounts of thefts, but in the long run a new balance of supply and demand should be reached which may not lead to much more theft than there was when addicts were not in the market.

Although there are some data available which show that auto theft and bank robbery may be subject to these kinds of market mechanisms (Gould, 1969, 1971), data are not available to establish clearly whether or not the presence of addict-thieves in this country adds to the total amount of theft or simply changes the composition of the labor pool of thieves. There is some indirect evidence, however, which can be brought to bear on the subject.

One might begin by observing that New York City, which by numerous estimates hosts half the addicts in the nation, accounts certainly for less than half the property crime in the country. In 1971, 465,888 burglaries, larcenies, and robberies were reported in New York City, only 10 percent of the nation's total (Uniform Crime Reports, 1972). Although the rate of property crime was high in New York City, which holds only 6 percent of the American population, the over-representation seems modest compared to its over-representation in terms of numbers of addicts.

Between 1960 and 1971 the number of arrests in the United States for narcotic drug law violations, according to the FBI, increased 765 percent (Uniform Crime Reports, 1972: 118-119.[7] Arrests for robbery increased 146 percent during this period, arrests for burglary increased 74 percent, and arrests for larceny 120 percent. [8] Arrests for theft, to be sure, have risen substantially, but not in proportion to arrests for narcotic law violations.

This is not to say, of course, that drug addiction might not account for those increases in theft which the nation has experienced or that New York's extremely high rate of narcotic use might not account for its higher-than-average rate of theft. It does seem, however, that the relationship between narcotic use and theft may not be as simple or direct as many people have recently been claiming.

The complexity of this relationship is illustrated by the work of Isidore Chein and colleagues (1964). These investigators carefully assembled data on 10,025 criminal charges against youthful offenders in two New York City courts from January 1, 1949, through December 31, 1952. Using these data to establish crime rates for 89 "health-areas," the authors compared crime rates with drug-use rates for the same geographical units. The correlation between crime rates and drug-use rates, by health-areas, was .63. Controlling for the ethnic composition of the neighborhood, however, reduced the correlation to .24.[9] Although there is some positive correlation between crime rates and drug-use rate, this correlation is low when controlling for ethnicity of the neighborhood, and in a statistical sense the drug rate can account for only about 6 percent of the variation in crime rates.

In a more recent and more extensive, although as yet unpublished, study covering all of New York City (reported here with permission of the author), Chein found similar results. Comparing the incidence of criminal activity with the incidence of narcotics law violation for males ages 16-19 within census tracts, Chein found moderately high correlations until he statistically controlled for certain socio-demographic variables. When controlled, the partial correlation coefficient between narcotics law violations and assault drops to .16 for 1950 and to .03 for 1960. The partial correlation between violations of the narcotics laws and major criminal offenses, excluding assault, is .12 in 1950 and .13 in 1960. Comparable partial correlation for minor crimes are .09 and .06.

These findings are by no means conclusive. Crime rates in the study are based on arrests of young offenders, which could be different than overall crime rates. The study also includes crimes against the person, and thus does not offer a direct test of the hypothesis that drug use increases theft. [10] Nevertheless, this study does suggest one very important thing about the relationship between addiction and crime: it may, to a large extent, be spurious. That is, it suggests that communities which support a lot of drug use may also support a lot of crime, but the former does not necessarily *cause* the latter.

The study contracted by the BNDD (1971) described earlier offers additional evidence pertinent to the question. Table 3 summarizes some of the findings from this study for each of the six cities included in the study sample.

One of the more astounding findings from the study is the percentage of those arrested for theft in New York City who are heroin users. Eighty percent of the arrestees for robbery were current users of heroin as were sixty percent of those arrested for other property crimes. The rates are also high in the other cities, but not nearly as high as in New York. The percentage of robbery arrestees who were current heroin users in New Orleans, the city with the next highest rate, was 36, and 24 percent of those arrested for other property crimes in New Orleans were heroin users. The lowest rate for robbery arrestees was found in St. Louis (17 percent), and the lowest rates for arrestees on other property crime changes (21 percent) were found in Chicago and Los Angeles.

Heroin users appear to dominate the labor market for thieves in New York City. Although it is possible that many of these addict-thieves were thieves first and became addicts second, it is equally possible that the entry of addicts into the labor market has been offset by the exit of non-addict thieves.

Hypotheses

Data pertinent to the relationship between drug addiction and crime are fragmentary, tangential, and often of dubious quality. We seem little better off than the President's Commission on Law Enforcement and Administration of Justice (Task Force on Narcotics and Drug Abuse) was in 1967 when it reported (p. 11): "The simple truth is that the addict's or drug users' responsibility for all non-drug offenses is unknown."

To a scientist, this should preclude further discussion except perhaps to suggest how the gross inadequacies in our knowledge about the subject might be remedied through further research. Those who must formulate drug control policy, however, cannot wait for further research. Therefore, it might be reasonable to state a few tentative hypotheses which seem to be most consistent with present data:

(1) Among those who commit crimes, heroin addicts are less likely than non-heroin users to commit crimes against the person.

(2) Heroin addicts are more likely than non-heroin users to commit theft.

(3) Heroin addiction per se does not increase the propensity to commit theft.

(4) Heroin addiction, where the cost of heroin is high, induces some heroin addicts to commit theft.

(5) Approximately 25 to 30 percent of the heroin users in the United States are engaged in theft.

Table 3. DRUG USAGE AND CRIMINAL ARREST CHARGES AMONG ARRESTEES IN SIX AMERICAN CITIES

	Serious Crimes Against the Person[1]		Less Serious Crimes Against the Person[2]		Robbery		Other Property Crimes[3]		All Other Crimes[4]		Total	
	N	%	N	%	N	%	N	%	N	%	N	%
Chicago:												
Current heroin users[5]	2	3	1	5	26	22	16	21	2	7	47	15
Past heroin users[6]	2	3	–	–	3	3	6	8	–	–	11	4
Other drug users[7]	25	38	8	42	43	37	31	42	11	37	118	38
Non-drug users	37	56	10	53	45	38	22	29	17	56	131	43
Total	66	100	19	100	117	100	75	100	30	100	307	100
Per cent of grand total		22		6		38		24		10		100
New Orleans:												
Current heroin users	–	–	–	–	11	36	29	24	–	–	40	17
Past heroin users	5	11	–	–	6	19	17	14	–	–	28	12
Other drug users	9	20	12	57	6	19	26	21	6	27	59	24
Non-drug users	31	69	9	43	8	26	51	41	16	73	115	47
Total	45	100	21	100	31	100	123	100	22	100	242	100
Per cent of grand total		19		9		13		50		9		100
San Antonio:												
Current heroin users	2	6	–	–	4	34	27	22	3	10	36	17
Past heroin users	1	3	2	18	1	8	8	7	2	7	14	7
Other drug users	4	12	1	9	4	33	32	26	13	43	54	26
Non-drug users	27	79	8	73	3	25	57	45	13	42	108	50
Total	34	100	11	100	12	100	124	100	31	100	212	100
Per cent of grand total		16		5		6		58		15		100

[68]

New York:												
Current heroin users	12	23	8	24	39	80	89	60	15	68	163	53
Past heroin users	3	6	1	3	3	6	9	6	–	–	16	5
Other drug users	13	25	4	12	5	10	12	8	2	9	36	12
Non-drug users	24	46	21	61	2	4	39	26	5	23	91	30
Total	52	100	34	100	49	100	149	100	22	100	306	100
Per cent of grand total		17		11		16		49		7		100
Los Angeles:												
Current heroin users	7	14	5	20	7	19	43	21	1	7	63	19
Past heroin users	2	4	2	8	4	11	28	14	1	7	37	11
Other drug users	23	45	9	36	24	65	100	48	9	59	165	49
Non-drug users	19	37	9	36	2	5	36	17	4	27	70	21
Total	51	100	25	100	37	100	207	100	15	100	335	100
Per cent of grand total		15		8		11		61		5		100
St. Louis:												
Current heroin users	7	14	–	–	7	17	33	22	5	12	52	16
Past heroin users	1	2	–	–	3	7	7	5	–	–	11	3
Other drug users	19	37	12	38	12	29	52	34	19	44	114	36
Non-drug users	25	47	20	62	19	47	60	39	19	44	143	45
Total	52	100	32	100	41	100	152	100	43	100	320	100
Per cent of grand total		16		10		13		48		13		100
All Cities:												
Current heroin users	30	10	14	10	94	33	237	29	26	16	401	23
Past heroin users	14	5	5	4	20	7	75	9	3	2	117	7
Other drug users	93	31	46	32	94	33	253	30	60	37	546	32
Non-drug users	163	54	77	54	79	27	265	32	74	45	658	38
Total	300	100	142	100	287	100	830	100	163	100	1722	100
Per cent of grand total		17		8		17		49		9		100

(6) Theft by heroin users increases the overall level of theft in the community.

(7) But, increases in theft due to the activities of heroin users is less than the total amount of theft committed by these users.

Hypothesis number one, although not consistent with the popular stereotype of the addict, is understandable on common-sense grounds. Addicts, at least many of them, are well known to the police and are usually under some form of surveilance. It behooves addicts, then, to "play it cool," for it is these crimes (murder, rape, assault, etc.) which most excite community concern and police action. That addicts avoid crimes of violence, then, seems quite understandable.

It is also quite acceptable on common sense grounds that addicts will steal to support their drug habits. What is not quite so readily apparent is why every addict does not steal. But this too makes sense when one stops to consider that theft is only one among a number of "hustles" that drug addicts have at their disposal. Selling drugs offers great opportunity for financial gain and some of the other vices, like prostitution, provide additional opportunities for addicts to make a living in ways other than theft. For some drug users, especially those who use only small amounts of heroin, legitimate sources of income should suffice. In total, then, it is not altogether surprising that studies to date find that only about a third of the heroin users in this country support themselves through theft.

In this light, hypotheses three and four would also seem to make sense. That is, it is not heroin per se or addiction to heroin which causes people to steal, but the fact that heroin costs so much in this country. It is these costs which the addict must meet, and he will do this however he best can. Theft is just one of a number of income sources American addicts use to afford heroin.

Hypotheses six and seven are the least readily explainable on common-sense grounds. Although the economic notions of supply, demand, and markets are common parlance in this country, these notions have not, generally, been applied to crime. There seems to be a very good reason for this which is that the prevailing notions of crime do not readily accommodate utilitarian notions like risks and gains and maximizing profits.

---

1. Includes: Criminal homicide, forcible rape, aggravated assault, and kidnapping.
2. Includes: Other assault, sex offenses (except forcible rape and commercialized vice).
3. Includes: Larceny, burglary, theft, auto theft, arson, forgery, counterfeiting, fraud, embezzlement, stolen property, and vandalism.
4. Includes: Weapons, prostitution, and commercialized vice.
5. Determined by positive answer during interview or positive urine analysis.
6. Determined by interview.
7. Marijuana, barbiturates, and amphetamines.

Americans think of crime as the action of criminals. To understand these criminal acts is to understand crime, and to understand the criminal is to understand why crimes occur. Among criminologists this is known as "positivism" (Matza, 1964: 1-30) and central to positivist criminological theory is the hypothesis that people commit crime because of psychological, biological, or social factors in their present makeup or personal backgrounds. Indeed, the most common form of criminological research in this country in the past half-century has been comparisons of known "criminals" with known "non-criminals" in order to identify "those characteristics which differentiate the two groups" and thus, presumably, are the causes of crime.

A more recent version of criminological positivism has come to be called "labeling criminology." Criminologists of this persuasion have abandoned the search for psychological, biological, and social causes of criminality, since it is their conception that criminals are not those who commit acts which are in violation of the law, but those who get caught at it and thus become "labeled" criminal. Almost everyone, these criminologists note, commits crime, but only a few are ever "labeled" criminals by society. The main task for criminology then, under this view, is to understand the processes by which society defines certain people as criminals.

Perhaps the single largest failure of positivist criminology has been its inability to explain differences in crime rates over time or across geographical regions. Indeed, positivist criminologists, if they do not ignore it altogether, dismiss data concerning differences in crime rates by noting the "obvious" deficiencies in the data. Such data, to be sure, are often deficient, but this is not reason in itself to ignore the issue altogether. The fact is that positivist criminologists, although they may have something to say about criminals, or even those who "label" people as criminals, have little to say about crime. When crime has been on the increase, all positivist criminologists have been able to do is recommend treatment and rehabilitation. When this has failed to halt the rise in crime, positivist criminologists have called for even more intensive treatment and rehabilitation (Gould and Namenwirth, 1971).

Many members of the general public have been less generous in these times. As crime increases, they have been heard to call for stiffer punishment. But this recommendation draws upon a completely different model of crime, one which criminologists call the "classical-utilitarian" theory. Although the theory has little currency among modern criminologists, it was the prevailing theory at the time our nation was founded.

"Classical-utilitarian" criminological theory focuses not on the actions of criminals but on infractions of the law (Beccaria, 1764; Bentham, 1843; Matza, 1964). Although such a distinction might seem trivial, it is important in that it emphasizes the law, and infractions of it, rather than criminals and their actions. The concern is not with why people commit criminal acts but with the justness and deterrent value of the laws.

The "classical-utilitarian" theory of crime assumes that anyone will commit infractions of the law if the conditions are right. Conditions are right if there is something to be gained from it. Laws, then, to be just and effective must call for punishments which are just sufficiently harsh to make the crime unrewarding but not so harsh as to cause a general breakdown in respect for the law or the state which embodies them. It is from this theory that we once got the slogan "punishment to fit the crime."

The blackmarket, supply-demand model of heroin use and theft, suggested in hypotheses six and seven, is quite compatable with the "classical-utilitarian" theory of crime. Addicts steal because there is profit in theft and addicts need considerable profits in order to afford the high costs of drug use. As addicts begin to compete for the profits available in theft, however, they not only take profits away from other non-addict thieves, but they probably also make theft a riskier, and thus more "costly" economic enterprise than it was previously. Thus, while addicts may, at least temporarily, expand the total amount of theft, market mechanisms operating in the world of crime should be expected, in the long run, to prevent theft from expanding in anything like direct proportion to the number of addicts there are in society.

Predictions

There is one aspect of the current drug crisis that neither positivist nor classical-utilitarian theories can explain. Why, beginning in the early to mid 1960s, did drug use begin increasing in epidemic proportions? Drug use is, after all, itself a crime, but neither positivist nor classical-utilitarian theories of crime seem well equipped to explain its sudden escalation. To do this one would need to identify either sudden increases in the nation's level of social pathology or sudden breakdowns in its legal system of deterrence. There is no compelling evidence that either has occurred.

To explain the epidemic qualities of drug use, one could turn to the works of Erikson (1966) and Durkheim (1958) who argue that crime becomes epidemic in form during periods of extreme social stress. Indeed, according to these sociologists, it is through the resolution of these epidemics that societies realign their normative boundaries and reaffirm the validity of their normative order.

Drug use today has all the earmarks of being a crime epidemic. As such, its etiology is probably to be discovered in the broad value conflicts of the 1960s, perhaps within the same complex of events which have surrounded the growth of the civil rights and youth movements and the reactionary countermovements which they generated. As an epidemic, however, heroin use (or at least social hysteria surrounding heroin use) should subside. It should subside in all communities, irrespective of whether or not the community offered treatment for heroin addicts and irrespective of whether the community instituted harsher penalties for heroin use.

As heroin use subsides, we might expect a modest decline in the overall amount of theft in American communities, especially those, like New York City, where heroin users have come to make up such a substantial proportion of that community's population of thieves. This prediction is based on the assumption that heroin users do expand the total market for theft somewhat. As addicts drop out of the market, which should happen as the heroin epidemic subsides, the market should shrink and total levels of theft should go down.

The decreases, however, will surely not be dramatic. The exit of addicts from the criminal marketplace will not eliminate the marketplace, it will only serve to readjust the equilibrium between supply and demand for criminal goods and services. This should mean less theft, but not the elimination of theft. Just how much less theft might remain is impossible to calculate or even guess. Perhaps it will be so little as to be completely indiscernible in overall crime statistics. More likely, it will be seen as a short-term drop in theft rates which will soon be reversed when the long-term trends, which have been increasing since the mid 1940s, take over again and theft will again be seen to be rising. How Americans will explain that rise when it can no longer be blamed on heroin addicts is interesting to contemplate. My guess is that they will blame it on someone. Crime in America must be someone's fault. That it might be the product of rather ordinary and otherwise respectable social processes, like a free market, is something few Americans are likely to accept.

NOTES

1. The FBI, in its Uniform Crime Reports, has traditionally included robbery as a crime against the person because it involves the use, or threat, of force. The object of robbery, however, is property, not violence to the person, and thus, it is legitimately one kind of theft.

2. The authors report findings on 1,889 arrestees. This number, however, includes people arrested for narcotics law violations in three cities and excludes them in the other three study locations. To maintain consistency, I have adjusted the original data to exclude cases of narcotics law violations from all cities.

3. In New York City, only cases from Brooklyn were studied.

4. Most heroin users, the authors determined, related to a single "copping" center. Although some users would make occasional journeys to other drug centers, their major center of activity was fairly easy to establish and by and large correspond to the area of town in which they lived.

5. There were 127 individuals in total in the "copping area" under study. Two of these were drug dealers who did not themselves use drugs. Information about occupational roles was unobtainable on 21.

6. Criminal markets may be the only major markets left which are essentially uncontrolled by the state and thus operate according to classic supply-demand economic principles.

7. Between 1970 and 1971 the increase was only 11 percent (Uniform Crime Reports, 1972: 121).

8. Between 1970 and 1971 increases were: robbery 15 percent, burglary 7 percent, and larceny 7 percent.

9. Chein and colleagues (1964), although arriving at this same conclusion via a different route, did not publish correlation coefficients controlling for ethnic composition of the neighborhood. They did, however, publish a scatter diagram (p. 58) with the appropriate control variable indicated. I have computed the partial correlation coefficient by reconstructing the original data from this diagram.

10. Chein's findings are also vulnerable to what Robinson (1950) refers to as the "ecological fallacy." That is, just because there is a correlation between two different rates in geographical areas does not mean that the same individuals are involved in generating the two rates. In this case, those using drugs and those arrested for other crimes might or might not be the same people. Unless they are, and unless we know that they are, it cannot be said that drug addiction leads to crime. The argument being developed here is not subject to this problem of interpretation, however, since it holds that the community as a whole, not individuals, is the proper unit of analysis.

REFERENCES

BECCARIA, C. (1764) "Essays on crimes and punishments." Reprint (1963). Indianapolis: Bobbs-Merrill.

BENTHAM, J. (1843) "Principles of penal law," in J. Bowring (ed.) The Works of Jeremy Bentham. Edinburgh: W. Tait.

CHEIN, I., P. GERARD, R. LEE and E. ROSENFELD (1964) The Road to H: Narcotics, Delinquency, and Social Policy. New York: Basic Books.

DURKHEIM, E. (1958) The Rules of Sociological Method. Translated by S. A. Solovay and J. H. Mueller. Glencoe: Free Press.

ERIKSON, K. (1966) Wayward Puritans. New York: Wiley.

GEARING, F. (1970) "Successes and failures in methadone maintenance treatment of heroin addiction in New York City." Proceedings of the Third Annual Conference on Methadone Treatment. Washington: Government Printing Office.

GOULD, L. (1971) "Crime and its impact in an affluent society," pp. 237-267 in J. Douglas (ed.) Crime and Justice in American Society. Indianapolis: Bobbs-Merrill.

GOULD, L. and J. NAMENWIRTH (1971) "Contrary objectives: crime, control and the rehabilitation of criminals," pp. 81-118 in J. Douglas (ed.) Crime and Justice in American Society. Indianapolis: Bobbs-Merrill.

――― (1969) "The changing structure of property crime in an affluent society." Social Forces 48 (September): 50-59.

HUGHES, P., G. CRAWFORD, N. BARKER, S. SCHUMANN and J. JAFFEE (1971) "The social structure of a heroin copping community." Amer. Journal of Psychiatry 128 (November): 43-50.

JAMES, I. and P. D'ORBAN (1970) "Patterns of delinquency among British heroin addicts." Bulletin on Narcotics 22 (April-June): 13-19.

MATZA, D. (1964) Delinquency and Drift. New York: Wiley.

MAY, E. (1972) "Narcotics addiction and control in Great Britain," pp. 345-394 in Dealing with Drug Abuse: A Report to the Ford Foundation. New York: Praeger.

NEWMEYER, J. (1972) "The junkie thief." Mimeographed. San Francisco: Haight-Ashbury Free Medical Clinic.

President's Commission on Law Enforcement and Administration of Justice (1967a) Task Force Report on Narcotics and Drug Abuse. Washington: Government Printing Office.

——— (1967b) Task Force Report: Crime and its Impact—an Assessment. Washington: Government Printing Office.

ROBINSON, W. (1950) "Ecological correlations and the behavior of individuals." Amer. Sociological Review 15 (June): 351-357.

SINGER, M. (1971) "The vitality of mythical numbers." Public Interest 23 (Spring): 3-9.

Uniform Crime Reports for the United States—1971 (1972). Washington: Government Printing Office.

U.S. Bureau of Narcotics and Dangerous Drugs (1971) Drug Usage and Arrest Charges. Washington: Department of Justice.

Chapter 4

COSTS, BENEFITS, AND POTENTIAL FOR ALTERNATIVE APPROACHES TO OPIATE ADDICTION CONTROL

WILLIAM H. McGLOTHLIN and VICTOR C. TABBUSH

INTRODUCTION

This chapter estimates the costs, benefits, and potential of various approaches to narcotics addiction control.[1] For each of several approaches, we wish to estimate the maximum number of addicts which may be treated, the cost of treatment, and the social benefits derived. The diagram in Figure 1 illustrates the method adopted. The horizontal axis indicates the number of addict or patient years for a given treatment modality, i.e., the average number of addicts in treatment during the year. On the vertical axis are plotted: (1) the total annual quantifiable social costs of an untreated addict, resulting from theft, anti-crime expenditures, and foregone production (unemployment); (2) the treatment cost per patient year; and (3) the treatment benefits per patient year, i.e., the

AUTHORS' NOTE: The research for this work was conducted under a contract from the U.S. Department of Justice Bureau of Narcotics and Dangerous Drugs (Contract No. J-70-33), and initially published in Alternative Approaches to Opiate Control: Cost, Benefits and Potential, Bureau of Narcotics and Dangerous Drugs, SCID TR-7, June, 1972. Interpretations or viewpoints expressed in this document do not necessarily represent the official position or policy of the Department of Justice or the Bureau of Narcotics and Dangerous Drugs.

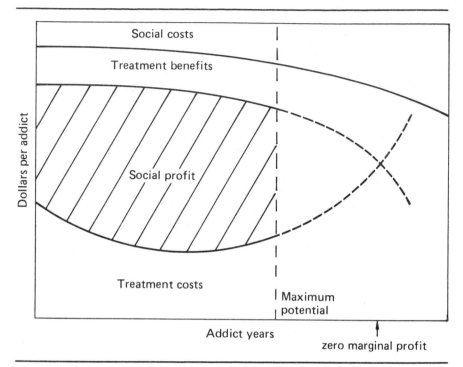

Figure 1.

reduction in social costs resulting from the treatment. Especially in volunteer programs, these variables can be expected to vary as a function of the ease with which addicts are attrac ted into treatment. In the illustrative diagram, treatment costs are shown first to decrease and subsequently to increase. Such a curve might result from the initial fixed costs, ultimately followed by the high cost of attracting and maintaining marginal patients as the program is expanded to maximum capacity. The social-cost curve is shown to decline as a function of increasing addict years (the average number of addicts in treatment), perhaps reflecting less theft among low-habit addicts who are reluctant to volunteer for treatment, or possibly a lower cost of heroin as the population of drug addicts decreases. The treatment-benefit curve is shown to decline as a function of increasing addict years, indicating lower benefits for the less-motivated addicts who are brought into the program as it nears its maximum potential.

At any point along the horizontal axis, the social profit derived from incorporating an additional addict in treatment is equal to the treatment benefit minus the treatment cost. When this value is zero (where the treatment benefit and cost curves cross), the program has reached its maximum theoretical potential for reducing the social costs of addiction, i.e., the profit represented by the area between the treatment benefit and treatment cost curves. In the diagram, the dashed vertical line represents an additional constraint determined by the proportion of the addict population accessible to the program. Theoretically, additional treatment funds could be profitably expended until the point of zero marginal profit is reached. In practice, however, society's goals for treatment often differ from those of the addict, and some volunteer programs are limited by the number of addicts attracted, independent of the available funds. For example, a program which only dispenses methadone in all probability could not attract volunteers beyond a given level because of the preference for illicit heroin. Further increases in participants would require a shift in approach rather than additional expenditures, e.g., the addition of direct compulsion or a change to heroin maintenance. Similarly, it is doubtful if the number of addicts participating in the therapeutic communities could be increased beyond a given level simply by spending more funds per participant. Another consideration is the possible attraction of new entries into the addict population via the existence of too-favorable treatment conditions. In short, the maximum potential of a treatment approach is usually subject to other constraints in addition to the equating of marginal treatment costs and benefits.

An essential factor in determining the proportion of addicts "volunteering" for treatment is the amount of enforcement pressure—not only directed at limiting the supply of heroin but also that aimed at the individual user. The latter will be treated as an independent variable in the portions dealing with civil commitment. Otherwise, enforcement pressure will generally be considered to remain at the present level. The decision not to introduce enforcement as an independent variable throughout the analysis resulted from the lack of quantitative data and the increased complexity resulting from the addition of another dimension.

The control approaches to be examined are:

   I. Methadone maintenance—strict control
  II. Methadone maintenance—dispensing only
 III. Heroin maintenance
 IV. Therapeutic community
  V. Detoxification
 VI. Civil commitment
VII. Combination civil commitment and other modalities

CURRENT STATUS OF ADDICT POPULATION

The available data only permit a very rough estimate of the size of the addict population in the United States. The only national register of addicts is that maintained by the Bureau of Narcotics and Dangerous Drugs (BNDD) and it listed 82,294 at the end of 1971. This list is compiled from voluntary data submitted by state and local enforcement authorities and is known to be markedly incomplete even in comparison with certain state enforcement data available from other sources. Greenwood (1971) has employed a statistical technique of determining the fraction of active addicts reported to the BNDD file in each of two successive time periods to estimate the addict population. This approach yielded an estimate of 315,000 addicts in the U.S. in 1969.

Additional data are available from which to estimate the New York City addict population. The New York City Narcotics Register shows 88,000[1] narcotic users for the six-year period 1964-69 (N.Y. City Dept. of Health, 1971), and Koval (1971) estimates the comparable number for the 1964-70 time period as 125,000. There are several factors which may lead to the inclusion of names of persons on the Register who are not addicts now living in New York City: (1) persons may be reported who use narcotics but are not physically addicted; (2) individuals who cease to use narcotics are not removed; (3) persons who die are not systematically removed except for those whose death is reported due to narcotics; (4) duplicates occur in spite of efforts to eliminate them; and (5) persons listed may no longer be residents of N.Y.C. On the other hand, while the Register has the advantage of receiving names from health as well as enforcement agencies, it obviously does not contain a complete listing of the addict population. Various studies of narcotic-related deaths in N.Y.C. have found that 33 to 60 percent of these individuals are listed in the Register prior to death (Koval, 1971; Larrier and associates, 1971; N.Y. City Dept. of Health, 1971). A check of known addicts living in one slum block in Manhattan showed that 78 percent appeared on the Register (Koval, 1970).

At the current rate of increase the Register probably contained the names of about 175,000 N.Y.C. residents at the end of 1971. If we assume that about 125,000 of these are active narcotic addicts and the list is 60 to 80 percent complete, the current estimate of addicts in N.Y.C. is about 150,000-200,000. Assuming the lower figure of 150,000 and that N.Y.C. contains 40 percent of the nation's addicts,[2] we obtain a nationwide estimate of 375,000 for the end of 1971. This estimate will be utilized in the remainder of the paper, but must be regarded as highly tentative. While there are perhaps sufficient data to estimate the addict popultion of N.Y.C. within 50,000 of the true value, no such data exist for the remainder of the country. Since the BNDD file lists only 22 percent of the estimated N.Y.C. addict population, the extent to which the

BNDD ratio (listed N.Y.C. addicts/listed addicts in remainder of country) reflects the true value may be subject to serious error. In short, we are able to make a rough estimate of the N.Y.C. addict population, and a highly tentative guess concerning the remainder of the country.

Table 1 lists the estimated addict population by current status. Forty thousand, or 11 percent, are estimated to be in methadone maintenance programs. Accurate data are available for New York state and federally financed methadone patients; estimates for other programs are based on data obtained by FDA in relation to the issuing of licenses (INDs). In addition to accounting for

Table 1. CURRENT STATUS OF ADDICT POPULATION (DEC. 1971)

Status		Number	%
Methadone maintenance		40,000	11
N.Y.C.[1]	18,000		
Remainder of country[2]			
Therapeutic communities		8,000	2
New York[3]	3,500		
California[4]	1,500		
Other	3,000		
Civil Commitment (non-methadone)		18,400	5
New York[5]	7,500		
California[6]	7,800		
Federal (NIMH)[7]	2,100		
Other	1,000		
Detoxification (in-patient)		2,500	1
Antagonist programs		200	–
Incarcerated		37,500	10
	Sub-Total	106,600	
On street		268,400	72
Temporary abstinent	40,000		
Addicted	228,400		
	Grand Total	375,000	101

1. New York State Narcotic Addiction Control Commission (NACC); unpublished monthly statistical reports, 1971. New York State financed—14,500; N.Y.C. financed—3,000, LEAA financed—500.

2. National Institute for Mental Health (NIMH) financed—8,000; LEAA financed—1,500; other 12,500 (interview with Dr. Barrett Scoville, FDA-BNDD, Dec. 22, 1971); currently approximately 300 IND's and 400 clinics.

3. NACC unpublished monthly statistics, 1971.

4. Interview with Dr. John Kramer, Special Action Office for Drug Abuse Prevention, Dec. 21, 1971.

5. NACC unpublished monthly statistics, 1971; does not include patients in abscondance.

6. California Civil Commitment monthly statistics, Dec. 1971; does not include patients in abscondance.

7. Narcotic Addict Rehabilitation Branch, unpublished statistics, 1971.

the largest segment in treatment, methadone maintenance is by far the most rapidly growing modality. At the time of the Second Methadone Maintenance Conference (Oct., 1969), the estimated number of methadone patients was only 3,000-4,000 (Zitrin, 1970).

Therapeutic communities in California and New York contain about 5,000 addicts. There are no good supportive data for the estimated 3,000 in the remainder of the country.

The data on civil commitment for federal, California, and New York programs are based on actual statistics and exclude those in abscondence. Overall about 40 percent are on inpatient status and 60 percent are outpatients. The number of addicts in civil commitment has stabilized in New York but is continuing to grow in California.

The annual number of addicts undergoing inpatient detoxification may be estimated from patient records. One study of 500 methadone patients in N.Y.C. found a mean of six detoxifications during an average of twelve years of addiction (Perkins and Bloch, 1970). Another N.Y.C. study found 81 methadone patients spent an average of nine inpatient days for detoxifications in the twelve months prior to admission (Cushman, 1971). Vaillant's (1966) sample of 100 underwent 270 known voluntary hospitalizations over a twelve-year period. The Bernstein Institute in N.Y.C. admitted nearly 8,000 for detoxification in 1970 with a mean hospital stay of twelve days (Richman, Clark, Bergner and Patrick, 1971). An estimate of one voluntary twelve-day inpatient detoxification per three years of street addiction yields an average inpatient detoxification population of about 2,500. [3]

The only direct information on the number of addicts imprisoned is provided by the Uniform Parole Reports. The 1967 data indicate that 13 percent of the 21,000 males paroled had histories of drug use. Applying this percentage to the 189,000 males in prison at the end of 1967 yields an estimate of 25,000 (National Prisoner Statistics, 1969). Some data on the incarceration rate are provided by follow-up studies. Early investigations of patients discharged from Lexington found 15 to 25 percent to be institutionalized at the time of follow-up. [4] A more recent follow-up of detoxification patients in New York City reported 11 percent of those living were incarcerated (Richman, Perkins, Bihari, and Fishman, 1971). The percentage of addicts imprisoned has probably dropped in recent years because of the number in civil commitment as well as in other treatment modalities. More lenient sentencing by the courts is also a factor (Curran, 1971). The estimated 37,500 incarcerated addicts in Table 1 represent 10 percent of the total population or 12 percent of those not in treatment.

Of the some 270,000 addicts shown as on the street in Table 1, 40,000 (15 percent) are estimated to be temporarily abstinent at any given point in time.

This estimate is necessarily imprecise because of the vague manner of defining the termination of the addiction status. Duvall and associates (1963) found the percentage voluntarily abstinent six months, two years, and five years after discharge from the Lexington hospital was 9, 17, and 25, respectively. Sixty percent had not been voluntarily abstinent for as long as three consecutive months during the five-year period. Vaillant's (1966) twelve-year follow-up provided comparable results up to five years, and 46 percent were voluntarily abstinent at the time of death or last contact. The follow-up by Richman, Perkins, Bihari, and Fishman (1971) of N.Y.C. patients first admitted for detoxification in 1961-63 located 84 percent in 1971 and found 18 percent of those living were "alleged abstinent." This represents 41 percent of those located who were not known to be in treatment or prison. Waldorf (1970) reported 55 percent of those addicted for ten years or more had been voluntarily abstinent at least one time for a period of eight months or more, compared to eight percent of those addicted fewer than ten years.

These and other studies strongly suggest that the proportion of the time voluntarily abstinent increases as a function of age and length of addiction. If the addiction career is defined as the period between the first and last physical addictions, excluding irregular use before and after, a rough estimate of percentage of time voluntarily abstinent outside of treatment is 10 percent for those addicted less than ten years and 30 percent for those over ten years.

ECONOMIC COSTS OF ADDICTION

The overall economic costs of addiction are treated in some detail in the appendix; however, the estimates required for the current analysis will be briefly examined here. For the present purposes, we are interested in the social profit derived from transferring addicts from the street to treatment status. Hence, the appropriate costs are for the average addict on the street rather than those for the total addict population.

Costs of Addict Related Crime

The extent of addict theft may be assessed by (1) estimating total theft and assuming a given proportion is committed by addicts, or (2) determining the average cost of heroin plus addict subsistence, and calculating the proportion acquired by theft. Unfortunately, neither method yields results in which much confidence can be placed. An estimate of $1.7 billion in addict theft per annum has been developed via the first method—an updating of the 1963 White House Conference on Narcotic and Drug Abuse assessment of $500,000,000 in addict theft for New York City (McGlothlin and associates, 1972). This represented an average annual theft of $6,300 per street addict.

The second approach involves a number of steps in addition to estimating the money spent for heroin, e.g., the portion of addict income obtained from theft of goods as opposed to cash; income from prostitution, welfare, jobs, and borrowing; discount value of stolen goods; and income from drug sales and its relation to habit size. Moore (1970) has estimated the average annual theft by addicts on the street to be $11,600 by this method. Of this, $3,400 is theft for subsistence costs.

Cushman (1971) utilized intensive interviewing of 64 male and 17 female methadone patients to estimate the cost of heroin and the means of acquiring funds during the twelve months prior to treatment. The average daily cost of heroin, for days actually used, was $35, or $12,200 per average year of street addiction. The reported amount of cash and goods (fair value) stolen per addict year was $10,900.[5] This sample of addicts had a mean age of 37 and an average of fourteen years of addiction. This relatively long addiction history probably accounts for their above-average habit and the fact that 51 percent of the amount spent on heroin was obtained via drug selling.

Table 2 summarizes the data from several studies on addict self-reported expenditures for heroin. From these data it would appear that the mean and

Table 2.   ADDICTS SELF-REPORTED EXPENDITURES FOR HEROIN

Reference	Year	Size of Sample	Cost per day ($) Mean	Median	Remarks
NACC (1968)	68	3,569	28	22	N.Y. civil commitments;
NACC (1969)	69	5,804	28	22	about 65% under 26 years;
NACC (1970)	70	9,321	29	21	expenditures for secondary drugs $3-5 per day
Wood (1970)	69	–		16	Calif. civil commitment
N.Y.C. Police (1967)	65	2,262	14		Arrested heroin users
Walter et al. (1972)	71	95		12	Random sample of N.Y.C. street addicts; med. age = 24
Perkins-Bloch (1970)	65-68	521	25		Methadone patients; mean age = 32
Cushman (1971)	69	81	35		Methadone patients; mean age = 37
O'Connor et al. (1971)	70	115		35	Methadone patients
Jones (1971)	71	201	31	24	Methadone patients; mean age = 36

median expenditures are about $25 and $20 per day, respectively. There are several reasons to expect addict-reported expenditures to be biased on the high side. They tend to report what they spend if money is available, but in practice they often have to manage on less (Moore, 1970). They frequently report in terms of the retail price for a given number of bags, although heroin is often bought at lower prices in larger quantities. Finally, data collected from methadone clinic patients are biased upward because such clinics tend to attract older addicts with long histories of addiction, which are correlated with larger drug expenditures (NACC, 1969). Methadone patients may also be motivated to exaggerate their habits in the hope of receiving larger maintenance doses.

From the standpoint of estimating the amount of theft, the most critical value is the percentage of addict income derived from stolen goods, as opposed to theft of cash, money from prostitution, or profits from selling drugs. This follows because of the multiplier of 3 or 4 usually applied to the income obtained from stolen goods in order to estimate the fair value of the property. Most observers agree that profits from drug selling are a major source of income for persons with large habits (Cushman's sample obtained one-half their funds in this manner). This means that the median expenditure for drugs is a better estimator for determining theft than is the mean, which is weighted by those with large incomes from drug selling. Theft of cash via robbery, picking pockets, check forging, etc., is generally estimated to represent no more than 10 to 20 percent of income obtained by theft (Inciardi, 1971; Moore, 1970); however, prostitution, pimping, numbers rackets, and legal sources are other means of addict income which do not involve theft. Cushman's sample obtained about 50 percent from drug selling, 25 percent from stolen goods, and 25 percent by other means. If it is assumed that the addict on the street obtains an average income of $10-15 per day from stolen goods, the market value would be $30-45. If the addict on the street is assumed to be addicted 85 percent of the time (see Table 1), this would amount to $9,300-14,000 per year. For the purposes of the present analysis, $10,000 has been adopted as the average theft per year for addicts on the street.

Costs of Anti-Crime Measures

In addition to the direct costs of addict-related crime, indirect costs are incurred by both the government and private citizens in terms of the expenses of law enforcement, courts, theft insurance, etc. The development of these cost estimates is provided in the appendix to an earlier version of this paper (McGlothlin and associates, 1972). In summary, the 1971 costs of anti-crime measures caused by narcotics addiction are estimated to be:

		Costs (millions)
Private		$233
Public		235
Police	$ 58	
Courts	27	
Corrections	150	
TOTAL		$468

Assuming an addict population of 375,000, this amounts to an annual cost of approximately $1,250 per addict.

Foregone Production

For the purposes of the present model addict unemployment, or foregone production, is considered to be a social cost. The rationale behind this assumption is that the unemployed addict burdens society in a number of indirect ways by failure to support dependents, cost of health care, etc. When the addict receives welfare payments, these costs are directly measurable, at least in part. However, welfare costs present a problem with respect to the present model, since only a small segment (4 to 6 percent) of the untreated addict population typically receives welfare payments (Babst and associates, 1969; Jaffe and associates, 1969; Wieland and Chambers, 1970), whereas the majority of unemployed addicts in treatment qualify for and receive welfare (Cushman, 1971; Gearing, 1971; Wieland and Moffett, 1970). Including both foregone production and welfare payments would result in double-counting. For this reason, foregone production will be used as the measure of social cost and welfare payments will not be included.

Table 3 summarizes the employment rates of untreated addicts, as reported in various studies. The first three listed are discharges from Lexington and prison parolees. With one exception, the remainder provides employment status at the time of admission to methadone maintenance clinics, as reported by the addict. In most cases there is no indication as to whether the data refer to fulltime or parttime employment. Higher employment rates tend to be found among older addicts applying for methadone treatment. For the purpose of the present model, we have assumed that 30 percent of patients currently applying for methadone maintenance are employed fulltime prior to admission. The overall population of addicts on the street is assumed to have a somewhat lower employment rate (25 percent).

The basis for estimating the productivity of addicts has been discussed elsewhere (McGlothlin and associates, 1972). It was concluded that the average annual productivity of fully employed addicts is valued at $4,600. Thus, the average annual loss or foregone production for an addict unemployed 75 percent of the time is $3,450.

Table 3. EMPLOYMENT RATES AMONG UNTREATED ADDICTS

Source	N	%	Remarks
Duvall et al. (1963)	453	55[a]	employable males discharged from Lexington
Babst et al. (1969)	424 201	34[b] 21[b]	N.Y. male parolees, prior to commitment (1966) N.Y. male parolees, prior to commitment (1967)
Gearing (1970)	1,974	34 (68)[c]	male; premethadone
Perkins-Bloch (1970)	712	17	methadone applicants-not accepted for treatment
Perkins-Bloch (1970)	521	27 (41)	82% male, premethadone
Jaffe et al. (1969)	48	58 (75)	premethadone
Wieland-Chambers (1970)	32	34 (78)	premethadone
Dobbs (1971)	100	41 (41)	premethadone
Maslansky (1970)	157	16 (49)	premethadone
Wieland-Moffett (1970)	104	45 (49)	premethadone
Cushman (1971)	81	57 (81)	premethadone

a. 37% full time, 18% part time.
b. Employed 25% or more of time.
c. Percentages in parentheses provide post-methadone employment rates, usually after 12 months.

METHADONE MAINTENANCE-1

Methadone maintenance-1 (MM-1) is the type of program currently being offered in a number of clinics imposing strict control. Urines are closely monitored and patients are confronted with evidence of illicit drug use. Take-home methadone is only permitted when there is continuing evidence of abstinence from heroin and other drugs, plus social stability. Patients are strongly urged to seek employment and are dismissed from the program for repeated illicit drug use, alcoholism, irregular participation, and illegal behavior.

Maximum Potential. A question currently very much in evidence is that of the number of addicts who can be enrolled and held in MM-1 type programs, given adequate services to satisfy the demand. As shown in Table 1, an estimated 40,000 addicts are currently in methadone programs. By no means all of the present clinics impose the discipline specified for an MM-1 type program; nevertheless, the demonstrated ability to attract large numbers of addicts off the street affords some basis for predicting its maximum potential. Although there are few data on the number of waiting lists, it is probably safe to predict that 40,000 volunteers could be added in MM-1 as soon as sufficient facilities become available. If the estimate of 375,000 addicts in Table 1 is reasonably correct, 80,000 MM-1 patients would be about 26 percent of the addict population not incarcerated or involved in other forms of treatment. Beyond the 80,000 level, the potential drawing power of MM-1 is less certain. One follow-up of 500 individuals detoxified in New York City during 1961-63 found that 23 percent had entered a methadone maintenance program by 1971 (Richman, Perkins, Bihari, and Fishman, 1971). The percentage of those available for participation was substantially higher, since 15 percent of the original sample was dead by 1971 and another 9 percent was in prison. On the other hand, the sample may not be representative of the general population of addicts since it was selected from a group initially seeking treatment. In addition, age at the time of entering methadone maintenance was substantially above the mean for the addict population, and this favors entry into this type treatment.

Some additional evidence is provided by the few cities whose methadone programs have been able to accommodate most of the applicants. In 1971 the New Orleans program contained 1,800 patients, estimated to be 30 to 40 percent of the addict population (Bloom, 1972). Most of the New Orleans clinics charge patients $10 per week, are quite strict, and receive some police referrals as patients. The Washington, D.C., program is another service which has attempted to operate without a waiting list. Their multi-modality service currently has 3,500 patients, estimated to be only about 20 percent of the active addicts (DuPont, 1972). Only 60 percent of the treatment population is on methadone maintenance. Of particular interest is the fact that methadone maintenance is by no means the most frequently requested service. Of new applicants only about 20 percent both request and are eligible for methadone maintenance; 60 percent are referred to a detoxification center, and 20 percent to abstinence programs. Similarly, Rosenberg and Patch (unpublished) found that most applicants in Boston requested gradual withdrawal rather than long-term methadone maintenance. On the other hand, Dole (1972) has reported that 80 percent of the addicts detoxified in the New York City detention facilities indicated interest in obtaining continuing treatment. Some argue that methadone maintenance will attract larger numbers as reluctance of addicts to participate is overcome because of recommendations of methadone patients, perhaps as many as 85 percent eventually volunteering.

The proportion of the population maintainable on methadone treatment is dependent as much on the ability to retain as to attract addicts. In general, about 70 to 85 percent are reported to still be in treatment after a period of one year. Data for some 8,000 admissions in New York City show about 85 percent retained for one year, 75 percent for two years (Gearing, 1971). The Washington, D.C. program retains 74 percent after one year (DuPont, 1972). The reasons for discharges in these two programs reveal larger discrepancies, however. In the New York data, 29 percent of those terminated during the first twelve months were voluntary and 8 percent due to death; the remainder are involuntary discharges primarily resulting from arrests, or alcohol and drug abuse (Gearing, 1970). In the Washington program, the majority of the first-year discharges are voluntary. Thus, the proportion voluntarily leaving the Washington program is much larger than that for New York City. The New York patients apparently seldom request detoxification—only 11 percent of those discharged during months 13-24 did so; and only 3 percent of those during months 25-36 (Gearing, 1970). On the other hand, Washington methadone patients often request detoxification after a period of successful maintenance (DuPont, 1972). Several factors may contribute to these differences; however, the major one seems to be availability of services. In New York City, the addict must usually wait several months for admission and, if he chooses to leave, must face another waiting list and additional uncertainty concerning readmission. In Washington, both the new patient and the dropout are admitted on a walk-in basis.

This aspect is even more clear in the Vancouver methadone maintenance program, which has been in operation for several years (Johnston and Williams, 1970). Of the 337 patients in treatment on January 1, 1970, only 38 percent remained after nine months. The time in treatment was substantially longer for older as opposed to younger addicts. A study of relapses and readmissions among patients initially admitted before 1966 showed a mean of 2.9 terminations of methadone maintenance followed by relapse to heroin use, and a range of 0-9. The mean period in treatment between relapse was 15 months with an average relapse to heroin use of three months.

It appears that the retention rates which can be expected for methadone maintenance will be strongly dependent on the alternatives available, and one important alternative is the ability to leave treatment and subsequently return at a later date. When sufficient methadone facilities are available to accommodate the demand, it seems likely that the proportion of admissions retained in continuous treatment for several years will be substantially lower than that currently found in the New York City program.

Another way of viewing the question of potential retention rates is from the standpoint of the individual addict. If the effects of oral methadone are simply to create a cross-tolerance to heroin and reduce or eliminate drug craving, the positive pull of the treatment must come from the opportunity to seek the usual satisfactions of the non-addict. A review of current methadone programs indicates that some 25 to 50 percent of the patients are indeed motivated by this aspect. They do want out of the addiction routine and are attracted by the normal rewards afforded by working, family, etc. They make minimum demands on the program staff, do not attempt to circumvent the treatment via substitution of other drugs, and often demonstrate a dramatic change in life style. These characteristics are more frequently found among older addicts who have apparently tired of the hazards of street addiction. On the other hand, about 25 to 50 percent of current methadone admissions appear to be largely motivated by the push of legal and other pressures. They come into treatment under legal pressure, the demands of relatives, the panic of withdrawal, the need for habit reduction, etc. They are not especially motivated to find employment and change their life style. They are more likely to continue to use heroin and other drugs during treatment, and when the pressure to seek treatment is reduced, often revert to heroin addiction. Of course, this dichotomy is an oversimplification—patients genuinely motivated to remain abstinent may relapse under stress, and some of the second group may be locked into treatment via their methadone addiction. However, it does point up the need to consider both the pull and the push of methadone maintenance and other forms of addiction treatment. It is clear the application of the term volunteer to addict patients is frequently a misnomer. We cannot assess the proportion of the addict population which can be enrolled and retained in treatment without first specifying the level of pressure exerted, both from within and without the program.

Returning to the question of estimating the maximum potential for an MM-1 type program, it is useful to think in terms of (1) the proportion who will enroll and (2) the percentage of time these individuals will spend in treatment—both initially and in subsequent readmissions. With regard to the first question, it appears that less than 50 percent of the addicts seeking treatment will choose methadone maintenance over simple detoxification—at least at first. Of course, addicts apply for treatment repeatedly, and a higher proportion might eventually accept a MM-1 type program. With regard to the second question, 50 to 65 percent appears to be a reasonable estimate for the proportion of time spent in MM-1 for those who ever enroll. Thus, the immediate potential for an MM-1 program is estimated to be a reduction of addict street-years by about 25 percent. Ultimately, the figure might increase to 50 percent, although this is probably an optimistic upper limit. For the present model, 125,000 addict years is taken as the maximum potential for MM-1 treatment, or about 40 percent of the addicts not presently incarcerated or in other forms of treatment. In making these estimates, it is assumed that the pressure directed against the addict remains at the present level. Increases or decreases in this dimension would have corresponding effects on the potential of MM-1.

Treatment Costs. The Annual reported costs of methadone maintenance programs per patient year range from a low of $500 (Davis, 1970; Goldstein, 1970; Stewart, 1970) to a high of $2,750 (Cushman, 1971). The current cost for the Beth Israel program in New York City is $1,900.[6] The differences in cost estimates are related to the extent indirect costs are included, geographic location, frequency of urine testing, and the offering of ancillary services.

For the purposes of the present model, the following treatment costs are assumed for a MM-1 program.

Addict Years	Cost per Patient
First 50,000	$1,500
Second 50,000	1,200
Next 25,000	2,500

It is assumed that some savings will result in the second 50,000 patients as a result of increased efficiency and spreading of overhead.[7] The estimate for the final 25,000 patients is increased to $2,500 per patient to allow for more expenditures for (1) outreach activities such as attempts to retrieve patients who drop out and become readdicted, (2) greater ancillary care for marginal patients, and (3) costs associated with a higher turnover rate.

Treatment Benefits. This is the extent to which the social costs of addiction are reduced via treatment. The *average* annual costs per addict street-year were estimated in the previous section in terms of theft, anti-crime measures, and foregone production. However, there are good reasons for expecting the costs of addiction are not uniform for addicts who volunteer for a given treatment program versus those who do not. Similarly, since motivation for treatment effects the order of volunteering, the first 50,000 patients are likely to have different characteristics from the second 50,000 and so on.

Theft is the largest quantifiable social cost, and the amount for addicts currently volunteering for methadone programs is probably substantially above that for the overall average. This follows because the mean age and years of addiction for methadone patients are some 4 to 7 years greater than those for the general addict population (Gearing, 1971), and years of addiction are known to be positively correlated with larger habits and greater expenditures for drugs. For example, among a sample of 3,600 addicts certified under the New York civil commitment program, 16 percent of those addicted for less than two years reported spending more than $30 per day for drugs, in comparison to 50 percent of those addicted five or more years (NACC, 1968). It is assumed that the first 100,000 addicts enrolled in MM-1 will have a substantially longer history of addiction than the overall addict population, and the annual cost of theft prior to treatment for this group is estimated to be $14,000 per addict. The mean age and years of addiction are expected to be lower for the final 25,000 enrolled, and the annual pre-treatment cost of theft is estimated to be $10,000 per addict. The amount expended on anti-crime measures is assumed to be proportional to the extent of addict-related crime, i.e., $1,750 for the first 100,000 and $1,250 for the final 25,000.

Whereas pre-treatment theft is estimated to decrease as a function of order of entry into the program, pre-treatment foregone production is expected to increase, i.e., the younger, less motivated addict is expected to show a higher unemployment rate.

In summary, the estimated pre-treatment annual costs per street-addict year as a function of order of volunteering for MM-1 are shown in Table 4. The next step is to estimate the reduction in addiction costs resulting from MM-1 treatment—the most important item being the reduction in addict theft. Since methadone maintenance presumably eliminates the necessity for large expenditures on illicit heroin, a sharp drop in the theft rate can be expected. Of course, the addict in MM-1 may still steal to support himself, or to obtain money to purchase substitute drugs. The long-argued question of whether criminal behavior precedes or follows addiction is relevant here, and some have suggested that methadone maintenance, by removing the urgency related to the avoidance of withdrawal, may simply result in a more careful and effective criminal. Since it is very difficult to collect reliable data on crimes committed before and after treatment, the available evidence is in the form of arrest rates. Gearing (1971) compared pre- and post-methadone arrest rates for the first 1,000 N.Y.C. methadone admissions. The mean number of recorded arrests during the four years prior to treatment was 0.6 per year. The reduction in arrests for patients in the first, second, third, and fourth year of treatment were 81, 92, 96, and 98 percent, respectively. Patients discharged from the program showed an arrest rate comparable to their pre-treatment level (Gearing, 1970). DuPont (1972) reported that 17 percent of methadone maintenance patients in the Washington, D.C. program were arrested on a new charge during their first year of treatment, in comparison to 39 percent of patients referred to their abstinence program. In a sample of 248, Cushman (1972) found a pre-methadone arrest rate of 0.42 per

Table 4.   COST PER STREET-ADDICT YEAR (PRE-TREATMENT)

| | Treated | | Untreated |
	0-100,000	100,000-125,000	125,000-300,000
Theft	$14,000	$10,000	$7,715
Anti-crime	1,750	1,250	965
Foregone production	3,220	3,450	3,600
Total	$18,970	$14,700	$12,280

year in comparison to 0.10 and 0.05 during the first and second year of treatment, respectively.

Accurate and complete information on arrests is difficult to obtain and the data cited in pre- and post-methadone arrest rates generally do not distinguish between drug and non-drug arrests. Since drug offenses typically constitute one-third of the total arrests among addicts, Vorenberg has suggested the reduction following methadone treatment may be partially an artifact resulting from fewer drug arrests (Vorenberg and Lukoff, 1972). In summary, adequate studies of the relationship between methadone maintenance and criminal behavior have not yet been conducted. The available evidence on arrests tends to indicate a substantial reduction following initiation of treatment. For the purpose of the present model, the reduction in theft and anti-crime measures is estimated to be 80 percent for the first 100,000 MM-1 patients and 70 percent for the next 25,000. These fairly optimistic estimates are based mostly on the assumption that a strict methadone program will largely eliminate illicit drug use and the accompanying requirement for fund-raising crime.

In addition to the question of treatment-related crime reduction, an estimate of the change in foregone production, or employment rate, is needed. Data on pre- and post-methadone employment rates are provided for several methadone programs in Table 3. Most have reported significant increases in employment. An employment rate of 60 percent (foregone production, $1,840) is estimated for the first 100,000 MM-1 patients in comparison to a pre-treatment rate of 30 percent. The estimated post-treatment rate for the next 25,000 MM-1 patients is 45 percent, reflecting less suitability for employment among those less motivated for treatment, as well as lower pre-treatment employment rates. As mentioned earlier, unemployed methadone maintenance patients generally qualify for and receive welfare; however, in the present model this cost is subsumed under the foregone production estimate.

Table 5 summarizes the pre- and post-treatment social costs per addict year for MM-1 type treatment. Figure 2 shows the estimated social profit resulting

Table 5. SOCIAL COSTS FOR MM-1 TYPE TREATMENT

	Number of addict years (000)				
Cost	0-100		100-125		125-300
	Pre	Post	Pre	Post	Untreated
Foregone Production	3,220	1,840	3,450	2,530	3,600
Theft	14,000	2,800	10,000	3,000	7,715
Anti-crime measures	1,750	350	1,250	375	965
Treatment costs	–	1,350	–	2,500	–
Total	18,970	6,340	14,700	8,405	12,280

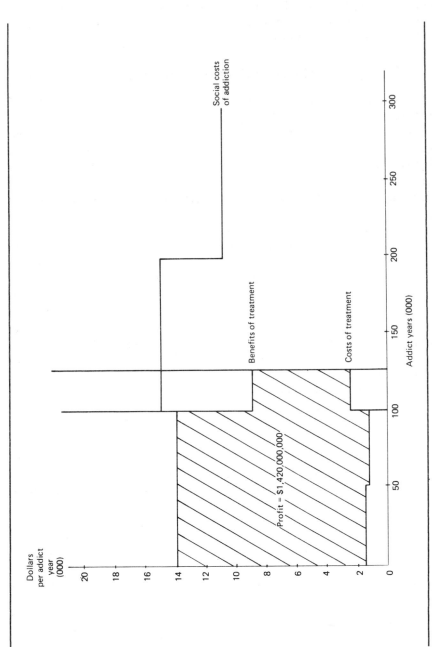

Figure 2.

from expanding MM-1 to 125,000 addict years. The area under the social cost curve to the right of the vertical dashed line represents the social costs of the remaining 175,000 addict years not in treatment.

METHADONE MAINTENANCE-2

Methadone maintenance-2 (MM-2) would dispense oral methadone to registered addicts without imposing controls on illicit drug use and other behavior. Take-home methadone privileges would be permitted to those voluntarily demonstrating abstinence from illicit drug use and social stability; otherwise, consumption would take place at the dispensing station. Other ancillary services could be provided either independently or as a reward for socially approved behavior; however, the availability of methadone would not be contingent on this aspect.

The essential difference between this approach and MM-1 is the lack of rehabilitative pressure exerted from within the program. Emphasis is placed on reducing the social costs of addiction by enrolling and maintaining as many addicts as possible. To further this goal, dispensing stations would be conveniently located and minimum demands would be made on the patient. Irregular participation would be permitted, and individuals could leave and re-enter the program with little difficulty. Adequate precautions would be taken to prevent the administration of methadone to ineligible persons, to avoid duplicate registration, and prevent diversion. Otherwise, the program would be geared to service a maximum number of addicts.

One advantage of this approach over MM-1 is the avoidance of the social costs incurred as a result of discharging methadone maintenance patients in violation of regulations covering illicit drug abuse, alcoholism, etc. Thus, discharges which result in a net economic loss due to the resumption of heroin addiction are not consistent with a policy of minimizing the social costs. A number of the current methadone maintenance programs are more or less following an MM-2 type policy, reasoning that a substantial reduction in heroin use is socially beneficial even though there is little evidence of individual rehabilitation. The major counter-argument is that enforced structure and discipline are essential components for maximizing social as well as individual benefits. The addict is viewed as the victim of a compulsive behavior who needs, and perhaps welcomes, the imposition of certain constructive external controls. According to this position, the social benefit derived from persons successfully treated in an MM-1 program would be significantly degraded by the removal of the coercive elements. Some preliminary investigations have confirmed that methadone maintenance patients do respond to the threat of expulsion by reducing illicit drug-using behavior

(Nightingale and associations, 1971). Further research is needed to adequately define the relationship between patient performance and the internal discipline imposed in methadone programs.

Maximum Potential. Presumably, addicts who participate in an MM-1 type program would continue in MM-2, although the results might be less socially desirable for the reasons discussed above. It also seems likely that the large majority of the remaining addict population would participate in an MM-2 type program at some time over a period as long as two or three years. The basis for this conclusion is the fact that most addicts periodically need to interrupt or reduce their heroin habit for various reasons, and an MM-2 program would provide this service more readily, and with less accompanying stress, than do the currently existing detoxification facilities. In addition, some investigations have found that substantial numbers of addicts are already protecting themselves against heroin shortages via a supply of black-market methadone (Walter and associates, 1972). The fact that a high percentage of addicts would at least pass through an MM-2 program in a relatively short period of time would provide an effective means of registering the addict population.

Another possible advantage of such a program is the clarification of addict responsibility for addiction-related theft and other crimes. At present, the courts are faced with the dilemma of whether to treat addiction and the associated fund-raising theft as a disease or a crime (Phillipson, 1971). Often this results in relatively short jail sentences, even though there is little doubt that the addict will continue his antisocial behavior as soon as released (Curran, 1971; Legislative Commission, 1971). With the existence of an MM-2 type program, the addict would have a viable alternative to heroin addiction, and the courts could take a more forceful position with respect to illicit narcotics use, and especially with regard to fund-raising crime. This in turn might result in greater long-term participation in MM-2 as a result of the increased external pressure against heroin use and its associated antisocial behavior.

In terms of estimating the maximum reduction in addict street-years resulting from a MM-2 type program, we may begin with the assumed 125,000 addict years for MM-1 and add (1) those lost to MM-1 via involuntary discharges, (2) the number contributed by addicts who would not enroll in MM-1 but do become involved on a continuing basis in MM-2 because of its ready accessibility and minimum demands, and (3) those resulting from the periodic participation of the remainder of the addict population.[8] For the purposes of the present model, it is assumed that MM-2 would provide treatment for an additional 50,000 addict years beyond that for MM-1, or a total of 175,000 addict years.

Treatment Costs. A purely dispensing and record-keeping service could probably operate for under $500 per addict year. However, it would likely be desirable to offer additional services aimed at maintaining addicts who are initially motivated to participate on a temporary basis, and to encourage rehabilitation beyond the simple discontinuation of heroin use. In order to expand the program to its maximum potential, additional funds could profitably be expended to provide greater accessibility via additional dispensing stations and through outreach efforts to retrieve persons discontinuing treatment. The following treatment costs were assumed:

Addict Years	Cost per Patient
First 50,000	$1,000
Next 100,000	750
Next 25,000	1,500

Treatment Benefits. As discussed earlier, the major contributor to social cost is addict theft. This in turn has been assumed to be closely related to the amount expended for heroin. Following this logic, the reduction in theft resulting from MM-2 treatment is largely a function of the reduction in heroin use. In the absence of the MM-1 type pressure against illicit drug use, it may be assumed that drug use and expenditures are somewhat greater for MM-2. On the other hand, except for special cases, MM-2 requires the methadone to be consumed under observation, and this should largely prevent the motivation for heroin use, at least when high methadone doses are used. For irregular participants, the days when methadone is not taken are not counted as treatment days. Thus, the cost of heroin consumed on days when methadone is not received would not be relevant for calculating MM-2 theft reduction as defined here. For these reasons, the reduction in theft and associated anti-crime measures for MM-2 treatment is estimated to be 75 percent for the first 100,000 addict years, or only slightly below the 80 percent assumed for this group under MM-1 treatment. The next 75,000 addict years treated under MM-2 are assumed to be made up of more marginal patients—hence, the theft reduction is estimated to be only 60 percent.

Employment rates under MM-2 are estimated to be 50 percent for the first 100,000 addict years and 40 percent for the next 75,000. Table 6 summarizes the pre- and post-treatment social costs per addict year for MM-2 type treatment, and Figure 3 shows the estimated social profit resulting from 175,000 addict years under MM-2 treatment.

HEROIN MAINTENANCE

The British System

The only significant information on heroin maintenance is provided by the British approach in dealing with a small population of narcotic addicts. Until

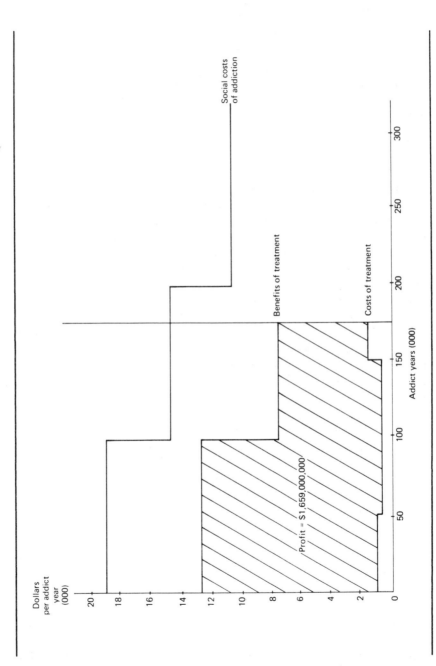

Figure 3.

Table 6.   SOCIAL COSTS FOR MM-2 TYPE TREATMENT

| | Number of addict years (000) | | | | |
| | 0-100 | | 100-175 | | 175-300 |
Cost	Pre	Post	Pre	Post	Untreated
Foregone production	3,220	2,300	3,450	2,760	3,650
Theft	14,000	3,500	10,000	4,000	6,800
Anti-crime measures	1,750	435	1,250	500	850
Treatment costs	–	875	–	1,125	–
Total	18,970	7,110	14,700	8,385	11,300

1968 addicts were largely maintained on their drug of choice by private physicians. Over-prescribing by a small number of physicians led to substantial leakage and resulted in prohibiting private physicians from prescribing heroin or cocaine for maintenance and the statutory requirement to notify the government of known or suspected addicts. A limited number of clinics were then authorized to prescribe narcotics to individuals demonstrating addiction. The committee on whose recommendations these changes were based also recommended permitting clinics to submit addict patients to compulsory hospitalization where necessary.[9] This provision was not enacted, however.

By the end of 1970 the number of addicts being served by the outpatient clinics had stabilized at around 1,150 (Bewley, 1971). This is less than 50 percent of the addict population, which is currently estimated at around 2,500-3,000 (Brill and Larimore, 1971). New admissions to the clinics now average about 30 per month (Bewley, 1971). Since the clinic population is stable, the twelve-month retention rate is about 70 percent.

The clinics initially prescribed primarily heroin. According to Bewley (1971), there has been a gradual shift to injectable methadone, but there is still relatively little oral methadone maintenance of the type employed in the U.S. At the end of 1970, the relative amounts of drugs being prescribed were 50 percent heroin, 40 percent injectable methadone, and 10 percent oral methadone. The drugs are obtained on a daily basis via prescriptions mailed to pharmacies.

The goals of the British approach are: (1) to treat the addict in a non-compulsory manner, (2) to prevent excessive leakage of narcotics to other persons; and (3) to discourage the establishment of a profitable black market. The goals are not entirely compatible since, to accomplish the third goal, the addict must be attracted into treatment with a form of maintenance acceptable to him—hence, the primary prescribing of injectable heroin or methadone. This, in turn, is not as compatible with the goal of resocialization as is oral administration. The avoidance of excessive leakage requires a conservative policy in terms of amount prescribed, since drugs are not injected under observation. This, in turn, may lead to the seeking of additional drugs in the black market, which tends to defeat the goal of preventing a profitable black market. On the whole, however, most observers agree that the current British system is functioning reasonably well. The relatively small population of addicts has apparently not increased over the past two years. Bewley and others cite the sharp rise in the price of black market heroin ($2.50 per 60 mg. in 1967 compared to $15.00 in 1971) as evidence that the clinic system has stemmed the substantial leakage resulting from overprescribing physicians. Of course, increase in black market prices may result from increased demand as well as shortages in supply. The current prices may also encourage the smuggling of illicit heroin, which has been minimal thus far. The current status of the estimated 1,500 addicts not enrolled in the clinics is also a question. Data on this group are not available, but some are probably being maintained on narcotics other than heroin by private physicians.[10] Others may be abstinent, dead, in prison, or substituting other drugs; but an unknown number are obtaining their drug supplies via the black market in preference to entering the official clinics.

Heroin Maintenance in the U.S.

Turning to the U.S., the principal argument for introducing heroin main-tenance is to increase the proportion of addicts volunteering for maintenance treatment. Instead of reducing the street addict population by an estimated 40 percent via MM-1 or 60 percent via MM-2, heroin maintenance would presumably attract virtually all. This did not occur in Britain. However, the reduced alternatives available in the U.S., the poor quality and high prices of illicit heroin, and the existing enforcement pressure, would likely result in a much higher proportion volunteering for and continuing in a heroin maintenance program.

For the purpose of the present model, a program similar to that currently existing in Britain will be assumed. Oral methadone maintenance would be encouraged but not required. Eighty percent or more would probably elect to take injectable heroin or methadone. Drugs would be available at pharmacies or dispensing stations on a daily basis. If leakage proved to be too great a problem, twice-a-day injection of methadone under observation might be required.[11] The maximum potential is estimated to be 250,000 addict years. The remaining 50,000 addict years would be made up of (1) persons ineligible because of age or too short a period of addiction, and (2) those who choose to obtain their drugs through illicit sources because of irregular use, light habits, or for other reasons.

Treatment Costs. As in the case of MM-2, treatment is assumed to include ancillary services for those requesting them. In addition, counseling and other efforts would be employed to encourage patients to participate in oral methadone maintenance. Perhaps new admissions would be required to accept a trial period of oral methadone prior to qualifying for injectable drugs. If a policy of only permitting consumption under observation were adopted, additional treatment costs would be incurred. For the present purposes, the following annual costs have been adopted:

Addict Years	Cost per Addict
First 50,000	$1,500
Next 100,000	1,000
Next 50,000	1,500
Next 50,000	2,000

Treatment Benefits. Predicting the impact of heroin maintenance on addict theft is highly speculative because of the lack of data. On the surface, it would appear that if the addict receives his drug of choice free there is no need to steal to buy it. On the other hand, stabilization at a given dose level is more difficult with heroin use than for oral methadone. The strong preference for the former is a function of the psychic effects which, to be maintained, require increasing doses. As discussed earlier, oral methadone produces little or no psychic effects after stabilization. Of course, the addict may seek the high effect via other drugs, but the fact that he does not experience it three or four times per day as a result of his maintenance treatment makes stabilization much easier. If heroin maintenance were not administered under observation, the problem of simultaneously preventing leakage through over-prescribing, and black market purchases from under-prescribing, would exist here as in Britain. Some data are provided by a British interview study of 111 patients being maintained on heroin (Stimson and Ogborne, 1970). The mean heroin dose was 135 mg. per day and 91 percent of the sample also received methadone.[12] In the month prior to the interview, 84 percent had used some illicit drugs other than cannabis and 38 percent admitted engaging in illicit activities.

The following table shows the estimated percentage reduction in theft for heroin maintenance in comparison to that assumed for MM-1 and MM-2:

Addict Years	MM-1	MM-2	Heroin
0-100,000	80	75	70
100,000-200,000	70	60	50
200,000-250,000	–	–	40

The 70 percent reduction for the first 100,000 addict years on the heroin maintenance program assumes that some portion of patients who are now functioning well in MM-1 programs would still choose oral methadone, and the staff efforts would strongly encourage this choice for all administrations. The lower reductions in theft for the next 150,000 heroin maintenance patients assume that the younger, less stable addicts will continue to engage in considerable antisocial behavior to purchase drugs and for other purposes. One reason for expecting this to occur more for heroin maintenance than for oral methadone is the anticipated lower level of employment and general rehabilitation for heroin maintenance. As stated initially, the basis for these estimates is quite speculative. One might argue equally well that, if tolerance were built up to point where satiation heroin doses of 500 mg. or more per day were administered under observation, this would eliminate both thefts for additional heroin and the problem of leakage.

The relative impact of heroin versus oral methadone maintenance on employment is more certain. The psychic fluctuation accompanying heroin use clearly impairs functioning more than does oral methadone. Stimson and Ogborne (1970) reported 40 percent of heroin-maintained patients were employed fulltime and 9 percent parttime. In general, British observers have found that the stabilized heroin addict who maintains steady employment, practices sterile injection procedures, and otherwise leads a normal existence represents only a small minority of the addict population (Edwards, 1969; Stimson and Ogborne, 1970). The following shows the estimated employment percentages for heroin maintenance in comparison to those assumed for MM-1 and MM-2:

Addict Years	MM-1	MM-2	Heroin
0-100,000	60	50	45
100,000-200,000	45	40	35
200,000-250,000	–	–	25

Table 7 summarizes the pre- and post-treatment social costs per addict year for heroin-maintenance type treatment. Figure 4 shows the estimated social profit resulting from 150,000 addict years under heroin maintenance.

Another advantage of a heroin maintenance approach not included in the model is the deep inroads which would be made in the illicit heroin market. With over 80 percent of the street-addict population in treatment, it might be possible to virtually eliminate the organized black market.

Table 7. SOCIAL COSTS FOR HEROIN-MAINTENANCE TYPE TREATMENT

	Number of addict years (000)						
	0-100		100-200		200-250		250-300
Cost	Pre	Post	Pre	Post	Pre	Post	Untreated
Foregone production	3,220	2,530	3,450	2,990	3,700	3,450	3,700
Theft	14,000	4,200	10,000	5,000	6,000	3,600	6,000
Anti-crime measures	1,750	525	1,250	625	750	450	750
Treatment costs	–	1,250	–	1,250	–	2,000	–
Total	18,970	8,505	14,700	9,865	10,450	9,500	10,450

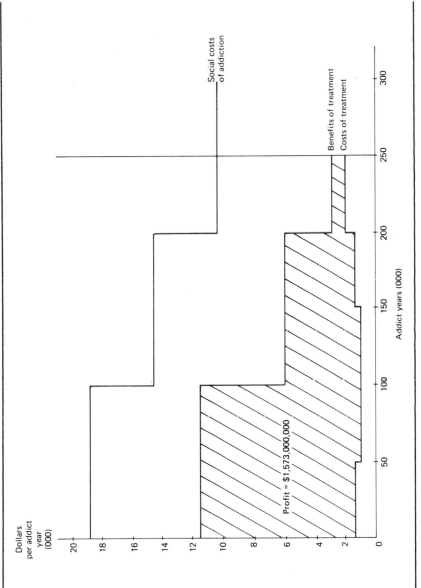

Figure 4.

There are also three potentially serious disadvantages which have not been discussed. First, the existence of a heroin maintenance program would remove some of the major hazards of becoming addicted and thus might increase the overall addict population. The fact that this has not occurred in Britain is no assurance that it would not happen here. In the extreme, it amounts to announcing that the choice to use heroin will result in society providing the drug of choice, *plus* spending money, i.e., welfare. A second disadvantage of heroin maintenance is that it would likely undercut other treatment programs which are more socially profitable on a per-addict basis. Oral methadone maintenance and therapeutic communities would undoubtedly attract fewer addicts when in competition with heroin maintenance. Finally, heroin maintenance would result in higher morbidity and mortality rates than those for oral maintenance because of the danger of disease and overdose resulting from the injection procedures.

THERAPEUTIC COMMUNITIES

The only other volunteer treatment program which has shown appreciable success on a continuing basis is the therapeutic community, e.g., Synanon, and other organizations modeled on its approach. Some participants have been assigned to these programs through the New York certification procedures; however, the basic treatment concept requires the evincing of strong motivation on the part of the individual. Some therapeutic communities view this form of treatment as continuing indefinitely, with the ultimate developing of industries and other requirements necessary for a self-contained micro-society. For others, the goal is to return the individual to the larger society after a prolonged in-residence period. The present model considers only the in-residence aspects.

Maximum Potential. These programs have generally provided few data on admissions and retention rates. One study found 20 percent of admissions were retained twelve months (Jaffe, 1970). Of 2,110 Addiction Services Agency-funded admissions to the New York City Phoenix House during 1967-70, only 79, or 3.7 percent, have completed the program.[13] Most observers agree that only a relatively small minority of the addict population is motivated to volunteer for therapeutic communities; selection processes further reduce this number; and the twelve-month retention rate for those accepted is no more than 25 percent. Eight thousand, or 2 percent, of the estimated addict population are currently estimated to be in therapeutic communities (Table 1). In California, where Synanon was founded in 1958, there are an estimated 1,500, or about 4 percent, of the addict population. Even if therapeutic communities were made widely available, admission requirements reduced, and no competing treatments existed, it is doubtful if more than 10 percent of the addict population could be maintained in this modality. For the present model, it is assumed that the maximum potential is 40,000 addict years.

Treatment Costs. This depends partly on whether or not professional staff are employed. With minimal or no professional participation, the annual cost per participant is estimated to be $4,000. Eventually, such communities can be partially self-supportive, so the annual cost used here is $2,500.

Treatment Potential. These programs generally demand complete abstinence, and available evidence indicates that drug use and criminal behavior are virtually non-existent in the more closely controlled communities. One study of 104 continuing participants with an average stay of 22 months found an arrest rate of 5 percent of the pre-admission level (DeLeon and associates, 1971). One-third of this sample was living in apartments outside the community. For the present model, treatment via therapeutic communities is estimated to reduce addict theft by 95 percent.

Employment is estimated to be 50 percent, including both in-house endeavors and external jobs. This is above the current level of employment for most therapeutic communities, but those continuing to function over a long period are expected to develop employment opportunities of the type now available to Synanon residents.

Table 8 summarizes the annual pre- and post-treatment social costs per addict year for the therapeutic community modality. Figure 5 shows the resulting social profit.

While the potential of therapeutic communities for reducing the street addict population is small relative to the chemotherapy approaches, it is nevertheless an important modality. For those addicts who find the approach acceptable, it produces good results at relatively low cost. It is also important to be able to offer a viable alternative for those who desire long-term treatment other than chemotherapy. Finally, since it is one of the most innovative developments in the field of addiction treatment, further exploration of its potential might yield valuable results.

Table 8. SOCIAL COSTS FOR THERAPEUTIC COMMUNITY TREATMENT

Cost	Number of addict years (000)		
	0-40		*40-300*
	Pre	*Post*	*Untreated*
Foregone production	3,450	2,300	3,450
Theft	10,000	500	10,000
Anti-crime measures	1,250	65	1,250
Treatment costs	—	2,500	—
Total	14,700	5,365	14,700

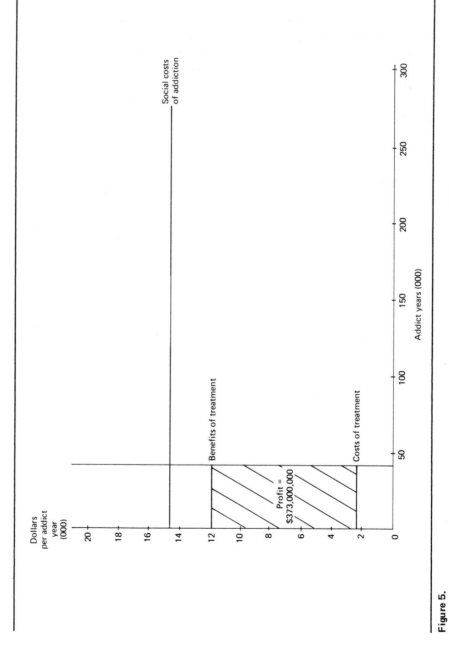

Figure 5.

DETOXIFICATION

Addiction treatment which involves only detoxification does not fit the model utilized in this paper; however, it deserves brief mention since it is the most frequently provided treatment service. Inpatient treatment is necessary to insure detoxification and is routinely accomplished with decreasing doses of methadone over a period of one to two weeks. As mentioned earlier, one hospital in New York City detoxifies some 8,000 addicts per year with an average stay of twelve days (Richman, Clark, Bergner, and Patrick, 1971). More recently, ambulatory detoxification has been attempted on a large scale. The N.Y.C. Addiction Services Agency currently provides a seven-day ambulatory methadone withdrawal which it projects will service some 25,000 addicts per year. There is no measure to determine the percentage of those who actually withdraw from illicit use of opiates; however, urine-monitored studies of ambulatory detoxification patients administered decreasing doses of methadone over periods of a few weeks to a few months have found about 25 percent are opiate-free at the completion of the detoxification period (Chambers, 1972; Wieland and Chambers, 1970).

Maximum Potential. In Table 1 it was estimated that addicts average one voluntary inpatient detoxification per three years. If sufficient in and outpatient detoxification facilities were available, this rate would likely be increased by a factor of at least two or three. A large number of involuntary detoxifications also take place in connection with incarceration. Recently, the New York City detention facilities have implemented a seven-day methadone withdrawal program and are currently detoxifying addicts at a projected rate of 45,000 per year (Malcolm, 1972).

Cost of Treatment. The average cost of an inpatient detoxification at the Beth Israel Center in N.Y.C. is $550. This figure may be somewhat higher for smaller programs. Outpatient detoxification costs depend on the length of the withdrawal period. With the exception of intake costs, outpatient costs are comparable to those for methadone maintenance for a similar time period.

Treatment benefits. One obvious benefit resulting from inpatient detoxification is the elimination of addict theft during the hospitalized period—an average of $27 per day under the $10,000-per-year assumption described earlier. Additional benefits result from the period of abstinence following discharge. A six-month follow-up study of 55 ambulatory detoxification patients by Moffett and associates (1972) found the following periods of abstinence from opiates:

Period	%
Using when discharged	53
1-5 days	14
6-30 days	6
31-90 days	6
91-181 days	11
No use	11

These data indicate a mean of 40 days of opiate abstinence per patient at the six-month follow-up, with 11 percent still abstinent at that time. Finally, some benefits result from habit reduction. If 30 days were required to return to the previous level of opiate use, this would amount to an estimated 50 percent reduction in cost during this period.

While detoxification does not provide a long-term impact for more than a small fraction of addicts undergoing this treatment, it still generates a net social profit, considering only temporary reduction in addict theft. A more important reason for maintaining detoxification facilities is to accommodate the addicts who are motivated to achieve and maintain an abstinent state: 15 percent of the street-addict population is estimated to be voluntarily abstinent at any given time (Table 1). In addition, availability of detoxification centers permits increased flexibility in treatment assignment, especially for young persons with relatively short periods of addiction. Such individuals may be detoxified one or more times before instituting methadone maintenance with its accompanying hazards for long-term addiction. Finally, detoxification provides an opportunity to establish contact with the addict and possibly initiate long-term treatment.

CIVIL COMMITMENT

Civil commitment of addicts normally involves a period of incarceration or compulsory hospitalization followed by a period of parole or outpatient supervision. During the latter period, detection of specified violations may result in additional compulsory confinement. There is considerable evidence that outpatient supervision combined with the threat of confinement results in longer periods of abstinence from opiate use than does release from prison or hospitals without such a program (O'Donnell, 1965; Vaillant, 1966). Other factors being equal, the success rate in the outpatient phase is a function of: (1) extent of drug use permitted; (2) closeness of outpatient monitoring; and (3) the certainty and degree of punishment following detected violations. In one program which provided daily urine testing of 327 parolees, 87 percent exhibited narcotics usage within twelve weeks (Kurland and associates, 1969). The criterion of failure in this program was more than five positive testings or unauthorized absences within any ten-day period. Using this definition, 71 percent either absconded or were returned to prison within six months after admission. Only 6 percent maintained complete abstinence for six months.

An earlier study of 344 parolees which did not utilize tests for narcotics use reported 35 percent were not delinquent for any cause after three years and 45 percent had not returned to opiate use (Diskind, 1960). A continued follow-up for an additional three years found 24 percent still demonstrated successful adjustment for the full six years and 32 percent had not relapsed to opiate use (Diskind and Klonsky, 1964). In another study of 30 parolees, Vaillant (1966) found 60 percent remained abstinent for one year.

The California program (CRC) has provided the most thorough recent test of a closely controlled civil commitment approach, using nalorphine testing to monitor opiate usage. During the initial years (1962-68), about 30 percent remained in outpatient status for one year after an average one-year inpatient confinement; 25 percent for two years; and 17 percent were defined as successes and discharged after three consecutive years on satisfactory outpatient status.[14] With the institution of more lenient conditions for remaining on outpatient status in 1970, the current percentages of one-year successes on first release are 45 percent for men and 50 percent for women (Sing, 1971b). At the end of 1971 approximately 25 percent of California commitments were on inpatient status and 75 percent were outpatients.[15]

A considerably more lenient approach termed "rational authority" maintained 91 percent of a sample of 95 parolees on outpatient status for eighteen months (Lieberman and Brill, 1968). This program only returned the individual to prison after exhausting various other alternatives including compulsory hospitalization for detoxification following relapse.

Maximum Potential. The legislative intent for establishing both the California and New York civil commitment programs was (1) to control the costs of addiction by getting the addict off the street, and (2) if possible, to provide relatively non-punitive rehabilitative services.[16] The estimated percentages of the addict population not incarcerated or in other forms of treatment who are presently on civil commitment status in California and New York are 23 and 7, respectively. Thus, neither program has fulfilled its primary goal. The principal reason is not an inability to apprehend the addict for various drug and non-drug offenses but a reluctance of the courts to commit addicts for long periods (three to five years in New York and seven years in California) when the rehabilitative aspects of the program have not demonstrated an effective cure for addiction, and when the alternative jail terms for most of the offenses are only a few months (Legislative Commission, 1971). If society, through the courts, were willing to fully implement a civil commitment program of the California type, it appears probable that the large majority of the addict population would be committed within two or three years. One study of over 4,000 heroin users found they averaged .84 arrests per year, 60 percent of which were for drug offenses.[17] The 45,000 detoxifications per year currently being conducted by the N.Y.C. detention facilities are a further indication of the rapidity with which addicts could potentially be civilly committed by the criminal justice system. By contrast, only about 2,800 were actually certified to civil commitment in New York via conviction in fiscal 1970 (NACC, 1970).[18]

Not all addicts who pass through the criminal justice system are viewed as potential candidates for civil commitment programs. In fact, both the California and New York laws are written so as to exclude most felons convicted of serious crimes. In practice, however, there are indications that the reverse is often true, at least in California. Felon addicts with long prison sentences are generally more likely to accept civil commitment than misdemeanants who face only a short jail time as an alternative (Katz, 1971; Wood, 1970). A study of California civil commitments found no difference in outpatient performance for felons versus misdemeanants (Sing, 1971a). On the other hand, this program has returned 5 percent of those committed as being "unfit" for treatment (Forden and Sing, 1970).

Another limiting factor for civil commitment programs is abscondence from outpatient care. In New York, 34 percent of those on outpatient status were in abscondence in October 1970 (Legislative Commission, 1971). The corresponding value for the California program was 20 percent for 1971 (California Rehabilitation Center, 1971). In the Diskind and Klonsky (1964) six-year follow-up of 34 parolees, 43 percent absconded at some time; all but 2 percent were apprehended. The mean period at large was 4.5 months.

For the purpose of comparing the maximum potential of a civil commitment program with those of the maintenance programs, it has been assumed that the base population available includes those now on methadone maintenance as well as the current civil commitment and stree-addict populations, i.e., approximately 320,000. It is estimated that 220,000 addict years could be included in a fully implemented California-type program, with 25 percent inpatient status and 75 percent outpatient.[19] The remaining 100,000 addict years would be made up of: (1) those who had never been committed—primarily young persons with a short addiction history; (2) those in abscondence from outpatient status, and (3) undetected persons who had relapsed after being discharged.

Treatment Costs. There is considerable variation in the reported costs of civil commitment programs. The New York annual inpatient cost per patient for 1970 was $7,000-9,250, depending on the facility; aftercare cost was $1,750 per patient. The federal program at Fort Worth and Lexington costs $12,000 for inpatient and $4,800 for aftercare (Chatham and associates, 1972). The corresponding reported costs for the 1971 California program were $4,000 and $850 (California Rehabilitation Center, 1971). For the purposes of the present model in- and outpatient costs were assumed to be $6,000 and $1,200, respectively. With a 25 to 75 percent ratio of in- to outpatients, the average annual cost per patient is $2,400.

Treatment Benefits. As in the case of the other programs, only benefits during treatment are considered. It may be argued that civil commitment is more likely to ultimately result in a drug-free state outside of treatment than are the chemotherapy programs; however, this has not yet been demonstrated. By the end of 1969, the California program had discharged some 600, or 16 percent of those in the program for at least 3.5 years (the minimum time required for discharge at that time), but no follow-up has yet been conducted (Forden and Sing, 1970). There is nothing unique in the inpatient treatment which would lead to above-average expectations; however, the prolonged outpatient phase may result in an increased probability of abstinence following discharge.

The extent of social benefits derived during treatment is favorable. Obviously, addict theft is eliminated during the inpatient phase, and since drug usage and other behavior are closely monitored in the outpatient status, crime rates also appear to be minimal in this phase. Of those returned to inpatient status in the California program, only 15 percent result from criminal involvement and only 5 percent are new felony convictions.[20] Data from the federal civil commitment program show that 29 percent are arrested during an approximate one-year outpatient period (20 percent excluding drug offenses and parole violation).[21] Eleven percent spent more than ten days in jail during the year. For the purposes of the present model, theft reduction is assumed to average 85 percent for the overall treatment.

Employment data for outpatients on the California program showed 44 percent fulltime and 13 percent parttime employment in December, 1971 (California Rehabilitation Center, 1971). Approximately 20 percent were receiving welfare payments. A follow-up of the New York aftercare patients showed 40 percent fulltime employment, 7 percent parttime, and 17 percent housewives or students (NACC, 1971). Data from the federal program indicate 65 percent employed at sometime during outpatient care but the equivalent fulltime employment rate was only 35 percent (days worked/available working days for total sample) (Chatham and associates, 1972). For the model, we have assumed 50 percent employment on outpatient status. Averaged over both in- and outpatient status, this amounts to 37.5 percent overall employment.

Table 9 summarizes the estimated pre- and post-treatment annual cost per addict year for the civil commitment program. Since the order-of-volunteering aspect of the maintenance programs does not exist for civil commitment, both

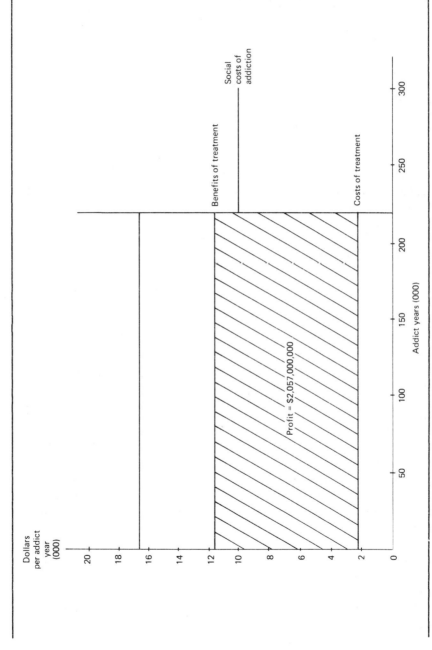

Figure 6.

Table 9.   SOCIAL COSTS FOR CIVIL COMMITMENT PROGRAM

Cost	Number of addict years (000)		
	0-220		220-320
	Pre	Post	Untreated
Foregone production	3,450	2,875	3,450
Theft	11,700	1,755	6,000
Anti-crime measures	1,450	220	750
Treatment costs	—	2,400	—
Total	16,600	7,250	10,200

the social cost and the percentage reduction are assumed to be uniform for the full 220,000 addict years. However, the social cost of the 100,000 addict years not in civil commitment is assumed to be less than the overall average since it consists of a disproportionate number of undetected young addicts with relatively small habits. Figure 6 shows the estimated social profit derived from 220,000 addict years under civil commitment.

COMBINED CIVIL COMMITMENT AND OTHER MODALITIES

As discussed above, the existing civil commitment programs have failed to accomplish their goal of controlling addiction because society is reluctant to deprive the addict of his freedom for such prolonged periods of time in the absence of an effective treatment (Kramer, 1970). One means of making civil commitment more palatable to the addict and the courts is to increase the flexibility of treatment by including other modalities, especially methadone maintenance. In the type of program envisioned, the committed addict would be initially assigned to inpatient status, if considered desirable, but would subsequently have a choice of entering an abstinence program, or, if eligible in terms of age and length-of-addiction requirements, a modified MM-1 type program.[22] Consistent with the privileges afforded other citizens, alcoholism would not be grounds for cancellation of outpatient status, and perhaps moderate usage of non-opiate drugs might also be tolerated. Violation of the conditions of abstinence or methadone outpatient status would result in reconfinement. However, with the alternative of methadone maintenance available, the proportion of time as an inpatient should be substantially reduced over that for straight civil commitment.

Three types of inpatient programs might be employed: (1) the kind presently used in California for initial intakes and psychotherapy; (2) work camps consistent with the concept of punishment for outpatient violations; and (3)

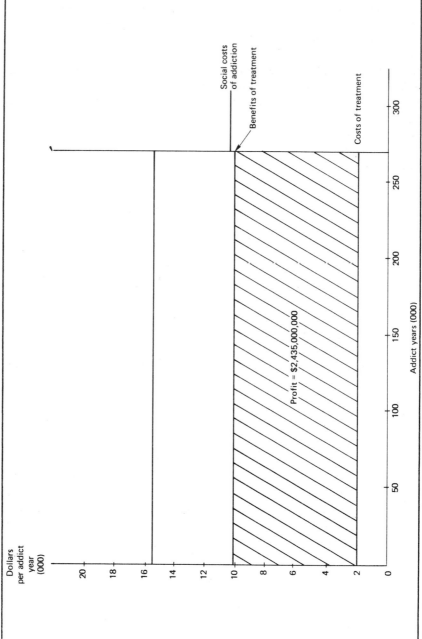

Figure 7.

heroin camps for those repeatedly failing in other approaches and who choose this in preference to other inpatient statuses.[23] In the future, compulsory administration of long-acting antagonists might provide an alternative to inpatient commitment for some individuals.

Maximum Potential. It is estimated that 270,000 of the total population of 320,000 addict years could be provided treatment by the combined programs, or 50,000 more than that for straight civil commitment. The expected increase would result from a much lower abscondence rate due to less dissatisfaction on the part of outpatients. Additionally, some of those who remained undetected under the straight civil commitment program would volunteer or be committed by relatives because of the increased treatment options.

The following breakdown by treatment status is assumed:

Status		Addict Years (000)
Outpatient		225
methadone maintenance	150	
compulsory abstinence	25	
optional abstinence	50	
Inpatient		45
TOTAL		270

The estimated number electing methadone maintenance is 25,000 more than that for the volunteer MM-1 program. The 25,000 in a compulsory abstinence program are ineligible for methadone maintenance because of age or length-of-addiction requirements. The 50,000 on optional abstinence status represent those initially choosing supervised abstinence or therapeutic communities plus those electing to withdraw from methadone.

Treatment Costs. Methadone maintenance costs are estimated at $1,500 per patient year, abstinence programs at $1,750, and inpatient costs at $4,000. The lower inpatient cost for the combined program, as opposed to the straight civil commitment, reflects the lower costs for that portion in work or heroin camps.

Treatment Benefits. The estimated treatment benefits are essentially the same as those for straight civil commitment, i.e., an 85 percent reduction in addict theft and a 50 percent employment on outpatient status. Table 10 summarizes the pre- and post-treatment annual costs per addict year for the combined program. Figure 7 shows the estimated social profit derived from 270,000 addict years treated under the combined program.

An additional advantage of the combined approach is that it appears to offer the best possibility of reducing the demand for illicit heroin to a point where distribution ceases to be a profitable activity. This is somewhat analogous to eradication versus containment of a contagious disease. If the source can be eliminated, the costs of future treatment efforts also cease.

Table 10. SOCIAL COSTS FOR COMBINED PROGRAM

| | Number of addict years (000) | | |
| | 0-270 | | 270-320 |
Cost	Pre	Post	Untreated
Foregone production	3,450	2,670	3,450
Theft	10,700	1,605	6,000
Anti-crime measures	1,350	205	750
Treatment costs	–	2,000	–
Total	15,500	6,480	10,200

It seems likely that the countermeasure resulting from decreased demand for heroin will be to make the illicit product more competitive by increasing its potency as opposed to lowering the price of the unit sales.[24] This appears to have already taken place in New Orleans where some 30 to 40 percent of the current addict population are estimated to be enrolled in methadone programs. The average potency of illicit heroin has reportedly increased from 3 percent in 1968 to 10 percent in 1971 (Bloom, 1972).

SUMMARY AND DISCUSSION

Table 11 lists the six programs providing continuing treatment in order of the estimated social profit. Also shown are the number and social cost of the addict years remaining untreated. While an effort was made to utilize empirical findings to the extent they were available, the calculations obviously include a number of speculative assumptions. In addition, the examining of the potential of each approach in isolation is somewhat artificial, since in practice it would be competing with other modalities. The major intent has been to provide a framework of reasonable internal consistency in order to examine the various approaches to addiction treatment and control.

Table 12 summarizes the advantages and disadvantages of each modality. Throughout, various results are obtained by combining treatment approaches with differing degrees of coercion. Detoxification, heroin maintenance, and MM-2 are largely free of coercive pressure from within the program; however, none of the approaches can be meaningfully considered outside the context of the coercive environment in which the addict exists. This is a point which is often overlooked when discussing the importance of self-motivation for treatment. Applying for oral methadone maintenance is typically not as much a volunteer action as an attempt to escape the pressures resulting from the vigorous enforcement against addiction—note the unwillingness to accept this

Table 11. ESTIMATED SOCIAL PROFIT BY TREATMENT PROGRAM

	Treated		Untreated	
Treatment	Addict years (000)	Profit (millions)	Addict years (000)	Social Cost (millions)
Combination civil commitment and other modalities	270	$2,289*	50	$ 510
Civil commitment	220	1,934*	100	1,020
Methadone maintenance-2	175	1,659	125	1,413
Heroin maintenance	250	1,573	50	523
Methadone maintenance-1	125	1,420	175	2,149
Therapeutic community	40	373	260	3,822

*Reduced to a base population of 300,000 to provide comparability with other programs.

type of treatment in Britain. When behavior changes are forced via threats of dismissal from a methadone maintenance program, the coercion differs from that of civil commitment only in terms of the probability and time of punishment. For example, Gearing (1970) found that 26 percent of methadone dismissals were arrested within six months; Stewart (1970) reported that 32 percent of dropouts were arrested almost immediately; and Perkins and Bloch (1971) reported that arrest and incarceration rates per annum among methadone dismissals were 0.8 and 0.6, respectively. From the standpoint of shaping behavior, a good case can be made for the efficacy of the certain and immediate action of civil commitment over the uncertain and delayed punishment connected with the methadone dismissals.

It is not the purpose of this paper to discuss political philosophy as it relates to drug addiction; however, it is useful to point out the logical fallacies resulting from society's ambivalence in dealing with the issue. It is perhaps best reflected in the Supreme Court's decision to invalidate the crime of being an addict, but continue the felony penalty for possessing the necessary material for addiction (Robison decision). Of particular relevance to the present paper is the failure to acknowledge and accurately identify the role of coercion in all forms of treatment and control of addiction. If society should decide to eliminate coercion as a means of controlling addiction, then heroin maintenance is the appropriate treatment. If it elects to continue coercion, then the isolation of treatment and coercive elements is often more illusory than real. If the goal is to achieve a given level of control with the minimum *overall* amount of coercion, then it seems necessary to integrate the elements of coercion and treatment into a single cooperative effort.

Table 12. SUMMARY OF ADVANTAGES AND DISADVANTAGES FOR SEVEN TREAT-
MENT APPROACHES

Treatment	Advantages	Disadvantages
Methadone maintenance-1	Patients show good social reha-bilitation; low illicit drug use and relatively high employment rate; encourages long-term participation.	Attracts fewer volunteers than other maintenance programs.
Methadone maintenance-2	Provides treatment for a relatively large portion of addict population and some contact with virtually all; relatively inexpensive.	Social rehabilitation is less than that for MM-1; participation is often on a sporadic basis.
Heroin maintenance	Results in the highest portion in treatment of all volunteer pro-grams; should sharply reduce demand for illicit heroin.	Stabilization of dose is difficult; administration is expensive if done at clinic; leakage is a prob-lem if self-administration is utilized; may attract additional persons into addict population; results in higher rates of morbidity and mortality as a result of intravenous use.
Therapeutic community	Produces good results for rela-tively low costs; provides alterna-tive to chemotherapy programs.	Attracts only a small fraction of addict population.
Detoxification	Provides means of withdrawal for persons motivated and capable of remaining abstinent; permits in-creased flexibility in treatment assignment, especially for recently addicted individuals; temporary reduction in illicit drug use and associated theft; pro-vides contact with most of addict population and the possibility of initiating long-term treatment.	Results in long-term solution for only small fraction of those treated.
Civil commitment	Effectively controls illicit drug use and associated crime; may offer higher probability of post-treatment abstinence than chemotherapy programs.	Involves long-term compulsory control without a compensatory high rate of permanent cures; courts are often unwilling to com-mit addicts under these conditions, so size of program is limited; ab-scondence rate is high in some programs; relatively expensive.

Table 12. Continued.

Treatment	Advantages	Disadvantages
Combined civil commitment and other modalities	Much more flexible than straight civil commitment; results in less dissatisfaction and abscondence on the part of the addict; has the largest treatment capability of any program examined and produces the greatest social profit; offers best opportunity to eliminate illicit heroin market.	Similar to straight civil commitment in sense of long-term compulsory control, but extent of confinement and dissatisfaction is less.

NOTES

1. This figure excludes those persons listed on the Register with residence outside New York City.

2. Forty percent of the 82,000 persons listed on the 1971 BNDD file were in New York City.

3. Malcolm (1972) reports an additional 45,000 detoxifications are annually conducted in New York City detention facilities.

4. See the early work of Duvall (1963) and Valliant (1966).

5. The annual cost of heroin and amount of theft reported by Cushman (1971) was increased to adjust for time incarcerated or hospitalized, i.e., to represent a full year on the street other than for periods of voluntary abstinence.

6. This figure was published by the Legislative Commission on Expenditure Review in New York State (1971).

7. Contributions of patients to treatment costs are not considered in this model; however, *some* methadone programs are currently funded by this means.

8. For the purpose of estimating addict years in treatment for irregular participants, only days on which methadone is received would be counted as treatment.

9. See the Second Report of the Interdepartmental Committee on Drug Addiction, H.M.S.O., London, 1965.

10. Physicians may still prescribe opiates other than heroin.

11. This is somewhat different from the heroin experiment currently being considered for New York City (Vera, 1971). That proposal seeks to determine if persons who fail, or do not volunteer for, oral methadone maintenance could be attracted into a short-term heroin program (up to six months) and later transferred to oral methadone. Heroin would be administered under observation in a day-care setting, and extensive efforts would be made to establish rapport in the hopes of continuing oral methadone maintenance.

12. Since the time of this study (1969) the heroin dose levels have been generally reduced. Few patients now receive more than 100 mg. per day. Also, the clinics initially continued the practice inherited from private physicians of prescribing cocaine and methamphetamine for some patients. This has now been largely discontinued.

13. See the 1971 Report by the New York State Legislative Commission on Expenditure Review.

14. See the Annual Report (1969) for the California Narcotics Rehabilitation Advisory Council.

15. Most of the data cited here were provided by Bruce Wilson, Research Analyst, Narcotics Addict Outpatient Program, California Department of Correction, Los Angeles and are unpublished.

16. See Kramer (1970) for California and the Legislative Commission on Expenditure Review (1971) for New York.

17. See the Task Force Report (1967) of the President's Commission on Law Enforcement and Administration of Justice.

18. The remaining 2,400 for 1970 were civilly committed by self or others.

19. This estimate is based on the assumption that the courts would be willing to fully cooperate in such a program, a condition which does not hold at present.

20. See the Annual Report (1969) of the California Narcotics Rehabilitation Advisory Council.

21. See Chatham and associates (1972) for a comprehensive report of this "federal" experience.

22. The federal civil commitment program currently includes a small methadone group, and the California program recently began a pilot methadone maintenance study (Chatham and associates, 1972; Jones, 1971). In addition, some methadone programs have established informal working relationships with enforcement agencies (Bloom and Sudderthe, 1970; Starkey and Egan, 1970). Antagonist programs would provide another alternative when this method becomes operational.

23. The latter two approaches have been previously suggested by Singer and Newitt (1970) and by Bejerot (1970).

24. The basis for this expectation is the profit-risk relationship. Given sufficient availability, potency may be increased by importation of larger amounts of heroin at the relatively low wholesale prices. Decreases in the unit price at the retail level, while maintaining the same low potency, would result in a greatly reduced total profit without a reduction in level of risk.

REFERENCES

BABST, D. V. et al. (1969) "Predicting post-release adjustment of institutionalized addicts: an analysis of New York and California parole experience and California civil commitment experience." Unpublished manuscript (November).

BAGANZ, P. C. and F. MADDUX (1965) "Employment status of narcotic addicts one year after hospital discharge." Public Health Reports 80 (July): 615-621.

BEJEROT, N. (1970) Addiction and Society. Springfield, Ill.: Charles C Thomas.

BEWLEY, T. H. (1971) "The treatment of opiate addicts in the United Kingdom, 1968-1971." Presented at the Fifth World Congress of Psychiatry (Nov. 28), Mexico City.

BLOOM, W. A. (1972) "Methadone in the street." Presented at Fourth National Conference on Methadone Treatment (Jan. 8-10), San Francisco.

BLOOM, W. A. and E. W. SUDDERTH (1970) "Methadone in New Orleans: patients, problems and police." International Journal of the Addictions 5 (3) (Sept.): 465-487.

BRILL, H. and W. LARIMORE (1971) "The British 'system,' an analysis: how Britain handles its drug problem." New York Law Journal (Dec. 6).

California Rehabilitation Center (CRC) (1971) Unpublished program statistics. Corona, Calif.

CHAMBERS, C. D. (1972) "A description of inpatient and ambulatory techniques," in C. D. Chambers and L. Brill, Methadone: Experiences and Issues. New York: Behavioral Publications.

CHATHAM, L. R. et al. (1972) "NIMH drug abuse treatment program evaluation reports, No. 1. The Federal Civil Commitment Program for Narcotic Addict Treatment and Rehabilitation: an assessment of the effectiveness of Titles I and III of the Narcotic Addict Rehabilitation Act of 1966." DHEW Publication No. 72 (HSM) in press (February): 9111.

CURRAN, P. J. (1971) "State commission reports on police and courts." New York Law Journal (Dec. 6).

CUSHMAN, P. (1972) "Arrest frequency before and during methadone maintenance: analysis of New York City police records." Presented at Fourth National Conference on Methadone Treatment (Jan. 8-10), San Francisco.

——— (1971) "Methadone maintenance in hard-core criminal addicts: economic effects." New York State Journal of Medicine 71 (14) (July 15): 1768-1774.

DAVIS, E. P. (1970) "The man alive program." International Journal of the Addictions 5 (3): 421-430.

DeLEON, G. et al. (1971) "The Phoenix therapeutic community: changes in criminal activity of resident drug addicts." Phoenix House Research Unit, New York. Unpublished (September).

DISKIND, M. H. (1960) "New horizons in the treatment of narcotic addiction." Federal Probation (December).

DISKIND, M. H. and G. KLONSKY (1964) "A second look at the New York State parole drug experiment." Federal Probation 28: 34-41.

DOBBS, H. (1971) "Methadone treatment of heroin addicts: early results provide more questions than answers." Journal of the American Medical Association 218 (10) (Dec. 6): 1536-1541.

DOLE, V. P. (1972) "Detoxification of 20,000 addicts in jail: medical procedure and plans for aftercare." Presented at Fourth National Conference on Methadone Treatment (Jan. 8-10), San Francisco.

DuPONT, R. L. (1972) "Trying to treat all of the heroin addicts in a community." Presented at Fourth National Conference on Methadone Treatment (Jan. 8-10), San Francisco.

DUVALL, J. et al. (1963) "Follow-up study of narcotic drug addicts five years after hospitalization." Public Health Reports 78 (3) (March): 185-193.

EDWARDS, G. (1969) "The British approach to the treatment of heroin addiction: hypotheses, difficulties and meeting the difficulties." European Committee on Crime Problems, Sub-Committee No. X. Council of Europe (March 18), Strasbourg.

FORDEN, F. W. and G. SING (1970) "Civil addict program effectiveness as measured by successful discharges: an administrative information report." California Rehabilitation Center. Corona, Calif. (March).

GEARING, F. R. (1971) "Methadone maintenance treatment program, progress report through March 31, 1971—a five year overview." New York: Narcotics Addiction Control Commission (May 14).

——— (1970) "Evaluation of methadone maintenance treatment program." International Journal of the Addictions 5 (3): 517-543.

GOLDSTEIN, A. (1970) "Blind controlled dosage comparisons with methadone in 200 patients." Proceedings Third National Conference on Methadone Treatment. National Institute of Mental Health.

GREENWOOD, J. A. (1971) "Estimating number of narcotics addicts." SCID-TR-3. Bureau of Narcotics and Dangerous Drugs.

INCIARDI, J. A. (1971) "The use of parole prediction with institutionalized narcotic addicts." Journal of Research in Crime and Delinquency 8 (1): 65-73.

INCIARDI, J. A. and C. D. CHAMBERS (1971) "Self-reported criminal behavior of narcotic addicts." Presented at the 33rd Annual Meeting of the Committee of Problems of Drug Dependence (Feb. 16-17) National Academy of Sciences-National Academy of Engineering. Toronto, Canada.

Interdepartmental Committee (1965) Drug Addiction. Second Report of the Interdepartmental Committee. London: H.M.S.O.

JAFFE, J. H. (1970) "Further experience with methadone in the treatment of narcotics users." International Journal of the Addictions 5 (3): 375-389.

——— (1970) Unpublished program statistics for Illinois drug abuse treatment program.

——— et al. (1969) "Experience with the use of the methadone in a multimodality program for the treatment of narcotics users." International Journal of the Addictions 4 (3) (Sept.): 481-490.

JOHNSTON, W. and H. R. WILLIAMS (1970) "Abstinence-relapse patterns among heroin addicts receiving methadone treatment on an outpatient basis." Proceedings Third National Conference on Methadone Treatment: National Institute of Mental Health.

JONES, A. (1971) "CDC methadone maintenance program: first statistical report on applications, rejections and participants." California Department of Corrections (Nov. 4).

KATZ, H. A. (1971) "California Rehabilitation Center: a critical look." International Journal of the Addictions 6: 533-542.

KNOWLES, R. et al. (1970) "Methadone maintenance in St. Louis." International Journal of the Addictions 5 (3): 407-420.

KOVAL, M. (1971) "Differential estimates of narcotics use in New York City." Unpublished manuscript (November). New York: State Narcotics Addiction Control Commission.

——— (1970) "Differential estimates of opiate use in New York City." Unpublished manuscript (February). New York: State Narcotics Addiction Commission.

KRAMER, J. C. (1970) "The state versus the addict: uncivil commitment." Boston University Law Review 50 (1) (Winter): 1-22.

KURLAND, A. et al. (1969) "The out-patient management of the paroled narcotic abuser: a four year evaluation." Committee on Problems of Drug Dependence: 5691-5723.

LARRIER, D. et al. (1971) "Deaths among known narcotics abusers in New York City." Committee on Problems of Drug Dependence I (Jan.-June 1970): 440-470.

Legislative Commission on Expenditure Review (1971) "Narcotic drug control in New York State." Program audit highlights. Albany, New York.

LIEBERMAN, L. and L. BRILL (1968) "Rational authority and the treatment of narcotic offenders." Bulletin on Narcotics 20 (1): 33.

MALCOLM, B. J. (1972) "Detoxification of 20,000 addicts in jail: reduction in incidence of violence and suicide in custodial institutions." Presented at Fourth National Conference on Methadone Treatment (Jan. 8-10), San Francisco.

MASLANSKY, R. (1970) "Methadone maintenance programs in Minneapolis." International Journal of the Addictions 5 (3): 391-405.

McGLOTHLIN, W. H., V. C. TABBUSH, C. D. CHAMBERS, and K. JAMISON (1972) "Alternative approaches to opiate addiction control: costs, benefits, and potential." U.S. Department of Justice Report SCID-TR-7, Bureau of Narcotics and Dangerous Drugs.

MOFFETT, A. D. et al. (1972) "Post-treatment behavior following ambulatory detoxification," in C. D. Chambers and L. Brill, Methadone: Experiences and Issues. New York: Behavioral Publications.

MOORE, M. (1970) "Economics of heroin distribution," in M. Singer and J. Newitt, Policy Concerning Drug Abuse in New York State, III. New York: Hudson Institute.

Narcotic Addict Rehabilitation Branch (1971) Unpublished program statistics (December), Washington.

Narcotic Addiction Control Commission (NACC) (1971) "A review of employment experience during the aftercare phase of treatment." Unpublished manuscript (November), New York.

——— (1970) "Third annual statistical report." (March 31), New York.

——— (1969) "Second annual statistical report." (March 31), New York.

——— (1968) "First annual statistical report." (March 31), New York.

Narcotics Rehabilitation Advisory Council (1969) "Fifth annual report." (April) State of California.

National Prisoner Statistics (1969) NPS Bulletin (44): (July).

New York Department of Health (1971) Narcotics Register Project. Statistical report for 1969. New York City.

New York City Police Department Statistical and Records Bureau (1967) "Statistical report of narcotic arrests and arrests of narcotic users, 1964-65." Cited in the President's Commission on Law Enforcement and Administration of Justice Task Force Report: Narcotics and Drug Abuse.

NIGHTINGALE, S. L. et al. (1971) "Clinical implications of urine surveillance in a methadone maintenance program." Committee on Problems of Drug Dependence 2: 1916-1934.

O'CONNOR, G. et al. (1971) "The economics of narcotics addiction: a new interpretation of the facts." Committee on Problems of Drug Dependence I: 397-424.

O'DONNELL, J. A. (1965) "The relapse rate in narcotic addiction: a critique of follow-up studies," pp. 226-246 in D. Wilner and G. Kassebaum (eds.) Narcotics. New York: McGraw-Hill.

PERKINS, M. E. and H. I. BLOCH (1971) "A study of some failures in methadone treatment." American Journal of Psychiatry 128 (1) (July): 47-51.

——— (1970) "Survey of a methadone maintenance treatment program." American Journal of Psychiatry 126 (10) (April): 1389-1396.

PHILLIPSON, R. (1971) "Drug dependence—opiate type and criminal responsibility." Committee on Problems of Drug Dependence I: 387-396.

President's Commission on Law Enforcement and Administration of Justice (1967) Task Force Report: Narcotics and Drug Abuse. Washington: Government Printing Office.

RICHMAN, A., J. E. CLARK, L. BERGNER, and W. PATRICK (1971) "Followup of 500 heroin users by means of a case register." Committee on Problems of Drug Dependence I: 853-890.

RICHMAN, A., M. E. PERKINS, B. BIHARI, and J. J. FISHMAN (1971) "Entry into methadone maintenance programs: a followup study of New York City heroin users detoxified in 1961-1963." Presented at the 99th annual meeting of the American Public Health Association (Oct. 11-15), Minneapolis.

ROSENBERG, C. M. and V. D. PATCH "Early dropouts from methadone treatment for heroin addiction." Unpublished manuscript. Boston City Hospital: drug dependency unit.

SING, G. E. (1971a) "Drug-free discharge recommendations by commitment type: felony, misdemeanor, no criminal charge." Unpublished manuscript (August 18). California Rehabilitation Center. Corona, Calif.

——— (1971b) "January-June 1970 releases: a one year followup civil narcotic addicts released to outpatient status." (November) California Rehabilitation Center. Corona, Calif.

SINGER, M. and J. NEWITT (1970) Policy Concerning Drug Abuse in New York State: The Basic Study, I (May 31). New York: Hudson Institute.

STARKEY, G. H. and D. J. EGAN (1970) "Combined treatment of the criminal opiate addict by medical and law enforcement professionals." Proceedings Third National Conference on Methadone Treatment. National Institute of Mental Health (Nov. 14-16).

STEWART, G. T. (1970) "A survey of patients attending different clinics in New Orleans." Proceedings Third National Conference on Methadone Treatment. National Institute of Mental Health (Nov. 14-16).

STIMSON, G. V. and A. C. OGBORNE (1970) "A survey of a representative sample of addicts prescribed heroin at London clinics." Bulleton on Narcotics 22 (4): 13-22.

Uniform parole reports (1967) National Data. National Council on Crime and Delinquency Research Center. Davis, Calif.

VAILLANT, G. E. (1966) "A twelve-year followup of New York narcotic addicts: IV. Some characteristics and determinants of abstinence." American Journal of Psychiatry 123 (5) (November): 573-583.

Vera Institute of Justice (1971) Heroin Research and Rehabilitation Program, Discussion Proposal (May). New York City.

VORENBERG, J. and I. F. LUKOFF (1972) "Problems of social and criminal evaluation and research concerning an inner-city methadone program." Presented at Fourth National Conference on Methadone Treatment (Jan. 8-10), San Francisco.

WALDORF, D. (1970) "Life without heroin: some social adjustments during long-term periods of voluntary abstention." Social Problems 18 (2): 228-243.

WALTER, P. V. et al. (1972) "Methadone diversion: a study of illicit availability," in C. D. Chambers and L. Brill, Methadone: Experiences and Issues. New York: Behavioral Publications.

WIELAND, W. F. and C. D. CHAMBERS (1970) "Methadone maintenance: a comparison of two stabilization techniques." INternational Journal of the Addictions 5 (4) (December): 645-659.

WIELAND, W. F. and A. D. MOFFETT (1970) "Results of low dosage methadone treatment." Proceedings Third National Conference on Methadone Treatment. National Institute of Mental Health.

White House Conference on Narcotic and Drug Abuse (1963) Washington: Government Printing Office.

WOOD, R. W. (1970) "Major federal and state narcotics programs and legislation." Crime and Delinquency 16 (January): 36-56.

ZITRIN, A. (1970) "Press conference." International Journal of the Addictions 5 (1): 563-580.

Chapter 5

NARCOTIC ADDICTION AND CRIME:
AN EMPIRICAL REVIEW

CARL D. CHAMBERS

INTRODUCTION

The professional literature contains a number of contradictions concerning the type, degree, and significance of any relationship between narcotic addiction and crime. For example, references are available which purport to demonstrate that drug use precedes any criminality *or* that criminality precedes any drug use. With a little searching, one can also secure references espousing the position that criminality and drug use are largely unrelated or at most accidentally related. Or, one can find references to a position advocating that criminality and drug use stem from the same causes and are so related that it is irrelevant to discuss the sequence of their occurrence. *All* of the positions are probably correct and a significant portion of the contradictions is attributable to the writers' attempts at projecting to a universe from an inadequate data base and their failure to control for those variables which would effect the relationship, e.g., age at onset of drug use, type of drug used, etc. For example, the health professional with a ready access to all forms of drugs who becomes addicted cannot be compared with the ghetto dweller who is exposed daily to crime *and* drug-taking opportunities.

This chapter was prepared to provide the reader with a review of the recent empirical attempts at assessing this relationship. The studies selected for review focus on: (a) pre- and post-addiction criminal activity; (b) supporting one's habit; (c) arrest/incarceration liability for criminal activity; and (d) treatment as an interrupter of criminal activity.

PRE- AND POST-ADDICTION CRIMINAL ACTIVITY

Most assessments of pre- and post-addiction criminal activity have been limited to analyses of the arrest/addiction sequence: which came *first* in the addict's career—his first arrest or the first addiction to narcotics. Based upon these greatly limited analyses, data has been obtained which indicate there has been a significant change in criminal activity associated with narcotic addiction: *addicts are much more likely to be criminally involved prior to using drugs than they were in the past.*

- In 1937, Dai reported that only 19 percent of his study population of 1,047 Chicago addicts had been arrested prior to becoming addicted. A study of 1,036 males from throughout the United States who were hospitalized for addictions during 1936-37 (Pescor, 1943) reported 25 percent had been arrested prior to becoming addicted. A study of 100 New York City addicts treated at Lexington during 1952-53 showed that 46 percent had been arrested prior to becoming addicted (Vaillant and Brill, 1965). This figure has remained relatively stable since that time.

The following is a review of studies which have pursued this issue with specific populations of narcotic addicts.

- O'Donnell (1966), reporting on Southern white addicts who had been residents of Kentucky, presents the following:

  •• Among 212 males, only 33 percent had been arrested prior to addiction but 60 percent had been arrested after becoming addicted.

  •• Among 54 females, only 6 percent had been arrested prior to addiction but 24 percent had been arrested after becoming addicted.

- Chambers (1973a), reporting on black addicts who had been residents of New York and Illinois, presents the following:

  •• Among 98 males, 25 percent reported being arrested prior to *any* drug use and 49 percent reported being arrested prior to any narcotic use. Some 97 percent had been arrested since becoming addicted and some 79 percent had been arrested for specific narcotic law violations.

Table 1.   ARREST HISTORIES BEFORE AND AFTER ADDICTION AMONG 266
WHITE ADDICTS

(Percentage of Subjects who Committed Specified Offenses Before and After
They Became Addicted)

| | Male (N=212) | | Female (N=54) | |
Offenses Against Persons	*Before Addiction*	*After Addiction*	*Before Addiction*	*After Addiction*
Murder and homicide	3%	2%	—	—
Assault	2	2	2	6
Weapons	1	1	—	—
One or more of above	6	5	2	6
Robbery	2	5	—	—
Other Offenses				
Burglary	6	10	—	—
Other theft	7	22	—	4
Liquor laws (moonshining)	7	7	—	—
Sex offenses	*	—	4	6
Other	25	38	4	11
One or more of above	30	47	4	15
Drug Offenses				
Sale of narcotics	—	11	—	—
Prescription forgery or fraud	—	14	—	6
Other narcotic offenses	—	18	—	11
Other drug offenses	—	2	—	—
One or more of above	—	33	—	15
One or more offenses of any type	33	60	6	24

*Less than 1%.
SOURCE: O'Donnell, 1966.

●● Among 57 females, 25 percent reported being arrested prior to any
drug use and 37 percent reported being arrested prior to any
narcotic use. Some 91 percent had been arrested since becoming
addicted and 67 percent had been arrested for specific violations.

● Chambers and Inciardi (1972), reporting on female addicts from New
York City, present the following:

●● Among 52 females, 10 percent had been arrested prior to becoming
addicted but 65 percent had been arrested after becoming addicted;
some 60 percent had been arrested for specific drug law violations.

Table 2.   ARREST AND INCARCERATION CHARACTERISTICS AMONG
             BLACK ADDICTS

Characteristic	Males (N=98)	Females (N=57)	Total (N=155)
A. Arrest history			
1. Percent with any arrest	96.9%	91.2%	94.8%
a. Range in number of arrests	1-9	1-13	1-13
b. Mean number of arrests	3.9	3.9	3.9
c. Median number of arrests	4	3	4
d. Percentage with narcotic arrests	78.9%	67.3%	74.8%
e. Mean number of narcotic arrests	1.9	1.9	1.9
f. Percentage with juvenile arrests	38.9%	17.3%	31.3%
B. Incarceration history (for those arrested)			
1. Percent with any incarceration	84.2%	82.7%	83.7%
a. Mean number of months	32.4	18.0	27.4
C. Sequential occurrence of events			
1. Of those arrested:			
a. Arrest preceded any drug use	24.5%	24.6%	24.5%
b. Arrest preceded narcotic use	49.0%	36.9%	44.5%
c. Mean age first arrest	19.8	21.2	20.3
d. Mean age first narcotic use	20.7	21.1	20.9
e. Mean age at interview (1965)	31.4	30.8	31.2

- Chambers, Cuskey, and Moffett (1970), reporting on Mexican-American addicts who had been treated at the National Institute of Mental Health Clinical Research Center at Lexington, Kentucky, present the following:

  •• Among 159 males, 64 percent experienced their first arrest at some time prior to their first use of narcotics, but all had been arrested at some time during their drug-taking careers.

  •• Among 10 females, 30 percent had been arrested prior to any narcotic use and all had been arrested at some time after the first use of narcotics.

- Ball and associates (1968), reporting on 2,213 narcotic addicts from throughout the United States, found that some 87 percent had been arrested and that the mean age at which the first arrest occurred was some two years prior to the mean age at which narcotic use began.

- Nash (1968), reporting on 422 institutionalized male heroin addicts in New York, found that 47 percent had been arrested prior to any heroin use.

- Lukoff (1973), reporting on some 765 heroin addicts undergoing methadone maintenance therapy in New York, indicated that some 44 percent had been arrested prior to any regular use of heroin.

- Bates (1965), reporting on 830 black male addicts residing in areas east of the Mississippi River, indicated that 47 percent had arrest histories prior to any narcotic use.

Although the consistency of these findings suggest their legitimacy as an index of criminality prior to addiction, they do little to satisfy the analyst who is concerned about the biases of arrest data. The preceding section has demonstrated the emptiness of most arrest statistics in trying to assess the content of criminal activity.

Plair and Jackson (1970), reporting on an interview study with District of Columbia addicts, have provided analysts with one of the most comprehensive assessments of pre- and post-addiction criminality. A brief summary of their more salient findings is as follows:

- At least 10 percent of the study population had committed crimes against persons prior to becoming addicted, but this increased by some 80 percent after addiction.

- Some 4 percent of the study population had committed property crimes prior to becoming addicted and this increased by some 70 percent after addiction.

- Some specific percentage increases are as follows:

  ●● Robbery increased by 61 percent;

  ●● Shoplifting increased by 77 percent;

  ●● Burglary increased by 56 percent;

  ●● Pickpocketing increased by 75 percent.

- Older addicts more frequently sell drugs than the younger addicts.

- Younger addicts commit four times as many assaults as older addicts, and they also appear to concentrate more frequently upon armed robbery, rolling drunks, and purse snatching as their "crime of choice."

For the first time, analysts have a data base for comparing pre- and post-criminality. Without question, this study needs immediate replication! The investigators have also provided some insights on the content of these changes as perceived by the addicts themselves. For example:

- 56 percent of the addicts reported they usually were feeling "good" from drugs when they "hustled."

- 22 percent of the addicts reported they were usually "hurting" when they "hustled."

- The younger the addict, the more likely he is to delay "hustling" until he begins to feel "bad."

- The majority of addicts reportedly believe that drugs "speed up" their "hustling" activities.

In summary, the contemporary addict is much more likely to be criminally involved prior to his addiction than not. Intensity and diversity increase sharply once the addict becomes involved with the drugs.

SUPPORTING ONE'S HABIT

There is a commonly held assumption that most addicts must steal or otherwise hustle most of the time in order to support their addictions. The basis for this assumption is, of course, the relatively high daily costs in maintaining the average "street habit" (see Chapter 4 for a comprehensive review of expenditures for drugs). The following studies indicate there are large numbers of addicts who do not steal most of the time.

- Chambers (1973a), while studying the criminal careers of black addicts, found that the primary means of support for addicts of both sexes during the six months *prior* to entering a treatment program was criminal activity: 68 percent were engaged in illegal pursuits *but* 25 percent were employed and reported this legal job as their primary means of support (see Table 3). The same study identified illegal activities as the dominant means of support since the onset of opiate use (see Table 4).

- Schut and associates (1972), reporting on 87 male heroin addicts entering a methadone maintenance program in Philadelphia, suggest a much "flatter" distribution (see Table 5):

Table 3. PRIMARY MEANS OF SUPPORT DURING THE SIX MONTHS PRIOR TO ENTERING TREATMENT

Primary Means of Support	Males		Females		Total	
	N	%	N	%	N	%
Illegal activities	66	67.3	39	68.4	105	67.8
Legal employment	30	30.6	9	15.8	39	25.2
Dependent on spouse	1	1.0	6	10.5	7	4.5
Dependent on parents	—	—	1	1.8	1	.6
Dependent on welfare	1	1.0	2	3.5	3	1.9
Total	98	100.0	57	100.0	155	100.0

Table 4.   MEANS OF SUPPORT SINCE ONSET OF OPIATE USE AMONG BLACK
            MALE ADDICTS

Dominant Since Onset of Opiate Use	Primary During Last Six Months	Black Male Addicts	
		N	%
Illegal	Illegal	61	62.2
Illegal	Legal-Dependent	5	5.1
Legal-Dependent	Illegal	5	5.1
Legal-Dependent	Legal-Dependent	27	27.6
Total		98	100.0

- In an earlier study, Chambers and associates (1970a/b) reported that among white female addicts the primary means of supporting oneself was somewhat different. For the six months prior to seeking treatment for their addictions, 104 addicts reported the following:

  - 32 percent supported themselves by criminal activities;

  - 23 percent were legally employed; and

  - 45 percent had been dependent upon their spouse or parents for their support.

- Plair and Jackson (1970), while studying black male heroin addicts in the District of Columbia, found that some 80 percent of the addicts derived their primary income from criminal activities, 14 percent from working, and 6 percent from family and friends.

These studies would suggest criminality as the primary means of support ranges from a low of about 30 percent (among white females) to a high of about 80 percent (among black males) in various addict groups. Several studies provide some awareness into the nature of this criminal activity.

- Chambers and Inciardi (1971) have reported that among female addicts prostitution and shoplifting are the most frequent means of supporting

Table 5.   MEANS OF SUPPORT AMONG ADDICTS ENTERING METHADONE
            PROGRAM

Illegal activities	27	31.0%	
Legal employment	27	31.0%	
Dependent on spouse	2	2.3%	
Dependent on parents	12	13.8%	34.5%
Dependent on welfare	16	18.4%	
No data/unknown	3	3.5%	

one's drug habit, some one-third of these females have committed burglaries, and some one-third have committed armed robberies and/or muggings.

- Chambers and associates (1968) reported the heavy involvement of black addicts of both sexes in the selling of drugs. Among males, 52 percent sold drugs, and of these "pushers" 31 percent supported themselves by selling. Among females, 40 percent sold drugs but 73 percent of these "pushers" supported themselves by selling drugs. Thus it was apparent that although female addicts as a group were less likely to resort to selling narcotics, if they did sell them, they frequently used this method as their primary source of income.

Table 6.   CRIMINAL INVOLVEMENT OF 52 FEMALE ADDICTS CERTIFIED TO NACC-NEW YORK

Offense	Number of Persons In Sample Commiting Offense	% of Sample Commiting Offense
Drug selling	26	50%
Boosting	21	40
Prostitution	15	29
Burglary	12	23
Forgery	11	21
Mugging	10	19
Robbery	8	15
Petit larceny	3	6
Procuring	3	6
Con games	3	6
Picking pockets	2	4
Stolen goods (receiving, possessing)	2	4
Grand larceny	2	4
Theft by prostitutes from clients	2	4
Lookout for robbery	2	4
Theft from auto	2	4
Loitering	2	4
Assault & robbery	1	1
Larceny	1	1
Public intoxication	1	1
Car theft	1	1
Possession of forgery instruments	1	1
Wayward minor	1	1
Disorderly conduct	1	1
Vagrancy	1	1
Probation violation	1	1

- Inciardi and Chambers (1972) found that 50 percent of a study population of 52 female addicts in New York reported themselves as drug sellers. More addicts in this study reported themselves as drug sellers than involved in any other criminal activity.

- Nash (1968) reported that among 422 male addicts, 48 percent stole as the primary means of supporting their habits and 41 percent sold or transported drugs as their primary means.

- Plair and Jackson (1970), reporting on the crime preference among 50 black male addicts, present the following distribution:

Drug Selling	12%	(N=6)
Shoplifting	50	(N=25)
Burglary and other Thefts	6	(N=3)
Robbery	16	(N=8)
Con Games	10	(N=5)
Pandering/Soliciting	6	(N=3)

- Inciardi and Chambers (1972) have provided the most extensive analyses of the nature and extent of the criminal activities of narcotic addicts (see Tables 7 and 8).

These data reveal a major change in the criminal involvement of narcotic addicts. *The contemporary narcotic addict is much more likely to commit crimes against persons than his counterpart of recent years.*

- 29 percent of the males and 28 percent of the females admitted committing assaultive robberies (muggings) and 32 percent of the males admitted committing armed robberies.

A recent report of two interview studies of the criminal involvement of female narcotic addicts (Chambers and Inciardi, 1971) highlighted significant changes in *how* female addicts support their addictions. Of these two studies, the first was conducted with 168 females consecutively admitted to the National Institute of Mental Health Clinical Research Center at Lexington, Kentucky, during 1965 (Chambers and associates, 1970b). The second study was conducted with 52 females consecutively admitted to the New York State Narcotic Addiction Control Commission during 1970. Although the authors recognized the limitations involved in comparing the two studies, both were reviewed in the interest of providing an empirical data base for comparison with the contemporary female addict.

Table 7.   CRIMINAL INVOLVEMENTS OF 38 MALE NARCOTIC ADDICTS CERTI-
FIED TO NACC–NEW YORK

Nature of Criminal Offense	Total Offenses During Median Period of 4 Yrs. No.	%	Percentage of Sample Committing Offense
Burglary[a]	2,341	35	74
Shoplifting[a]	1,272	19	39
Theft from vehicle[a]	1,053	16	21
Other larcenies[a]	570	8	16
Sneak theft[a]	500	7	3
Vehicle theft[a]	411	6	13
Assault & robbery[b]	292	4	29
Armed robbery[b]	184	3	32
Purse snatching[a]	85	1	32
Picking pockets[a]	58	<1	16
Property crimes	6,290	93%	97
Personal crimes	476	7%	60
Loitering	*	–	8
Disorderly conduct	*	–	5
Procuring	*	–	5
Policy (numbers)	*	–	3
Total	6,766		

a. Property crimes.
b. Personal crimes.
*Total number of occurrences not known since activities were often carried out on a routine daily basis, and respondents were unable to accurately estimate.

Female Addicts as Drug Sellers

In 1965, 25.0 percent (N=42) of the 168 respondents admitted to having been drug sellers, and 71.4 percent (N=30) of these reported that this activity had at some time been the complete means of supporting themselves and their drug habits. The *arrest liability* for selling drugs was high but the *conviction liability* was low: 28.6 percent of these admitted drug sellers had been arrested specifically for the selling of drugs, but most of these arrests did not culminate in convictions; at least 75.0 percent of those arrested for selling drugs had legally maneuvered these charges to a reduction or dismissal.

The second study was conducted five years later, during 1970. In this study 38.5 percent (N=20) of the 52 respondents admitted to having been drug sellers but only 20.0 percent (N=4) of these (or 7.7 percent of the total) reported the selling of drugs as having been their complete means of support at any time. The

Table 8. CRIMINAL INVOLVEMENT OF 32 FEMALE NARCOTIC ADDICTS CERTI-
FIED TO NACC—NEW YORK

Nature of Criminal Offense	Total Offenses During Median Period of 3 Yrs.		Percentage of Sample Committing Offense
	No.	%	
Boosting (shoplifting)[a]	2,556	39.8	46.9
Picking pockets[a]	1,650	25.7	6.3
Forgery[a]	1,030	16.1	15.6
Burglary[a]	556	8.7	37.5
Theft by prostitutes from clients[a]	239	3.9	6.3
Mugging[b]	250	3.7	28.1
Robbery[b]	58	<1	12.5
Con games[a]	40	<1	3.1
Theft from auto[a]	30	<1	6.1
Lookout for robbery[a]	6	<1	3.1
Property[a]	6,118	95.4	78.1
Personal[b]	297	<1	42.5
Total	6,415		

a. Property crimes.
b. Personal crimes.

arrest liability for drug selling among these contemporary addicts was low: only 10.0 percent or 2 of the 20 who had admitted selling drugs had been arrested for this activity, and both had also been convicted on these charges.

Projecting from these relatively small sample analyses, it would appear the incidence of drug selling among female narcotic addicts has significantly increased (25.0 to 38.5 percent) but the incidence of selling as the means of complete support among female addicts has significantly decreased (17.7 to 7.7 percent).

Female Addicts as Prostitutes

In 1965, 47.0 percent (N=79) of the 168 respondents reported that they had been prostitutes after the onset of drug use. Of these 79 subjects, 87.3 percent (N=69) reported that this activity had at some time been the complete means of supporting themselves and their drug habits. Not unexpectedly, the arrest and conviction liabilities associated with prostituting was high: 43.1 percent (N=34) of the admitted prostitutes had been arrested for this activity and the majority of these arrests had culminated with a conviction for that offense.

In 1970, only 28.8 percent (N=15) of the female addicts interviewed reported having been prostitutes. Of these 15 respondents, 20.0 percent (N=3) reported that this activity had at some time been the complete means of support. Such support had admittedly required that they "turned" an average of six "tricks" per day. Quite unexpectedly, the arrest liability for this activity among these prostitute addicts was very low: only 26.7 percent (N=4) had been arrested for prostitution. Arrest clearance by conviction was 100 percent.

Projecting from these two relatively small sample analyses, it would appear that the incidence of prostituting among female narcotic addicts significantly decreased (47.0 to 28.8 percent) as did the incidence of prostitution as the means of complete support (41.1 to 5.7 percent).

Female Addicts as Both Drug Sellers and Prostitutes

In the 1965 sample, 17.3 percent (N=29) of the 168 female addicts reported that during their drug-taking careers they had both sold drugs and prostituted themselves. This incidence figure had not changed significantly by 1970; for in the later sample, 13.5 percent (N=7) of the 52 female addicts admitted engaging in both activities. During the same time interval, the data also suggest no significant change in the incidence of persons engaging in neither of the activities. For example, in the 1965 sample 45.8 percent (N=77) reported neither selling drugs nor prostituting as compared with 46.2 percent in the 1970 sample.

The preceding data may be summarized as follows:

	1965 (N=168)	1970 (N=52)
Some drug selling	25.0% (42)	38.5% (20)
Drug selling—Complete support	17.7 (30)	7.7 (4)
Some prostituting	47.0 (79)	28.8 (15)
Prostituting—Complete support	41.1 (69)	5.7 (3)
Both drug selling and prostituting	17.3 (29)	13.5 (7)
Neither drug selling nor prostituting	45.8 (77)	46.2 (24)

Subsequent analyses of the 1970 data, controlling for the ethnicity of the respondent, have suggested that at least in New York City:

● The female narcotic addict population is approximately 50 percent black, 25 percent white, and 25 percent Puerto Rican. Within these groups, Puerto Ricans were more likely to be drug sellers than either the whites or the blacks, and the proportion of drug sellers among white and black addicted groups was about the same. Fifty percent of the Puerto Ricans sold drugs as compared with 35 percent of the whites and 35 percent of the blacks.

- Once an addict began to sell drugs, however, all ethnic group differences disappeared, with some 15 to 20 percent of all sellers doing so as their primary or complete means of support.

- The arrest liability was significantly higher among the whites who sold drugs when compared with the blacks (25 percent and 10 percent respectively). Arrests among Puerto Rican drug sellers in this study were almost nonexistent.

- The incidence of prostitution was not significantly different between the whites and Puerto Ricans. Approximately 40 percent in both addict groups prostituted, but both more frequently reported themselves as prostitutes than did the black addicts (25 percent). Black prostitutes, however, more frequently used this as their primary or complete means of support and therefore were more often arrested for this activity.

- White addicts were more likely to combine drug selling and prostitution in order to support themselves and their drug habits (whites—25 percent; blacks and Puerto Ricans—10 percent).

ARREST/INCARCERATION LIABILITY FOR
CRIMINAL ACTIVITY

There are a number of studies which indicate that both the arrest and incarceration liabilities are *low* for the criminal activities of narcotic addicts.

- Inciardi and Chambers (1972), studying a population of male and female heroin addicts undergoing treatment in New York, found that less than one percent of all self-reported crimes had been cleared by arrest. Within this study population there was a ratio of one arrest for every 120 crimes perpetrated; less than half who were arrested were convicted for that offense; less than half who were convicted of that offense were incarcerated as the end product of the conviction.

- Other researchers (Plair and Jackson, 1970) have also suggested the following offense-specific ratios:
  - •• Drug Selling   = 1 arrest per *2000* offenses
  - •• Prostitution   = 1 arrest per *500* offenses
  - •• Armed Robbery = 1 arrest per *180* offenses

While neither of the two studies is precise, they do reflect the very low arrest clearance rates.

- Plair and Jackson (1970), studying a population of black male heroin addicts undergoing treatment in Washington, D.C., found that a greater proportion of these addicts had been "let off" by the police and the courts than had not been: 66 percent had been "let off" by the courts for crimes which they had committed. Moreover, 98 percent admitted crimes for which they had not been arrested.

- Chambers and Inciardi (1971) found that among female narcotic addicts less than one-half of those with arrest histories had been incarcerated as a result of those arrests.

- Collier (1972), reporting on the histories of 627 addicts within a residential therapeutic community program, found that only 64 percent had *ever* been arrested and only about half of those who had been arrested had ever been convicted.

- Chambers (1973b), studying the careers of some 1,200 addicts in treatment in Miami, Florida, found that 80 percent had been arrested at some time during their careers but that only 60 percent of those who had been arrested had been convicted.

The more one probes for reasons for such low risks in such gross amounts of criminal activity, the more it becomes obvious that conspiracies exist to insure that they remain low. For example, prostitution and drug-selling rarely produce a "victim" who is inclined to report the activity to the authorities, and in one study (Cushman, 1971), the addicts obtained some 50 percent of their income from drug selling. Another conspiracy involves the willingness of persons to purchase obviously stolen merchandise. A study in the District of Columbia (Plair and Jackson, 1970) indicated:

- 26 percent of all stolen goods were sold on the street;
- 20 percent were sold to regular customers;
- 2 percent were sold to friends/neighbors;
- 2 percent were sold to businessmen, and
- 42 percent were sold to "fences"

TREATMENT AS AN INTERRUPTER OF CRIMINAL ACTIVITY

It seems reasonable to assume and it is generally acknowledged that providing treatment for narcotic addicts significantly reduces the *amount* of criminal activity among the "patients" as well as produces changes in the *nature* of the criminal activity which is retained. For example, if one accepts the high incidence of socioeconomic criminal involvement prior to addiction described in the preceding sections, then one must also assume that these same socio-economic needs will persist after treatment has begun. Such is indeed the case. Since not all crime is drug produced, treatment for drug use cannot eliminate it all.

The author's experiences in methadone maintenance programs in Phila-delphia, New York, and Miami suggest one can expect about 75 to 80 percent of addict-patients to cease almost all of their socioeconomic-motivated criminality *if* the program adequately addresses this socioeconomic issue, e.g., by placing addict-patients in jobs, on training programs, on public assistance, etc. Fortunately, those who persist in their criminal involvements tend to retain involvements in the "victimless crime" areas such as gambling, running numbers, pimping, etc. Investigation in other geographical areas (Plair and Jackson, 1970) have reported similar reductions in criminality.

The arrest liability for addict-patients who continue criminal involvements after entering treatment *appears* to be very high. In one program, for example, where criminal involvements ran around 20 to 25 percent of the patient population, some 19 percent were arrested while still in the program (Wieland and Chambers, 1970).

Although it seems reasonable to assume significant decreases in criminality as the result of treatment, such decreases have not been carefully documented. Most "studies," for example, demonstrate decreases by comparing total arrests during a given addiction career with arrests during treatment, with no regard for variances in at-risk times. Or, they rely solely on the self-reported arrest data provided by their patients. Or, they assume arrests have a greater relationship to actual criminal activity than they have in reality. For these reasons, analysts can usually disregard most "studies" produced by a program.

A number of studies do, however, deserve some mention due primarily to their contrasts:

- Moffett and associates (1972), reporting on the post-treatment behavior of addicts in an *ambulatory detoxification* program, indicate that some 42 percent of the addict-patients had been arrested at some time during the treatment process, and some 47 percent had been arrested within one year of leaving treatment.

One can compare the risk for arrests in such an ambulatory program which keeps their patients on the streets, with the experiences of a residential program:

- DeLeon and associates (1971), reporting on the post-treatment behavior of addicts from a 24-hour *residential, therapeutic community program,* indicate that some 45 percent of their clients had been arrested during the year preceding the time when they entered the program; some 8 to 10 percent were arrested while in the program; and some 25 percent were arrested within one year after leaving the program.

Not unexpectedly, the arrest liability was considerably lower when the addict was completely removed from his "hustling" environment. This risk factor is reinforced by the New York State Civil Commitment experience where some 33 percent of 1,900 males and some 19 percent of 245 females released to *Aftercare* for the first time during 1970 were arrested during that first year following release (Chambers, 1971).

- Brill (1968) has provided analysts with probably the best data relative to arrests while on methadone maintenance. His statistics indicate annual arrest rates ranging from 22 percent to 26 percent during the first year and 6 percent to 16 percent during the second year.

After reviewing the "studies" it becomes obvious that treatment reduces criminality among narcotic addicts. It is equally obvious we do not know by how much or with whom. One can only assume that as we begin to apply cost-benefit and cost-effectiveness frames of reference to our treatment efforts, the data will become more specific and meaningful.

CONCLUSIONS

This review of empirical studies focusing upon the relationship between drugs and crime has identified a number of unrelated conclusions:

- At least for most of the contemporary narcotic addicts, criminal involvement is a part of their life style prior to becoming addicted to narcotics but not necessarily prior to some drug experimenting.
- The vast majority of the contemporary narcotic addicts support their addictions by committing crimes. Although the majority of crimes committed to support addictions involve the theft of goods which are then sold or traded to secure drugs, the rate at which addicts are turning to crimes against persons to secure money rather than goods and to the selling of drugs are both alarming.
- The risk of arrest and incarceration for drug related criminal activity are both extremely low.
- The younger narcotic addicts appear to be criminal opportunists —whatever criminal opportunity presents itself attracts this contemporary addict.

- Treatment does reduce the extent of criminal involvement of addicts but it certainly does not eliminate this activity and in most cases the curtailment is probably transitory.

The profession sorely needs well designed studies to address these and other related issues. Quite probably these assessments need to be done by competent and truly independent researchers.

REFERENCES

BATES, W. M. (1965) Unpublished program statistics from the NIMH Clinical Research Center program at Lexington, Kentucky.

BALL, J. C., C. D. CHAMBERS and M. J. BALL (1968) "The association of marihuana smoking with opiate addiction in the United States." Journal of Criminal Law, Criminology and Police Science 59 (June): 171-182.

BRILL, H. (1968) "Progress report of evaluation of methadone maintenance treatment program as of March 31, 1968." Journal of the American Medical Association 206 (12): 2712-2714.

CHAMBERS, C. D. (1973a) "Criminal behavior and black narcotic addicts." Unpublished manuscript.

——— (1973b) Unpublished program statistics from treatment settings within Dade County, Florida.

——— (1971) "Onset activity on aftercare." Unpublished report from the New York State Narcotic Addiction Control Commission.

CHAMBERS, C. D., W. R. CUSKEY and A. D. MOFFETT (1970) "Demographic factors associated with opiate addiction among Mexican-Americans." Public Health Reports 85 (June): 523-531.

CHAMBERS, C. D., R. K. HINESLEY and M. MOLDESTAD (1970a) "Narcotic addiction in females: a race comparison." International Journal of the Addictions 5 (June): 257-278.

——— (1970b) "The female opiate addict," in J. C. Ball and C. D. Chambers (eds.) The Epidemiology of Opiate Addiction in the United States. Springfield: Thomas.

CHAMBERS, C. D. and J. A. INCIARDI (1971) "Some aspects of the criminal careers of female narcotic addicts." Paper presented at the 34th annual meeting of the Southern Sociological Society (May 6-8), Miami Beach.

CHAMBERS, C. D., A. D. MOFFETT and J. P. JONES (1968) "Demographic factors associated with Negro opiate addiction." International Journal of the Addictions 3 (Fall): 329-343.

COLLIER, W. V. (1972) The 1971 Profile/Statistical Report on the Therapeutic Community Program of Daytop Village, Inc. New York: Satellite Litho Corporation.

CUSHMAN, P. (1971) "Methadone maintenance in hard-core criminal addicts: economic effects." New York State Journal of Medicine 71 (July 15): 1768-1774.

DAI, B. (1937) Opium Addiction in Chicago. Shanghai: Commercial Press.

DeLEON, G., S. HOLLAND and M. S. ROSENTHAL (1971) The Phoenix Therapeutic Community: Changes in Criminal Activity of Resident Drug Addicts. New York: Phoenix House Monograph.

INCIARDI, J. A. and C. D. CHAMBERS (1972) "Unreported criminal involvement of narcotic addicts." Journal of Drug Issues 2 (Spring): 57-64.

LUKOFF, I. F. (1973) "Issues in the evaluation of heroin treatment." Paper presented at the Epidemiology of Drug Abuse Conference (Feb. 12-14), San Juan, Puerto Rico.

MOFFETT, A. D., I. H. SOLOWAY and M. X. GLICK (1972) "Post-treatment behavior following ambulatory detoxification," pp. 215-227 in C. D. Chambers and L. Brill, Methadone Maintenance: Experiences and Issues. New York: Behavioral Publications.

NASH, G. (1968) Unpublished material from the Columbia University Bureau of Applied Social Research study supported by the New York State Narcotic Addiction Control Commission.

O'DONNELL, J. A. (1966) "Narcotic addiction and crime." Social Problems 13 (Spring): 374-385.

PESCOR, M. J. (1943) "A statistical analysis of the clinical records of hospitalized drug addicts." Public Health Reports Supplement No. 143. Washington: Government Printing Office.

PLAIR, W. and L. JACKSON (1970) Narcotic Drug Use and Crime: A Report on Interviews with 50 Addicts Under Treatment. District of Columbia: Department of Corrections.

SCHUT, J., T. W. WOHLMUTH and K. FILE (1972) "Low dosage methadone maintenance: a re-examination." Paper presented before the Canadian Society of Chemotherapy (July 6-7), Quebec.

VAILLANT, G. E. and L. BRILL (1965) "A twelve year follow-up of New York City addicts: the relation of treatment to outcome." Paper presented at the American Psychiatric Association Annual Meeting (May 3), New York City.

WIELAND, W. F. and C. D. CHAMBERS (1970) "Methadone maintenance: a comparison of two stabilization techniques." International Journal of the Addictions 5 (December): 645-659.

Chapter 6

SOME REFLECTIONS ON COMPULSORY
TREATMENT OF ADDICTION

DAVID M. PETERSEN

Of an estimated 200,000-300,000 narcotic addicts in the United States, available data suggest that large segments of these are processed through various phases of the criminal justice system at one time or another. For example, a study of the extent of heroin use among offenders in the District of Columbia jail (Kozel et al., 1972) noted that almost one out of every two new admissions (45 percent) during August and September 1969 were heroin addicts. Further, the President's Commission on Crime in the District of Columbia (1966) stated that 15 percent of all convicted felons in the District during 1965 were drug addicts. Of 5,221 felony offenders newly received at the various California Department of Corrections institutions during 1968, some 16 percent (N=810) had histories of narcotic addiction (California Department of Corrections, n.d.). Similarly, the President's Commission Task Force Report on Narcotics and Drug Abuse (1967b) reported that an average of 8 percent of all persons committed to federal prisons and other penal institutions admitted a history of drug use (mostly heroin). Finally, *Uniform Parole Reports* data indicate that some 13 percent of the nation's annual releasees have histories of drug use (National Council on Crime and Delinquency, 1967). These data would suggest that the criminal justice system occupies a significant role in the control and treatment of narcotic addicts.

Specialized narcotic addict rehabilitation programs have emerged during the past two decades at various levels of the criminal justice structure, including local detention facilities, prisons, and the community-based settings of parole, probation, and halfway houses. This paper examines the treatment of addicts within these structures in terms of program availability, retention, and relapse, and offers a summary assessment of the nature, extent, and effectiveness of this *compulsory* order.[1]

The number of existing programs for the treatment and rehabilitation of narcotic addiction within criminal justice facilities in the United States is not readily known. It is probable, however, that those identifiable through a systematic review of the professional literature on narcotic addiction and its treatment represent only a segment of the total currently operative.[2] There are some 400 institutions for adult felons in the United States, more than 300 facilities for juvenile offenders (President's Commission on Law Enforcement and Administration of Justice, 1967a: 4), an estimated 4,000 county jails and city workhouses, some 11,000 village and city lockups (Reckless, 1967: 633), and probation and parole agencies providing services at the county and local level in all 50 states. There is no reason to assume that more than a small minority of these facilities have any specialized treatment program for narcotic addicts beyond the services offered to non-addicts entering their programs.

However, it seems equally clear that a number of programs are likely to exist—such as Narcotics Anonymous groups in penal facilities—that have not been reported in the professional literature, thus tending to obscure the extent to which the criminal justice system has made efforts to provide such services. One such program involves a voluntary group established in 1968 by prisoners and treatment staff at the Federal Penitentiary at Lewisburg, Pennsylvania, entitled the Road Back Anti-addiction Group. To the author's knowledge no published or unpublished reports have ever resulted from this program. This paper will consider, then, the major studies which have been reported.

INSTITUTIONAL PROGRAMS

Treatment or Punishment: Contrasting Viewpoints

For more than a half century, the appropriateness of incarceration in the treatment of addiction has been actively debated. This argument will endure for as long as this nation's legislative approach to the management of the drug problem remains enforcement-oriented.[3]

The arguments for imprisonment of narcotic addicts can be summarized as follows. First, and perhaps most important, incarceration prevents addicts, at least for a time, from using drugs and committing crimes. Not only is the addict removed from a source of supply, but he is also prevented from contaminating others (Anslinger and Tompkins, 1953: 161). There is no doubt but that the present penalty system does, in fact, suppress a degree of narcotics use by removing some from their sources of supply. Statistics on length of stay in prison indicate, however, that sentences in long-term penal institutions are notably short (Reckless, 1967: 699). As a consequence, violators are removed from both the larger society and drugs for only a short period. Second, criminal penalties are seen as a necessary punishment for the commission of criminal acts. Punitive action against an offender is made so that he will atone for his crime by suffering. It is assumed that the addict has been acting in his own best interests, that he is not sick, and that sentencing him for his offenses will allow him to assume responsibility for his actions.[4] Third, imprisonment is thought to serve as a deterrent against future criminal acts. Stated differently, it is expected that criminal penalties will lower the probability that an offender will repeat his violation. These arguments taken together form the basis for the belief that imprisonment *is* a form of treatment. Under the present control system the addict is viewed as a criminal; but he is sent to either jail or prison not only as punishment but in an attempt to rehabilitate him.

On the alternative side of this debate are those who oppose the imprisonment of narcotic addicts.[5] Individuals arguing against criminal penalties for addicts have stressed the view that the addict is a sick person. As such, they argue that he is unable to protect himself from the consequences of his own actions; he should not be held responsible. Also, the attention required for his rehabilitation—medical and otherwise—should occur at some location other than prison. Furthermore, addicts committed to penal settings receive long sentences which not only serve as punishment but, in addition, are not conducive to rehabilitation (Lindesmith, 1965: 77-98). A variety of alternatives to imprisonment have been offered over the years—hospitals, civil commitment programs, and so on—but forced imprisonment for treatment has been held unacceptable.[6]

The ineffectiveness of imprisonment in dealing with a wide range of other offenders is of some import to those who object to the sentencing of addicts to penal institutions. A number of general critiques of the penal or correctional system have been made by others which bear directly on the issue of the efficacy of incarceration as a penalty procedure for addicts (see, for example, Clark, 1970; Jackson, 1971; Zimbardo, 1972; Menninger, 1969).

It has been variously noted that imprisonment is not an effective deterrent to future criminal behavior. Prisons have not only failed to meet the objective of lowering the probability of repetition of crime, but they have served to perpetuate criminal behavior. In a review of the recidivism literature Glaser (1964: 13-35) indicated that roughly one-third of prison parolees are returned to penitentiaries within five years of their initial release.

Secondly, it has been pointed out in numerous quarters, including from within the correctional system, that it is considerably more expensive to maintain an offender in an institution than in the community. The President's Commission Task Force Report on Corrections (1967a: 5) reported that well over three-fourths of the national investment in corrections went for such management of offenders. Moreover, the greatest proportion of this money was spent to feed, clothe, and guard prisoners.

The prison experience has been identified as a major obstacle to treatment efforts (Irwin, 1970). The origin of the resistance to staff attempts for treatment of offenders has been attributed to a prison value system—the so-called "inmate code." This code demands peer group loyalty while discouraging any liaison with staff. Two maxims of the code emphasize "doing your own time" and "not informing on another convict" (Irwin, 1970: 62). Informal peer group pressures within an institution operate as a major obstacle to attempts to modify behavior. Those prisoners who adhere to a prison value system more often resist treatment attempts such as group therapy (Tittle and Tittle, 1964).

Finally, it has been suggested that the realities of prison administration are such that little can be done for the addict in a correctional setting (Adams, 1955). Since addicts are but one type of offender among many, and perhaps only a minority, the disproportionate amount of attention their treatment and care would require is often nullified by the realities of inadequate staffing and facilities. Again, the President's Commission Task Force Report on Corrections (1967a: 57) indicated that the management of special offender groups—such as the narcotic addict—is one of the most ignored areas of corrections.

Narcotic Treatment in Prisons: 1920s-1970s

Specific programs for the treatment of drug addiction in correctional institutions over the last half century have been as diversified as programs within the free community, ranging from detoxification to methadone maintenance. In this respect, however, the prison is a microcosm of treatment trends in the larger community. Treatment modalities in the correctional setting include group therapy (Rosenthal and Shimberg, 1958; Dwyer, 1971), chemical detoxification (Dole, 1972), therapeutic communities (Petersen et al., 1969; Farkas et al.,

1970), ex-addict counseling (Farkas et al., 1970), methadone maintenance (Dole et al., 1969), and the use of psychedelic drugs (Leary and Clark, 1963; Lyle, 1968; Duncan, 1972).

During the 1920s the treatment of choice in prisons was withdrawal of the drug in conjunction with supportive treatment when necessary. Nellans and Massee (1929: 1154) described their treatment program at the Federal Penitentiary at Atlanta in this manner:

> Our usual method of treatment is what is known in the parlance of the drug addict, or "junker," as "cold turkey." It consists essentially of absolute withdrawal of the drug. . . . Perhaps our most powerful therapeutic agent is the absolute certainty which the patient has that he will not receive any more "junk," regardless of contingencies.

In describing the withdrawal program at Clinton Prison in New York, Kossef noted (1925: 18):

> Some have stated that sudden withdrawal of the drug is dangerous and cruel. I have never seen a patient die from such procedure and I believe that the memory of their misery has deterred a great many addicts from resuming the habit when released.

In addition to the withdrawal of the narcotic drug Hamilton (1922: 125) identifies the provision of graded exercise and sufficient nourishment to be vital parts of any penal treatment program; it is here he argues that there is hope for future rehabilitation. As in the larger community, treatment personnel in prisons have searched for new and improved methods of combating addiction when faced with the fact that the number of individuals cured by withdrawal was not particularly promising.

As previously noted, a wide variety of treatment methods have been attempted in penal settings. Prison addiction programs in the 1960s and '70s have kept pace with innovations in treatment techniques, and this is reflected in the application of these new modalities in the correctional environment. Specific examples include methadone detoxification in the detention jails of New York City (Dole, 1972), methadone treatment in prison (Dole et al., 1969), and the NARA Program (Narcotic Addict Rehabilitation Act of 1966–Title II) implemented in the Federal Bureau of Prisons (Petersen et al., 1969; Farkas et al., 1970; Rapkin, 1971).

The U.S. Bureau of Prisons Narcotic Addiction Treatment Program is illustrative of the rehabilitative efforts that have been attempted in correctional settings in recent years. Prior to the opening of the first NARA treatment unit at the Federal Correctional Institution at Danbury, Connecticut, in 1968, no specialized treatment program for narcotic addiction existed in the federal correctional system.[7] By July 1970 four NARA treatment units were operational with an overall capacity of 600 patients.

  ˙ Living arrangements within these institutions stress community living; each unit has a NARA dormitory separated from the rest of the institutional population, and all units utilize the therapeutic community approach. Treatment emphasis is focused on the here-and-now; attention is focused upon behavior rather than on thoughts and feelings. Beyond these general directions each treatment unit has developed its own specific treatment modality; the NARA treatment program is not a single program. For example, staffing patterns of the units vary. Although all programs are headed by professional personnel, either social workers, psychologists, or psychiatrists, some units utilize ex-addict paraprofessionals (incarcerated prisoners) in staff positions and as cotherapists. Releasees or "graduates" from the institutional program have been returned as consultants to the treatment process at one unit. Another program employs a committee system (patient self-government) involving patients in all phases of the treatment program as well as in decision-making processes. A number of other innovations to the correctional setting have been attempted, including videotape feedback therapy, marathon groups, and a tier system for patient advancement.[8]

The point is not that the approaches utilized in the NARA program or by Dole in New York are new developments to the field of addiction treatment, but rather that they are innovations to the treatment of addiction within the correctional setting. (Some of these approaches are, of course, more new than others to the addiction treatment field.) Few correctional practitioners would have been aware several years ago, however, that ex-addicts (prisoners), methadone, or psychedelic drugs would be utilized as treatment techniques in correctional settings.

Treatment Outcome: The Need for Research

Despite a considerable body of descriptive and/or philosophical writing on the treatment of addiction in prison, a paucity of evaluation research has appeared in print.[9] Only three studies could be identified that provided actual data descriptive of such addict rehabilitation.[10]

Rosenthal and Shimberg (1958) report on a group therapy program at the Cook County Jail in Chicago which was designed to (1) aid the prisoners make and "adequate adjustment" upon release, and (2) induce them to seek further therapeutic help at a medical counseling clinic after release. At the end of one year's experience, 21 percent (N=15) of the 70 patients seen during this time appeared at one of three clinics following their release. Also, the authors state (1958: 142): "It should be noted that the number continuing in treatment was very low." Further, at this time 23 percent (N=16) of those patients seen had been rearrested subsequent to release from jail. In the second year of the study and with a new group of 17 patients, the authors failed to obtain enough information to make any determination of post-institutional adjustment.

A study conducted by Dole et al. (1969) was also a two-foci research effort. The study design attempted to ascertain (1) how motivation for entering treatment could be induced in a sample of inmates without prior interest, and (2) whether methadone treatment initiated in a jail would be effective in rehabilitation.

Opportunities for interviews with the researchers regarding methadone treatment were made available to addicted prisoners in the jail. One hundred sixty-five inmates accepted interviews, and the methadone program and its general procedure were explained to them; during the seventeen-month interview experience 70 percent (N=116) of the inmates applied for the treatment program. In the second part of the study 12 randomly selected applicants were started on methadone treatment approximately ten days prior to their release, and their outcomes after release from jail were compared to sixteen inmates who had applied for but were not given treatment and four inmates who were offered treatment and refused. Seven to ten months following release of these addicts, half of the treatment group were employed or in school. Of the remaining six subjects, half were characterized as unemployed and poorly motivated and half had been rearrested and returned to jail. Three of the four untreated individuals who declined and fifteen of sixteen of the controls had been reinstitutionalized following release. All twenty of the untreated group became readdicted to narcotics, whereas none of the treatment groups became regular daily users (although ten of twelve used heroin at some time following release).

The data reviewed here, and the analyses and comparisons presented, are not too enlightening concerning the effects or consequences of incarceration for the treatment of narcotics addiction. There is no means of determining from these studies the impact of the overall institutional experience, if any, on subsequent behavior upon release. It is difficult to be critical of these studies on this basis, however, since the investigators were oriented toward demonstrating the efficacy of a particular modality for addict rehabilitation. Nonetheless, the most basic problem concerns the failure to identify the factors which distinguish the "successes" from the "failures," including pre-treatment, treatment, and post-treatment characteristics. [11]

A follow-up of 359 releases [12] from the NARA program (U.S. Bureau of

Prisons, n.d.) from August 1, 1968, through June 30, 1971, provides some evidence regarding institutional variables that differentiate between successful and unsuccessful performance of the releasee in the community. The study results indicate that 55 percent of these subjects had remained in satisfactory status in the community from at least six months to as long as three and one-half years of aftercare supervision.[13] More importantly, however, the research examined nearly 100 items of information for possible relationships to parole performance.

The NARA follow-up study cannot be considered as a measure of the effectiveness of the program as there were no direct controls or comparison groups. It is, however, an adequate descriptive survey of program performance for these 359 releasees. Moreover, as far as can be determined, it is the only study which has reported on in-care variables and their relation to community performance.

Information was gathered in this study on 20 variables that summarized the institutional experiences of the inmate-addicts, including items such as the following: length of stay in the institution, previous institutional commitments, counselor assessment of inmate's counseling progress, improvement in academic skills, disciplinary infractions, participation in voluntary activities, and participation in vocational training. Only one of 20 in-care variables—staff assessment of patient's counseling progress—was found to be significantly related to aftercare performance. The major finding from this study is that in-care "treatment" variables are *not* related to post-incarceration performance in the community (U.S. Bureau of Prisons, n.d.: 134).[14]

To what extent does compulsory treatment for addiction in prison alter the subsequent criminal behavior, drug use, and drug-seeking behavior of prisoner-addicts upon release? What number of these individuals again come to the attention of agencies of the criminal justice system? Little hard data are available which bear directly on these points. The studies reviewed here have not provided any conclusive data relative to the impact of the correctional system in the treatment of the addict.

Of the three available studies, only the NARA research is an attempt to assess the efficacy of in-care treatment of the narcotic addict, and this study indicates that institutional experience is negatively related to outcome success upon release. The NARA in-care experience was apparently of little help in preparing the prisoner-addict for his return to community living.[15]

Unfortunately, the measure of post-institutional performance for the NARA study was remaining in the community without being returned to institutional care. It is, of course, highly probable that many of those individuals not returned to a correctional institution have had difficulties of one sort or another which are undetected.[16] Moreover, there is no way of determining why specific individuals were returned to prison, whether it was for technical violation of parole, drug use, or the commission of a new criminal offense. In short, with the existing data, there are no means of assessing what impact a specific program has had relative to subsequent drug use and criminal behavior. The data indicate that over half (55 percent) of the releasees have managed to remain in the community, but not whether they were drug-free or if they have had further contact with components of the criminal justice system. Both the Dole study and that of Rosenthal and Shimberg, however, provide some limited data on further contacts with social control agencies following release from prison. Roughly one-fourth of the experimental subjects in both studies were subsequently rearrested following their release. It is not known, however, what number of these were later convicted. Regarding narcotic use, Dole reports that no individual under methadone treatment became readdicted, although almost all had used heroin at some time.

In sum, the limited data that are available is not supportive of treatment for addiction in the prison setting. Despite the concern that incarceration of addicts has generated over quite a number of years, we can say nothing conclusive about penal institutions and addict treatment. At the moment it is still an issue of some debate, with sufficient candidates to argue for either side of the issue. What is perhaps most surprising is that little work has been done in this area. It is becoming a cliché to make note of it, but nevertheless more research is needed if this issue is ever to progress beyond the arena of philosophical debate.

COMMUNITY-BASED PROGRAMS

Quite a number of studies have examined the treatment of criminal-addicts in community settings such as praole and probation programs and the halfway house. These investigations do not lend themselves easily to comparative analysis, although most of them provide data relevant to the efficacy of compulsory treatment of addiction.

Enforced supervision of addicts in the community after release from an institutional program or in lieu of commitment to an institutional program has received support from a number of quarters in recent years (Vaillant, 1966; Diskind, 1960; Diskind and Klonsky, 1964a; Joint Committee of the American Bar and Medical Associations, 1961). These reports emphasized that a major shortcoming of institutional programs—hospitals, prisons, etc.—was their failure to provide for the patient's aftercare following his release to the community.

Upon his release from institutional care, the addict most often returns to the same general area of residence where he lived prior to his treatment. As Winick (1957: 26) has noted, the ex-addict returns to his home under difficult circumstances:

> He has no money and is back in the same community which helped to spawn his addiction, with the additional handicap of being known as a former addict. Employers are often wary about hiring a person who has been an addict, and since he is often unskilled to begin with, his legitimate employment is likely to be difficult. His family situation is likely to have been strained by his long absence. Social agencies are often reluctant to help the former addict in his attempt at rehabilitation, especially in the vocational retraining which he is likely to need. His nonaddict friends may be suspicious of him, and his addict friends may be all too available.

Recognition was given to the fact that the addict needed additional supportive help and services after his release from institutional treatment. Acknowledging the importance of community aftercare in the treatment of addiction, Congress incorporated mandatory aftercare supervision in the Narcotic Addict Rehabilitation Act of 1966 for all patients committed under the provisions of the act, including voluntary hospital patients and involuntary prisoner patients.[17] Concomitant with the recommendation of intensive supervision in the community, then, was the notion that this aftercare should be compulsory.

The process of reintegrating the criminal offender into the community has long been a concern of the probation and parole services. However, programs specifically designed to provide the offender with special services and supportive therapy have been scarce. As Moeller has noted (1969: 83): "Before 1960, corrections had developed no substantial aftercare services and had limited access to community resources supportive to the needs of the probationer or the parolee." The organization of treatment services in the community for the narcotic addict were, of course, no better than the opportunities open to other offenders. With the increased attention being given in the late 1950s and early 1960s to the importance of community aftercare for the addict, special treatment projects began to appear (Diskind, 1960; Petersen et al., 1969; Brill and Lieberman, 1969; Geis, 1965; Shelly, 1966; Carrick, 1967).

Although the specific programs that have been introduced for the community treatment of addiction have appeared in a variety of settings and have emphasized various techniques and treatment approaches, they share in common the rehabilitation of addicts on an involuntary basis. The authoritative or compulsory approach is advocated because many addicts will not seek treatment unless the service is imposed upon them; it is a means of holding the patient in treatment. It has been pointed out that addicts are not self-motivated for treatment and that unless the addict is engaged in treatment he cannot be expected to change. Once the addict is forced into treatment, it is argued, he will become self-motivated and a satisfactory relationship can be established between patient and treatment personnel. Compulsion has a legitimate place in the treatment of addiction (Diskind, 1960; Diskind and Klonsky, 1964a). Brill and Lieberman (1969: 13) use the term "rational authority" to refer to this rehabilitation of addicts on an involuntary basis:

> We prefer the term "rational authority"... because these programs derive their legitimate coercive powers through the *authority* of the courts, and these are *rational* in the sense of utilizing it in a humane, constructive manner by relating the *means* of authority to the *ends* of rehabilitation.

It is important to stress that those advocating the authoritative approach believe that effective treatment of addiction can be conducted on a mandatory basis. Of central concern to this paper, then, is an assessment of the effectiveness of compulsory treatment of the addict in the community. To that end treatment programs in parole, probation, and the community treatment center will be reviewed.

Parole

In an early study, Bailey (1956) tested the relative effectiveness of two therapeutic techniques—individual parole counseling and psychoanalytically oriented group psychotherapy—with paroled drug addicts. Exposure time to the experimental treatment regimens was for a five-month period utilizing two sample groups of eight parolees. Comparison of the two sample groups on an index of parole failure (Parole Violation Index) revealed that those addicts exposed to psychoanalytically oriented group psychotherapy (Group II) violated parole at a higher rate than those exposed to individual parole counseling (Group I). Further indices of parole failure were supportive of the above finding. Individuals in Group II relapsed to the use of opiates more often than Group I (62 percent versus 25 percent), were arrested one or more times with greater frequency (75 percent versus 37 percent), and committed one or more major parole violations more often (62 percent versus 25 percent). In addition, one year after the termination of the treatment program 63 percent of Group II had been returned to prison as compared to 25 percent of Group I.

In 1964 Diskind and Klonsky provided a comprehensive report on a special narcotic project for parolee-addicts in the New York State Division of Parole that emphasized the authoritarian approach, aggressive casework, and small caseloads (Diskind and Klonsky, 1964a/b).[18] Follow-up results from the project were presented in three separate analyses with varying sample numbers and time spans. The first study involved 695 parolees who had been under supervision between November 1, 1956, and December 31, 1961. The follow-up period extended for one year beyond December 1961. The study results indicated that 185 parolees out of 695, or 27 percent, made a "successful adjustment." A warrant for arrest was issued for 510 cases (73 percent) and they were adjudged to be delinquent. The "successful-adjustment" category included the following: those 173 cases that never evidenced any delinquent bahavior, four individuals who committed minor technical violations, five individuals who were arrested but charges were dismissed, and three cases who were charged with informal delinquency (misconducts where a warrant is not issued). In addition, there were 62 non-drug-using individuals categorized as delinquents who were not counted among the 185 successes above. Diskind and Klonsky added these 62 subjects to the previous 185 and noted that 36 percent of all parolees refrained from drug use.

The second sub-study was a follow-up of 344 parolees who had been under supervision during the first three years of the project ending October 31, 1959. Data for these cases as of December 31, 1962, showed that 83, or 24 percent, made a successful adjustment (including five subjects still under active supervision). Again, 29 non-drug-using delinquent cases were added to the 83 successful adjustments, indicating that 32 percent abstained from drug use.

The final study was an examination of the above 83 subjects who were successfully discharged from parole supervision. This restudy was designed to determine the degree of post-parole adjustment of these discharged parolees. For the purposes of this sub-study the researchers defined successful adjustment as the ability to refrain from drug usage. For a variety of reasons 17 cases were eliminated from the study, leaving 66 discharged cases to be followed up in the community by home visits, contacts with relatives, and so on. It was learned that 36, or 55 percent, of the subjects had continued to refrain from the use of drugs in the post-parole period. Seven subjects who had used drugs but not in the three months prior to the follow-up contact were added to the above 36, yielding a 65 percent abstinent rate for the study group.

Also, Diskind and Klonsky examined arrest record and employment status during the post-parole period for these 66 parolees. It was determined that 95 percent of those cases readdicted had had at least one arrest, while only approximately 20 percent of the abstainers had such contact with the police. In the area of employment, 93 percent of the abstainers had regular jobs, while only 31 percent of the drug users were so employed.[19]

Adams and McArthur (1969) in a District of Columbia study provide information relative to the effects of three types of community experience for paroled narcotic offenders. The three groups and modes of experience were: (1) 36 parolees who were released to the D.C. Public Health Department Drug Addiction Treatment and Rehabilitation Center, where they were involved in a group-oriented therapy program with referral to social services on an outpatient basis; (2) 57 parolees and conditional releasees who were provided supervision and counseling services through parole officers in the D.C. Department of Correction Division of Parole, and (3) 49 mandatory releasees who were unsupervised releases to the community.

The three groups were followed up through official records to determine the extent to which members of each group were arrested and booked after release to the community. Six months after their release to the community, the 36 parolees in the special treatment program showed a 27.8 percent arrest and detention rate. The 57 parolees and conditional releasees had a 28.0 percent rate, while the mandatory release cases had a 44.5 percent rate. In short, straight releasees from prison show higher failure rates than either the parolees or the special treatment group. Further, all three groups show higher failure rates when compared with data on the general population of prison releases.

As noted earlier, an analysis of the NARA Program under the U.S. Bureau of Prisons revealed that of 359 releases prior to June 30, 1971, 55 percent remained in the community in satisfactory status. The study attempted to identify those variables that differentiated the successful cases from the unsuccessful ones; in the main, these were "community variables." Items showing statistically significant differences and strong associations were those in aftercare treatment rather than the institutional treatment program. Few variables traditionally associated with parole outcome, such as admission characteristics, were significant for the NARA cases. Aftercare variables showing a significant relationship to outcome included the following: occupational level obtained following release, earnings from employment, employment in one particular job—that of a case aide (ex-addict counselor), no difficulty in finding leisure activities, conducive events (such as job promotions, pay raises, and so on), and keeping appointments with aftercare supervisors in the agency providing community supervision.

Joseph and Dole (1970) identified in a recent report some 269 methadone patients known to parole and probation authorities among the 1,800 patients retained in the New York methadone treatment program over the six-year period January 1964 to December 1969. Of these patients 193, or 72 percent, maintained satisfactory adjustments and were retained in treatment. Discharges from treatment for other drug or alcohol abuse or for continued criminal activity and subsequent revocation of parole and probation status were made for 76 individuals, or 28 percent of the cases. Patients on probation and parole have a lower rate of success on methadone than for the program as a whole—72 percent and 82 percent respectively.

Probation

Brill and Lieberman (1969) analyzed the adjustment of 86 addicts involved in a specialized treatment program emphasizing rational authority and aggressive casework techniques at the Washington Heights Rehabilitation Center, in which service was given jointly by the Center and the Special Narcotics Unit of the New York Office of Probation (Group I). Outcome comparisons were made at the end of a one year period with a control group of 73 addicts receiving traditional probation attention but in small case loads, from the Special Unit of the Office of Probation (Group II). Comparisons between the two groups were recorded for reduced drug use and criminality and improvement in employment and social adjustment. Although there were some differences between these indices for the two groups, they are not large enough to indicate that either group was more successful in any given area. However, there were indications that a good deal of success was achieved in all four areas for probationers in both groups.

Patients were categorized as successes for the purposes of this study if they "improved" (moved in the direction of improvement for the index used) or if they "stayed well" (did not deteriorate over the course of the study). The following are the results of this comparison: (1) heroin use—61 percent of Group I were found to be successes, as compared to 58 percent of Group II; (2) criminality—77 percent of Group I and 78 percent of Group II were categorized as successes; (3) work—for Group I 52 percent were identified as successes and 38 percent of Group II; (4) social adjustment (conventionality)—71 percent of Group I as opposed to 60 percent of Group II were identified as successful cases. Further, at the end of the study year only 22 percent of Group I and 21 percent of Group II did not use heroin at least once during the year. Also, during the treatment year 49 percent of the Group I probationers and 47 percent of the Group II probationers were rearrested, although only half of the arrests resulted in convictions.

English and Monroe (1972) examined the relationship between personality type and type of outpatient supervisory system on "success rate" in post-institutionalized narcotic addicts. The study design included 190 male prisoner addicts on probation compared to a group of 289 civilly committed addicts under aftercare supervision. All cases were treated at the Lexington facility. The primary purpose of the study was to establish interaction between treatment modality and personality, but the results for overall success rate indicate that 64.2 percent of the probationers were successes—remained in uninterrupted outpatient treatment—as compared to 47.4 percent of the civil cases. The cutoff date on which this study was based was the actual date of termination of obligation to the court for the probationers, while for the civil cases the cutoff date represents the date the information was collected, up to seven months from discharge.

The Halfway House

Although considerable literature is available on the community treatment center or halfway house for narcotic addicts, only one center has received a thorough evaluation (Geis, 1966; Fisher, 1965).[20] The opening in 1962 of the East Los Angeles Halfway House, a temporary residence for narcotic addict parolees, provided the researchers with an opportunity to evaluate its effectiveness over straight parole in reducing recidivism of this offender. Some 116 residents (experimental group) were randomly selected from a pool of parole placements in the East Los Angeles area for residence at the halfway house, as were 109 individuals who were placed on straight parole (control group).

At the end of a twelve-month period a follow-up comparison was made between the two groups. The results indicated that the halfway house experiment was no more successful than regular parole in its ability to deter subsequent involvement in criminal behavior or subsequent use of narcotics. At the end of the first year of the study, 33 members of the experimental group (28 percent) and 34 members of the control group (31 percent) had not used narcotics or encountered "serious difficulty." Additional information was provided by Geis (1966) regarding correlates of success for both experimental and control group subjects; thirty-eight variables in the areas of education, work, family, associations and narcotic-related items were found related to success in abstaining from drug use or avoiding serious difficulty.

Compulsory Aftercare and Effectiveness

At issue in this section has been whether the compulsory treatment of narcotic addicts in community criminal justice facilities is effective. Some research findings suggest that individuals directly released to community supervision are more successful than those individuals exposed to incarceration, but that individuals who are incarcerated and then paroled do even better upon final release (Vaillant, 1966). There has been, however, very little research on the criminal justice system which has documented the effectiveness of different community experiences relative to the treatment of the narcotic addict. Further, it is difficult with the existing research studies to distinguish which component of criminal justice—prison, parole, etc.—has a greater impact relative to outcome following treatment (see U.S. Bureau of Prisons, n.d.).

Three of the eight studies reviewed in this section have provided some information on this issue. Adams and McArthur (1969) provide data which demonstrate that releasees from prison to the community without any aftercare supervision do more poorly in terms of rearrest than individuals receiving community supervision—either parole supervision or special narcotic treatment through a public health facility. Geis (1966), in his study comparing parolees with individuals released to a community treatment center (halfway house), found no difference in outcome between the two groups. Finally, Brill and Lieberman (1969) compared addicts released to straight probation with those involved in intensive rehabilitation in addition to probation; they found no significant differences between the two groups in terms of several indices of improvement. Some type of community supervision appears to be better than none at all, but nothing conclusive can be inferred from these studies as to which modality has a greater impact. However, "special" treatment programs have not faired well compared to standard criminal justice programs such as parole and probation.

What can be said regarding treatment outcome for the studies reviewed here in terms of traditional indices of success, that is, drug use, arrest record, and so on? Studies of criminal justice programs have tended to depend more upon relatively crude measures of outcome than those existing follow-up studies of hospital programs (Vaillant, 1966; O'Donnell, 1965: 228-230). Five of the eight studies reviewed in this section utilize some measure such as "successful adjustment" or "satisfactory status" as the primary index of treatment outcome.[21] This usually means that the patient has *not* been returned to institutional care and is currently residing in the community. Four of the studies provide information on rearrest and three on subsequent drug use. The range of results reported in these studies is quite variable and comparisons are fraught with hazards.[22] A mechanical summing up with reference to these variables is not an entirely satisfactory procedure, but it is preferable to no procedure at all.

In terms of the measures of successful community adjustment, outcome rates vary from a low of 24 percent under intensive parole supervision in the New York Parole Project to a high of 72 percent in the New York methadone program. Rearrest rates vary from 20 percent for the successful cases in the New York Parole Project to 49 percent in the Washington Heights Project. Measures of freedom from narcotic use among the success cases indicate a range from a low of 22 percent in the Washington Heights Project to a high of 55 percent in the New York Parole Project.[23]

It seems that compulsory treatment of the narcotic addict in the community, whether in a parole, probation, or halfway house setting, is less than successful. None of these treatment modalities is dramatically effective in improving the adjustment of addict patients in these settings. Further, it is not established in existing studies that compulsory or authoritarian supervision in the community is more effective than other treatment modes.

DISCUSSION

The foregoing critique, which is an attempt to assess the efficacy of narcotic addict treatment in the criminal justice system, suggests that a number of observations are in order. These will include consideration of the methodological limitations of those studies reviewed herein. They are set forth to place in some perspective the findings of these studies. It should be acknowledged at the outset that the aforesaid review does an injustice to the wealth of significant data reported in these investigations. It is also apparent, however, that a complete assessment of the methods and findings of each individual study was precluded.

It was previously noted that most of the studies used "satisfactory status," "successful adjustment," or some equivalent term as the primary classification for successful outcome. In these studies individuals are usually classified as successful if they have not been removed from the community and placed in an institutional setting. The use of this operational definition of performance is problematic. There is, of course, the possibility of hidden deviance; individuals may continue to use narcotics or engage in other deviance but this is not detected (Lewis et al., 1972). More importantly, supervising officials can detect violations that they do not report either because they do not consider them serious or for some other reason, such as program policy. In the NARA Program of the Federal Bureau of Prisons the decision to violate an individual detected through urinalysis to be using drugs is left to the discretion of the probation officer (Farkas et al., 1970: 56-57) [my emphasis] :

> Should there be two positive urine tests in succession, it is the probation officer's responsibility to report this to the Board of Parole. Upon notifying the Board, the probation officer either recommends continuation under community supervision or revocation of parole. . . . It should be noted that parole violation warrant is not recommended or issued automatically when a NARA case has two positive urine tests in succession. *Much depends upon the individual case in question.*

Further, variations in supervision by parole region which might affect performance have been identified in a national study (U.S. Bureau of Prisons, n.d.: 133).

Some of the studies reviewed here make no note of the possibility of these occurrences, while others carefully document that a classification of successful community adjustment can include individuals who committed technical violations of parole, or who were rearrested but not convicted and so on (Diskind and Klonsky, 1964a: 76). Not only does this type of classification make comparisons between different studies difficult, it makes it impossible to isolate separately for study the types of success or failure (O'Donnell, 1965: 235).

What does it mean that an individual remains in the community in "satisfactory status"? One can only conclude that in most studies it means nothing more than the individual hasn't had a warrant issued against him for his arrest and return to an institution. Although he remains in the community, with this measure of outcome we really know little of his adjustment. The individual may be using narcotics or he may be involved in a number of other possible difficulties. It becomes evident, then, that there is little consistency in the process of classifying individuals as successful for those utilizing this measure. In short, the use of such a crude classification of findings is unfortunate because it often masks more information than it reveals.

A point can be made regarding the type of time frame utilized in these studies for the determination of treatment outcome. At least half of the studies evaluated treatment effects during the course of treatment itself rather than determining post-treatment outcome following the discontinuation of treatment. Nothing is known in these studies regarding the long-range effects of these programs on their participants. It is, of course, a legitimate procedure to utilize only immediate treatment effects for program evaluation. Indeed, the stated goals of a program may identify such a period of time as appropriate. It would seem, however, that a period of post-treatment follow-up is particularly important to the evaluation of criminal justice programs. For example, every individual involved in community supervision in the criminal justice system is aware that his behavior will be monitored and that inappropriate behavior can result in revocation of his freedom to remain in the community.[24] This has a powerful incentive for the addict to remain in treatment which voluntary treatment programs lack—the ability to remove an individual from the community and place him in prison. It is suggested, then, that because of the enforcement power inherent in criminal justice programs that in-program evaluation occurs under conditions quite different from those following the discharge of an individual from treatment. Only post-treatment evaluation can determine if the effectiveness of treatment has carried over after patients have been discharged from a program.

In any analytic research endeavor, a most crucial methodological issue involves the determination that the nature of any change in patients will be measurably different from what would have been present if the treatment had not taken place. In order that a valid assessment of program effectiveness can be made, some basic comparison measure needs to be established. Ideally, one would use a research design in which individuals were randomly selected for treatment and control groups from a common base population. By this procedure one is assured that any differences in outcome are the result of the effect of differences in exposure to the specific treatment regimens. Only two studies (Geis, 1966; Dole et al., 1969) reviewed in this paper utilized this design. [25] Limited numbers of narcotic-involved offenders and other conditions precluded the development of an adequate control group for most of the studies; two investigations (Diskind and Klonsky, 1964a; U.S. Bureau of Prisons, n.d.) did not utilize any comparison group. Alternative designs to the classical experimental approach exist, and while each of these has disadvantages, they may be used in instances where it is not possible to assign subjects randomly to treatment and experimental groups. It is not our intention to criticize these studies for their inability to use random assignment of subjects, but rather to point out that the comparisons which have been made in these studies are subject to various kinds of errors. The extent to which any of the various comparison groups utilized in these studies are comparable to the study groups is not precisely known.

Finally, few studies have attempted to identify factors that differentiate between the successful cases and those who fail (Geis, 1966; U.S. Bureau of Prisons, n.d.). In the main, these investigations have concentrated upon establishing the efficacy of one treatment technique, approach, or program over another. Studies of criminal justice participants have added little to our knowledge of the processes of success and failure.

CONCLUSION

A wide variety of studies have been reviewed here, and some interesting findings have been presented on the treatment of the narcotic addict in the criminal justice process. But what implications may we draw from these investigations? *The findings suggest that neither incarceration nor compulsory community supervision are highly effective in the rehabilitation of the narcotic addict.* Moreover, it would not appear that the addition of more intensive treatment to incarceration and aftercare supervision has been demonstrated to be very promising. Stated differently, despite good intentions, generous expenditures, and attempts at innovative programing, it is not evident that treatment in criminal justice facilities brings marked improvement in performance. Nevertheless, it must be recognized that criminal justice management does serve as an effective supervisory system for *some* individuals. There are offenders who are likely to have a greater probability of success under compulsory supervision than with some alternative approach, such as voluntary hospitalization. Unfortunately, research findings have not as yet identified which forms of institutional and aftercare treatment are most effective with different kinds of patients.

As a final point, it appears relevant to mention that a new way of dealing with the problem of the addict in the criminal justice system is diversion of the drug-dependent individual to treatment before he has been convicted. Referral to treatment at some point in the criminal justice process has been cited as a major development in the nonpunitive approach to narcotic addiction (Bellassai and Segal, 1972).

N O T E S

1. The term "compulsory" must be viewed with some caution here since few addicts who voluntarily seek treatment manifest conscious desires for self-improvement and behavioral change. There is general agreement throughout the literature that addicts approach the treatment setting with varying degrees of readiness for help, and the initial impetus to embrace treatment is typically spirited by some crisis situation, for example, marital difficulties, familial pressures, loss of drug supply, peer coercion, and so on (see Brill, 1968; Brill and Jaffe, 1967; Brill and Lieberman, 1969). As such, elements of compulsion do indeed exist, but nevertheless, the addict is not necessarily constrained from exercising his freedom of choice and his decision is voluntary. By contrast, treatment initiated by the criminal justice system is grounded in some legal authority and participation becomes mandatory regardless of the addicts' personal wishes. It is in this latter sense, when the decision to move in or out of treatment is governed by some political body, that the notion of "compulsory treatment" is being utilized throughout this paper.

2. In this respect it might be noted that data are also incomplete regarding the extent of active treatment programs in other settings throughout the United States. A recent commentary identified some 165 governmental and nongovernmental programs in the United States (Winick and Bynder, 1967), but this is likely to be a gross underestimation of the total number of programs existing today. Data from the Special Action Office for Drug Abuse Prevention (1972) describing seven federal agencies indicate some 321 federally funded drug treatment programs as of June 30, 1972, a substantial increase from the 16 federally supported programs identified in January, 1969. However, the number of civil programs in the United States at this time remains unknown.

3. Writings on America's position of handling drug abuse as a criminal problem rather than a medical or social one have been numerous. See Lindesmith (1965), Duster (1970), and King (1972) for excellent general treatment of the subject.

4. For a general discussion of the several justifications for punishment by society, see Reckless (1967: 501-508).

5. As previously indicated, the literature on this topic has been voluminous. The following selections are reasonable representations of this position: Kolb (1939a/b), Reichard (1939), Stachnik (1972), and Goode (1972: 181-210).

6. The original act establishing the U.S. Public Health Service Hospitals at Lexington and Fort Worth contained a provision for treatment of convicted federal prisoners who were granted probation in lieu of incarceration if they entered treatment at one of the hospitals. At these facilities the prisoner-addicts were actually held under forced confinement, but the opponents of the incarceration of addicts felt this means for handling the addict appropriate. It was noted by Kolb (1939a: 25) [my emphasis]: "A certain measure of forced confinement of addict violators for treatment is justifiable and when administered *as treatment* is accepted without the resentment that precludes cooperation." Bloch and Geis have suggested (1970: 440-442), however, that a distinction between reformation and punishment is often a very difficult one to make. They suggest (1970: 441) that "Whether a program is 'punishment' or 'reformation,' therefore, probably must derive from a subjective evaluation of the intent of the program as well as a review of its operating character-istics. . . . To the extent that an individual does not prefer to be part of such a program, then the program contains an element of punishment and of deprivation of liberty." While the addict has been confined in various settings the debate has continued as to which of these is the more appropriate for his welfare.

7. Prior to the passage of the Narcotic Addict Rehabilitation Act of 1966, federal prisoner addicts were sent on a selective basis to one of the U.S. Public Health Service Hospitals at Lexington or Fort Worth for treatment of their addiction.

8. For further information on the NARA program, see Petersen et al., (1969), Farkas et al., (1970), and Rapkin (1971).

9. Although this paper is concerned with addict-offenders in prison, probation, and parole settings, and in related criminal justice programs, there have been several follow-up studies of patients treated at the U.S. Public Health Service Hospital at Lexington that contain data relevant to prisoners (Pescor, 1943; Hunt and Odoroff, 1962; Vaillant, 1966). Of the 87,800 total admissions to the hospitals at Lexington and Fort Worth from 1935 through 1964, 27 percent (N=23,700) were federal prisoners who were also narcotic addicts (Rasor and Maddux, 1966: 28). These addicts were convicted in federal courts for violation of federal laws and were subsequently sent to either Lexington or Fort Worth to undergo treatment for their addiction during the term of their sentences in lieu of placement at a federal penal facility.

The research reports from the Lexington facility have consistently shown that nonvoluntary patients—prisoners—released to the community have done better from the standpoint of continued abstinence from drugs than voluntary patients. Pescor's study (1943) of 4,766 male patients discharged from January 1, 1936, to December 31, 1940, recorded information for 60 percent of the sample group; over 74 percent of the patients had relapsed. Paroled prisoners made the best record of freedom from drug use (55.7 percent), probationers the second best (38.6 percent), and voluntary patients completing treatment were third (24.5 percent). Three other types of patients had lower rates of abstinence than the above.

The study by Hunt and Odoroff (1962) was a follow-up of 1,912 male and female patients discharged from Lexington to the New York City area during the period from July 17, 1952, to December 31, 1955; some degree of contact was made with 98.4 percent of these patients. Lower readdiction rates were found for all nonvoluntary patients—prisoners and probationers—as compared to voluntary patients—85.7 percent and 91.2 percent respectively.

Vaillant's study (1966) reports on a twelve-year follow-up of 100 New York City male addicts admitted to Lexington between August 1952 and January 1953. The results of the study indicated that at some time during the follow-up period 90 percent of the patients returned to drug use; however, 46 percent were drug-free and in the community at the time of the study contact or at the time of their death. The findings indicate that 96 percent of the voluntary patients had relapsed within a year but that 67 percent of those who served at least nine months of prison time and a year of parole were abstinent for a year or more.

The data from these investigations are *suggestive* that community supervision—compulsory supervision—may help to account for the differential performance of voluntary and prisoner patients. For example, the results from Vaillant's study lead him to conclude (1966: 736): "The writer believes that both prison sentences without provision for parole and purely voluntary programs are often contraindicated in the treatment of urban addiction." Data relevant to the performance of narcotic addicts in compulsory settings following institutional care are presented in this paper under the section on community based programs.

10. I have excluded studies such as that of Feldman and Mulinos (1970) where researchers have used a sample of prisoners for the purpose of testing the medical properties of certain drugs (in this case a test of the addictive properties of Tybamate).

11. There are a wide variety of criteria that can be used for the determination of the success-failure outcome of a program. Hopefully, the criteria chosen for evaluation relative to the effectiveness of a program will be related to the goals and means of the program. Abstinence from drug use, although a highly desirable goal, is only *one* possible measure of improvement. Other success-failure parameters include improvements in social, familial, educational, and occupational functioning. Freedom from arrests and incarceration are also important data for measurement of improvement. Indeed, some treatment programs do not identify freedom from drug use—abstinence—as a primary goal (see Brill and Lieberman, 1969: 133-134).

Making outcome comparisons between various treatment programs is at best a risky undertaking. Many studies are not directly comparable; they have used different measures of outcome and/or they vary in their operational definition of similar measures. A number of the studies reviewed in this paper use measures of outcome that do not allow the reader to identify the specific factors as to why an individual is classified as a success or a failure. For example, a differentiation between successes and failures on parameters such as abstinence or criminal activity may not be made, but instead cases will only be classified as successfully or unsuccessfully participating in the program. O'Donnell (1965, 1967) and Glaser (1967) have well documented a number of the theoretical and methodological difficulties in follow-up study of addicts, not the least of which is varying definitions of outcome.

Despite the above most researchers feel compelled to use freedom from drug use as a major criterion for measuring the success of a treatment program, even when abstinence may not be a *main* program goal. This paper will, like most others, look at abstinence from drug usage as a major success-failure parameter. When it is appropriate and possible, other comparisons will be made.

12. Ten patients were released from NARA units more than once during the study period, thus the sample size of 359 refers to releases and not individuals.

13. A releasee was designated as successful—in "satisfactory status"—for the purposes of this study if he was currently participating in aftercare with no indication of an imminent parole violation or if he had satisfactorily been released from parole supervision. An individual was classified a failure if he had been returned to one of the NARA institutions or if he was scheduled to be returned. No designation was made in this study as to why cases were determined to be failures.

14. Nearly one-fourth (N=24) of the 100 variables examined in this study were related to community performance at a statistically significant level. In sum, the variables related to performance were found to be in community aftercare following discharge from prison. These results will be covered later in the paper.

15. There are a number of methodological limitations in this study, as well as in others reviewed in this paper, that are certainly relevant to the acceptance of outcome findings. I have chosen not to discuss any possible shortcomings of each individual investigation but rather will make some general comments in the concluding section of this paper.

16. A preliminary report on the NARA program would indicate that this is the case. Farkas et al., (1970: 59) report that 85 of 145 patients (59 percent) under community supervision and in satisfactory status had at least one positive urinalysis test for drug use.

17. Public Law 89-793, 89th Congress, H.R. 9167, November 8, 1966.

18. Additional information relative to this project can be found in Travers (1957), Diskind (1960, 1967), and Klonsky (1965).

19. An additional follow-up study has been done with this special narcotic project (see Inciardi, 1971).

20. Two other halfway houses have received considerable attention in the fields of correction and drug addiction, namely, Daytop Village—formerly Daytop Lodge—(Shelly and Bassin, 1964; Shelly, 1966, 1967; Bassin, 1968) and Southmore House (Carrick, 1967; Wiener and Muehlberger, 1968). Unfortunately, the final evaluation report on Southmore House (Wiener and Muehlberger, 1968) indicates that of 113 residents during the three and one-half years of its operation only 13 were releasees from correctional facilities, and in the data analysis the researchers did not separate these cases from noncorrectional residents. Although highly publicized, Daytop Village has never been the subject of an adequate evaluation. A number of interim reports on this facility have appeared (Shelly, 1966, 1967), but Glasscote et al. (1972: 244) have noted that Daytop Village "has yet to publish a methodologically sound evaluation study of the effect of its programs on its clients."

21. Only one of these studies also provides separate data on drug use and rearrest, while it is noted in one study that drug use was included in a determination of community adjustment.

22. See note 11.

23. This excludes the study by Bailey (1956) in which he indicates that six of eight patients (75 percent) were drug free at the end of five months.

24. In addition to the general conditions imposed by the court for guidance of the probationer or parolee in the community, the narcotic offender is frequently required to submit to urine surveillance or some other technique to determine if he has returned to drug use. The use of such testing procedures has a number of consequences for both the patients and social control officials (see Lewis et al., 1972).

25. Geis (1966: 249-250, 255-256) has documented some of the problems of random assignment of inmates to treatment in his study of the East Los Angeles Halfway House.

REFERENCES

ADAMS, M. E. (1955) "The state narcotic patient at the Florida state prison." Journal of the Florida Medical Association 42 (December): 467-469.

ADAMS, S. and V. McARTHUR (1969) "Performance of narcotic-involved prison releasees under three kinds of community experience." Research Report No. 16. District of Columbia Department of Corrections.

ANSLINGER, H. J. and W. F. TOMPKINS (1953) The Traffic in Narcotics. New York: Funk and Wagnalls.

BAILEY, W. C. (1956) "Individual counseling and group psychotherapy with paroled drug addicts: a pilot field experiment." Research Studies, State College of Washington 24: 141-149.

BASSIN, A. (1968) "Daytop Village." Psychology Today 2 (December): 48-52.

BELLASSAI, J. P. and P. N. SEGAL (1972) "Addict diversion: an alternative approach for the criminal justice system." Georgetown Law Journal 60: 667-710.

BLOCH, H. A. and G. GEIS (1970) Man, Crime, and Society. New York: Random House.

BRILL, L. (1968) "Three approaches to the casework treatment of narcotic addicts." Social Work 13 (March): 25-35.

BRILL, L. and J. H. JAFFE (1967) "The relevancy of some newer American treatment approaches for England." British Journal of Addiction 62: 375-386.

BRILL, L. and L. LIEBERMAN (1969) Authority and Addiction. Boston: Little, Brown.

California Department of Corrections (n.d.) California Prisoners: 1968. Sacramento: Human Relations Agency.

CARRICK, R. W. (1967) "Southmore House: use of a 'halfway' house and integrated community approaches in the posthospital/correctional institution rehabilitation of narcotic addicts," pp. 219-224 in Rehabilitating the Narcotic Addict. Washington: Government Printing Office.

CLARK, R. (1970) Crime in America, Observations on Its Nature, Causes, Prevention and Control. New York: Simon and Schuster.

DISKIND, M. H. (1967) "The role of the parole officer or the use of the authoritative casework approach," pp. 285-292 in Rehabilitating the Narcotic Addict. Washington: Government Printing Office.

——— (1960) "New horizons in the treatment of narcotic addiction." Federal Probation 24 (December): 56-63.

DISKIND, M. H. and G. KLONSKY (1964a) Recent Developments in the Treatment of Paroled Offenders Addicted to Narcotic Drugs. Albany: New York State Division of Parole.

——— (1964b) "A second look at the New York State parole drug experiment." Federal Probation 28 (December): 34-41.

DOLE, V. P. (1972) "Detoxification of sick addicts in prison." Journal of American Medical Association 220 (April): 366-369.

DOLE, V. P., J. W. ROBINSON, J. ORRACA, E. TOWNS, P. SEARCY and E. CAINE (1969) "Methadone treatment of randomly selected criminal addicts." New England Journal of Medicine 280 (June): 1372-1375.

DUNCAN, D. F. (1972) "Psychedelic drugs in correctional treatment." Crime and Delinquency 18 (July): 291-297.

DUSTER , T. (1970) The Legislation of Morality. New York: Free Press.

DWYER, J. (1971) "Volunteers help prisoner addicts." Rehabilitation Record 12 (March-April): 12-14.

ENGLISH, G. E. and J. J. MONROE (1972) "A comparison of personality and success rates of drug addicts under two outpatient supervisory systems." International Journal of the Addictions 7 (Fall): 451-460.

FARKAS, G. M., D. M. PETERSEN and N. I. BARR (1970) "New developments in the federal bureau of prisons addict treatment program." Federal Probation 34 (December): 52-59.

FELDMAN, H. S. and M. M. MULINOS (1970) "Nonaddictive psychotropic medication for imprisoned narcotic addicts." Journal of the Medical Society of New Jersey 67 (June): 278-283.

FISHER, S. (1965) "The rehabilitative effectiveness of a community correctional residence for narcotic users." Journal of Criminal Law, Criminology and Police Science 56 (June): 190-196.

GEIS, G. (1967) "The East Los Angeles Halfway House: two years later," pp. 231-237 in Rehabilitating the Narcotic Addict. Washington: Government Printing Office.

––– (1966) The East Los Angeles Halfway House for Narcotic Addicts. Sacramento: Institute for the Study of Crime and Delinquency.

––– (1965) "A halfway house for narcotic addicts." British Journal of Addiction 61: 79-89.

GLASER, D. (1967) "Problems in the evaluation of treatment and rehabilitation programs," pp. 335-341 in Rehabilitating the Narcotic Addicts. Washington: Government Printing Office.

––– (1964) The Effectiveness of a Prison and Parole System. Indianapolis: Bobbs-Merrill.

GLASSCOTE, R. M., J. N. SUSSEX, J. H. JAFFE, J. BALL and L. BRILL (1972) The Treatment of Drug Abuse—Programs, Problems, Prospects. Washington: American Psychiatric Association.

GOODE, E. (1972) Drugs in American Society. New York: Alfred A. Knopf.

HAMILTON, J. A. (1922) "The treatment of drug addiction at the correctional hospitals in New York City." Journal of the American Institute of Criminal Law and Criminology 13 (May): 122-126.

HUNT, G. H. and M. E. ODOROFF (1962) "Followup study of narcotic drug addicts after hospitalization." Public Health Reports 77 (January): 41-54.

INCIARDI, J. A. (1971) "The use of parole prediction with institutionalized narcotic addicts." Journal of Research in Crime and Delinquency 8 (January): 65-73.

IRWIN, J. (1970) The Felon. Englewood Cliffs, N.J.: Prentice-Hall.

JACKSON, B. (1971) "Beyond Attica." Trans-action 9 (Nov.-Dec.): 4, 6-7, 10.

Joint Committee of the American Bar and Medical Associations (1961) Drug Addiction: Crime or Disease? Bloomington: Indiana University Press.

JOSEPH, H. and V. P. DOLE (1970) "Methadone patients on probation and parole." Federal Probation 34 (June): 42-48.

KING, R. (1972) The Drug Hang-Up, America's Fifty-Year Folly. New York: Norton.

KLONSKY, G. (1965) "Extended supervision for discharged addict-parolees." Federal Probation 29 (March): 39-44.

KOLB, L. (1939a) "Addicts on probation." Federal Probation 3 (February): 25.

––– (1939b) "The narcotic addict: his treatment." Federal Probation 3 (August): 19-23.

KOSSEF, A. (1925) "Study drug addicts in New York state prisons." Nation's Health 7 (January): 16-18.

KOZEL, N. J., R. L. DUPONT and B. S. BROWN (1972) "Narcotics and crime: a study of narcotic involvement in an offender population." International Journal of the Addictions 7 (Fall): 443-450.

LEARY, T. and W. H. CLARK (1963) "Religious implications of consciousness expanding drugs." Religious Education 58 (July-August): 251-256.

LEWIS, V. S., D. M. PETERSEN, G. GEIS and S. POLLACK (1972) "Social-psychological observations on urinalysis to detect heroin use," pp. 248-253 in F. Adler and G.O.W. Mueller (eds.) Politics, Crime and the International Scene: An Inter-American Focus. San Juan, P.R.: North-South Center Press.

LINDESMITH, A. R. (1965) The Addict and the Law. New York: Vintage Books.

LYLE, W. H. (1968) "A new psychotherapeutic technique for the sociopathic offender." Correctional Psychologist 3: 6-9.

MENNINGER, K. (1969) The Crime of Punishment. New York: Viking Press.

MOELLER, H. G. (1969) "The continuum of corrections." Annals of the American Academy of Political and Social Science 381 (January): 81-88.

National Council on Crime and Delinquency (1967) Uniform Parole Reports. Davis, Calif.

NELLANS, C. T. and J. C, MASSEE (1929) "Management of drug addicts in United States penitentiary at Atlanta." Journal of the American Medical Association 92 (April): 1153-1155.

O'DONNELL, J. A. (1967) "Research problems in follow-up studies of addicts," pp. 321-334 in Rehabilitating the Narcotic Addict. Washington: Government Printing Office.

––– (1965) "The relapse rate in narcotic addiction: a critique of follow-up studies," pp. 226-246 in D. M. Wilner and G. G. Kassebaum (eds.) Narcotics. New York: McGraw-Hill.

PESCOR, M. J. (1943) "Follow-up study of treated narcotic drug addicts." Public Health Reports, Supplement No. 170. Washington: Government Printing Office.

PETERSEN, D. M., R. M. YARVIS and G. M. FARKAS (1969) "The federal bureau of prisons treatment program for narcotic addicts." Federal Probation 33 (June): 35-40.

President's Commission on Crime in the District of Columbia Report (1966). Washington: Government Printing Office.

President's Commission on Law Enforcement and Administration of Justice (1967a) Task Force Report: Corrections. Washington: Government Printing Office.

––– (1967b) Task Force Report: Narcotics and Drug Abuse. Washington: Government Printing Office.

RAPKIN, R. M. (1971) "The NARA unit at Danbury: a short history of a unique treatment program for heroin addicts." American Journal of Correction 33 (March-April): 24-26.

RASOR, R. W. and J. F. MADDUX (1966) "Institutional treatment of narcotic addiction by the U.S. Public Health Service." Health, Education and Welfare Indicators (March): 27-40.

RECKLESS, W. C. (1967) The Crime Problem. New York: Appleton-Century-Crofts.

REICHARD, J. D. (1939) "The narcotic addict before the court." Federal Probation 3 (November): 21-25.

ROSENTHAL, V. and E. SHIMBERG (1958) "A program of group therapy with incarcerated narcotic addicts." Journal of Criminal Law, Criminology and Police Science 49 (July-August): 140-144.

SHELLY, J. A. (1967) "Daytop Lodge—a two year report," pp. 239-246 in Rehabilitating the Narcotic Addict. Washington: Government Printing Office.

——— (1966) "Daytop Lodge—halfway house for addicts on probation." Rehabilitation Record 7 (May-June): 19-21.

SHELLY, J. A. and A. BASSIN (1964) "Daytop Lodge: halfway house for drug addicts." Federal Probation 28 (December): 46-54.

Special Action Office for Drug Abuse Prevention (1972) "Federally funded drug treatment programs." (mimeo)

STACHNIK, T. J. (1972) "The case against criminal penalties for illicit drug use." American Psychologist 27 (July): 637-642.

TITTLE, C. and D. TITTLE (1964) "Social organization of prisoners: an empirical test. Social Forces 43 (December): 216-221.

TRAVERS, P. D. (1957) "An experiment in the supervision of paroled offenders addicted to narcotic drugs." American Journal of Correction 19 (March-April): 4.

U.S. Bureau of Prisons (n.d.) "The NARA II program after four years: some variables related to outcome." (mimeo)

VAILLANT, G. E. (1966) "A twelve-year follow-up of New York narcotic addicts: I. the relation of treatment to outcome." American Journal of Psychiatry 122 (January): 727-737.

VAILLANT, G. E. and R. W. RASOR (1966) "The role of compulsory supervision in the treatment of addiction." Federal Probation 30 (June): 53-59.

WIENER, F. and H. MUEHLBERGER (1968) "Southmore House, use of a 'halfway' house and integrated community approaches in the post hospitalization/correctional institution rehabilitation of narcotic addicts." Houston, Texas: Vocational Guidance Service.

WINICK, C. (1957) "Narcotics addiction and its treatment." Law and Contempory Problems 22 (Winter): 9-33.

WINICK, C. and H. BYNDER (1967) "Facilities for treatment and rehabilitation of narcotic drug users and addicts." American Journal of Public Health 57 (June): 1025-1033.

ZIMBARDO, P. G. (1972) "Pathology of imprisonment." Society 9 (April): 4, 6, 8.

Chapter 7

THE ROLE OF CIVIL COMMITMENT IN
MULTIMODALITY PROGRAMMING

HAROLD MEISELAS and
LEON BRILL

During the 1960s, civil commitment was used by a number of states—California (McGee, 1965) and New York (Meiselas, 1971) among others—as a means for structuring the treatment of narcotic users and other drug-dependent individuals. The federal government similarly instituted its Narcotic Addict Rehabilitation Act (NARA) Program, which entailed a six-month stay at the National Institute of Mental Health Clinical Research Centers at Lexington, Kentucky, and Fort Worth, Texas, followed by care in the patient's own community for a period up to three years (Conrad, 1972; Kay, 1973).

As a consequence of this activity, a considerable body of experience pertaining to civil commitment has accrued. In this chapter, the authors will explore the meaning of the technique and the role it should play in a comprehensive, multifaceted approach to treatment.

BACKGROUND CONSIDERATIONS

Basic to any understanding of drug dependence is the fact that it presents a wide variety of ways and encompasses different groups of drugs and individuals (Brill, 1971a/b). That is to say, there are many kinds of drug users who use a variety of drugs in different ways and in varying degrees. Our society for some time focused primarily on the *drug*—usually heroin—and devoted far less effort to understanding the person involved and the role drugs were playing in his life. It did not, in brief, view drugs as a "people thing." Today, it is better understood that drug use is neither uniform nor monolithic: it subsumes a variety of categories, ranging from experimental and social-recreational to more serious dysfunctional use as embodied in the terms "street addict" or chronic alcoholic. It also includes use for adaptive reasons, i.e., to maximize functioning within a conventional framework, for life-adjustment rather than "deviant" or delinquent reasons.

Many of the treatment techniques or modalities developed to date evolved in response to the various ways drug dependence presents itself, and reflect the diverse approaches required to cope with it. Historically, the gradual accumulation of different treatment modalities, including the use of narcotic antagonists (Geis, 1972), methadone maintenance (Chambers and Brill, 1973; Dole and Nyswander, 1966; Dole et al., 1968), rational authority concepts (Brill and Lieberman, 1969), religious identification, ex-addict-directed therapeutic communities (Brill, 1971c; Yablonsky, 1965), and the use of day centers (Brill, 1971a), among others, eventually culminated in the concept of a multimodality approach which has been pursued by the New York State Narcotic Addiction Control Commission (NACC) since 1967, and by other programs in different parts of the country. This approach derives from the belief that there is no universal such as "the addict," but rather a variety of addicts with different characteristics, backgrounds, states of addiction, and degrees of readiness for help. By evaluating which characteristics can be treated by specific modalities, it is hoped that objective criteria for the screening and treatment of patients can be developed. This would permit patients, after an initial evaluation, to be referred to the modality best equipped to reinforce treatment and cover different phases of their rehabilitation.

The multimodality concept is increasingly being advanced today through the provision, at the community level, of a comprehensive range of services geared to encompass all drug abusers in treatment. This is particularly true in New York state where approximately $70,000,000 was spent in fiscal 1972-73 to support services delivered at the county and municipal level. In a given region in New York, such a comprehensive system of care may include intervention services such as case-finding in courts, police stations, health centers, school and business infirmaries; centers for detoxification and emergency treatment where case-finding, counseling, and referral are built into the procedures used; residential care centers for those who require this degree of structure, be they professionally-led or ex-addict-directed; and the offering of assistance on an ambulatory basis to those whose functioning and social ties permit them to be approached constructively while they remain in the community. These latter services include day-care centers and clinics which provide counseling and casework services as well as individual and group therapy. In most communities, chemotherapeutic assists such as methadone maintenance are also available.

Such a diversity of approaches, which permits discriminations to be made on the basis of a differential diagnosis, is at wide variance with the earlier rationale of advocating a single approach for all addicts. This view was primarily oriented to the institutional-aftercare model, which stipulated that all patients must first be admitted to an institution for an extended period and returned to the community only when they were deemed to be "cured"—a goal the authors view as impossible to achieve for most addicts in light of the chronic relapsing nature of confirmed heroin addiction (Brill and Meiselas, 1973). Indeed, it is increasingly recognized today that criteria other than abstinence—such as improvement in interpersonal relationships, changes in self-image, employment, better use of leisure time, reduction in drug use and criminality, and general movement towards conventional behavior must be applied to assess treatment success. Of importance, it is also recognized that, if a multimodality system for programing is to be comprehensive, it is necessary to have available not only a wide variety of techniques to help different kinds of patients but the means for involving them in treatment. That is, the approach must recognize that, while a large number of individuals may be sufficiently community-embedded and motivated to relate to a program on a voluntary basis, others will not come into treatment of their own accord. Methods therefore need to be found to engage the latter in treatment. For some, the use of authority and compulsion through civil commitment represents one such technique (Brill and Meiselas, 1973).

CURRENT PERSPECTIVES

Civil commitment has been condemned in many quarters because its meaning and proper place in treatment were widely misunderstood. One source of criticism stemmed from its association with the institutional-aftercare model of service. This approach originally sought to produce an abstaining, functioning person within the institutional setting and then return him to the community for continued care, with the understanding that he could be readmitted to the institution for a further stay if he resumed drug use. This in turn led to the "patient movement" method of evaluation, which has been used by program administrators and research personnel in the following way: patients released to the aftercare phase of treatment who relapse and are returned to the hospital or institution are considered "treatment failures," and their number is listed as the "percentage who failed." When measured in this way, the New York State NACC programs, which served addicts civilly-committed to its care within an institutional-aftercare model, were described as having a 75 to 80 percent failure rate by the end of one year. Or, stated differently, only 20 to 25 percent of those released remained continuously in aftercare for a one-year period. However, retention in aftercare constitutes an unsuitable single criterion for measuring program success, since it is, to a considerable extent, a function of how treatment is structured. For example, if a very loose structure were maintained in a methadone program, it might be possible to increase the retention rate to almost 100 percent by totally ignoring acting-out behavior, such as drug abuse and other antisocial or dysfunctional activity. By the same token, a very tightly structured program would show a far smaller "retention rate." Variations exist in the statistics reported by different methadone programs—part undoubtedly related to the competence and experience of the administrators, but much also depending on where they choose to draw the line (Brill, 1972).

At its inception, many of the counselors in the New York State NACC program returned patients to the institution if they "slipped" even briefly. This did not mean that these patients were to be considered failures forever for not being "retained in aftercare"; but should rather be viewed in terms of the chronic nature of drug addiction, with "relapses" to be anticipated along the way as they participated in treatment. This aspect constitutes one of the major sources of misunderstanding about the treatment of drug abuse. To reiterate: the "success" of a patient depends on a wider number of parameters, including employment, reduction of criminality and drug abuse, improvement in interpersonal relationships, changes in self-image, better use of leisure time, and general movement towards conventional behavior.

What cannot be emphasized sufficiently is that growth toward these goals occurs only gradually and may require a period of years for its accomplishment. Any expectation that a patient will have "made it" fully after a period of six months or even a year or more of institutionalization is naive in light of our present understanding. The goals established need to be relative and flexible; allowing for differentiation among different kinds of patients, and anticipating relapses, lost-to-contact phenomena, abscondences, and continued regressive behavior for extended periods of time.

In short, what patient-movement data emphasize is that the hospital-aftercare model of care as originally conceived is far too simple a model, and its expectations are unrealistic. Residential settings where individuals can pause to take stock, be detoxified or stabilized on methadone, plan for the future, and begin to reconstitute their lives, certainly have a place in a total approach. It is not essential, however, that the individual begin his treatment with a residential stay or, conversely, that he be limited to only one residential experience. The residential setting should rather be used flexibly, as required. The task thus becomes one of sustaining addicts in the community at various levels of functioning by bringing to bear all our knowledge and supports (Brill, 1971b; Brill and Lieberman, 1969; Brill and Meiselas, 1973). Experience to date indicates that long-term institutional stays, in and of themselves, do not facilitate this process. However, we are not prepared to say that periods of residential care should arbitrarily be brief since early return to the community may be premature in some cases.

Only gradually and with difficulty have we begun to understand the factor discussed thus far, namely, that the concept of medical quarantine is inappropriate for drug addiction since it grossly distorts and oversimplifies the complex nature of the problem. What must be stressed instead is that there are all kinds of drug abusers, involved in varying degrees with drugs. Some may be "deviant" only in the area of involvement with drugs and conventional in all other respects; while others are totally submerged in all aspects of living as subsumed under the term "street addict" (Brill, 1971a/b; Brill and Meiselas, 1973).

A uniform or single approach to drug abuse—such as a universal civil commitment procedure for all users—doesn't make sense in light of the heterogeneous composition of this population. Our goals need to be clearer: we cannot insist on total immediate abstinence in view of the chronic relapsing nature of drug addiction. We must also establish different goals for different kinds of addicts, depending on their strengths, capacities, and degree of involvement with drugs. Civil commitment would be best equated with the use of rational authority, and not be viewed as a treatment in itself but rather a procedure for involving addicts in a variety of treatment approaches. From this standpoint, civil commitment cannot be the answer for everybody as it was believed to be some years ago, but rather a technique for involving selected recalcitrant patients in a comprehensive approach to treatment. Through the use of a differential diagnosis, different kinds of addicts would be helped to find the treatment most appropriate for them. Within this framework, civil commitment would be used to engage those individuals who do not come into treatment voluntarily but can respond to a structured treatment program.

OTHER ISSUES

As indicated, there has been considerable criticism of civil commitment procedures emanating, as the authors believe, from misunderstanding of its real role and wider possibilities. Much of this misunderstanding related to stereotyped thinking about civil commitment as a uniform procedure for *all* addicts, and as a reinforcement for the institutional-aftercare or parole model of treatment (Ausubel, 1970; Brill and Meiselas, 1973). As noted, this approach was bound to fail, among other reasons because there are different kinds of addicts who require different approaches. Civil commitment, like any component of a multimodality program, must define its true role and usefulness for a selected segment of the addict population. If it draws into treatment those individuals who do not come in voluntarily, it should contribute to the overall effectiveness of the multimodality approach.

The question confronting us is how to make authority from such a source rational *and* multifaceted enough to involve the different kinds of recalcitrant drug-dependent persons in treatment. For example, methadone maintenance has already proven its effectiveness for certain addicts (Chambers and Brill, 1973; Dole and Nyswander, 1966; Dole et al., 1968), and the problem now is to extend its usefulness to still more patients. With authority, too, experience reveals that some addicts clearly do better when their treatment is structured (Brill and Lieberman, 1969; Brill and Meiselas, 1973). How to enhance its usefulness for additional users who seem to require it? In considering this problem, we shall need to draw upon all possible sources of rational authority-civil commitment as well as court deferment and other procedures yet to be devised.

Court deferment, while not entirely new, is currently receiving considerable attention through support by the President's Special Action Office for Drug Abuse Prevention (SAODAP) (Jaffe, 1972; Perito, 1972; Special Action Office, 1972a/b). As implied by the name, the technique involves interruption of the court process and referral of the defendent to a community-based treatment program in lieu of prosecution. It seeks to interrupt the cycle of street crime-jail-street crime; protect society through the reduction of drug-related crime; treat hard-core addicts who do not have motivation to seek treatment; use the lever of the criminal justice system to get the addict into treatment and hold him there; decrease the tensions in jails due to withdrawal symptoms; and reduce the burdens the addicts place on the criminal justice system (police, judiciary, and penal institutions).

The approach as conceptualized by SAODAP in its "Treatment Alternatives to Street Crime" (TASC) program, generally begins in jail, where all arrestees are screened for drug addiction after police processing. Types of offenders ineligible for referral to treatment are determined by the local judiciaries. The screening process includes a brief interview during which the program is explained to the arrestee. The arrestee is told that information given in these proceedings or obtained from the urinalysis may not be the subject of any court proceedings or prosecution against him other than in determining bail. With the arrestee's permission, urinalysis is performed, followed by a more intensive counselor interview to determine drug-related history. Results from the urinalysis (obtained in 24 hours) and interview findings are compiled in a report which is sent to the presiding justice, the prosecutor, and the individual's attorney or the public defender.

The judge then determines whether to send the arrestee to detention or set treatment as a condition of bail and divert him to the TASC system. If the former procedure is followed, an arrestee sent to detention who is currently intoxicated on drugs is given medical assistance in the detention facility (or a secure detoxification unit as permitted by local statutes and procedures). If the latter is followed, an arrestee currently on drugs is sent to a detoxification unit where medical aid and counseling services are provided.

An evaluation is then performed by the diagnostic unit for each individual, with referral to a holding unit. The individual is treated in this facility until he can be transferred to a community treatment program. During the treatment period, a tracking system functions to ensure that each individual is following the conditions set at bail. This system reports drop-outs from treatment to the judiciary, which treats the individual as if he had violated conditions of bail. When the individual case comes up for trial, the presiding judge may take into account his cooperation and success in the treatment program thus far, and determine that he should remain in that program as an alternative to prosecution or possible incarceration subsequent to prosecution.

The TASC approach makes the court the locus of authority, a factor which poses many problems that will need to be addressed. To begin with, courts are generally not equipped to make decisions that entail diagnosis and referral of defendants to treatment programs. In addition, judges frequently are caught up in an ambivalent stance: on the one hand, they wish to appear as wise arbiters aware of a wide range of sociological issues; on the other, as strong and firm agents of the law.

However, the use of civil commitment as a means for placing authority with the treatment agency presents still other kinds of problems since civil commitment is a cumbersome process against which addicts often struggle to avoid supervision of their behavior (Hogan, 1972). Attempts to achieve effective application of authority thus tend to be caught between the Scylla of civil commitment's unwieldiness and the Carybdis of the deferred prosecution procedure's inability to maintain a rational, consistent posture with addicts through its court base.

Some of these problems are mitigated when addicts accept and are suitable candidates for a community-based program such as methadone maintenance. They are exacerbated when the patient becomes involved with a therapeutic community whose ability to hold patients on a continuing basis is, at best, limited (Brill, 1971c; Brill and Meiselas, 1973). If authority is vested in an agency with structured institutional facilities such as NACC, this may also prove problematic: NACC can indeed return patients to the institution, but finds it difficult to deal with more serious acting-out behavior which tests limits unbearably or subverts the program for other, more amenable, patients. This in fact constitutes the dilemma for programing on a global scale since not all patients can be helped by, or respond effectively to, treatment services structured by authority.

Court deferment procedures pose similar problems since they tend to select out those patients who wish to be treated. These constitute only a small portion of the total addict population. A surprisingly large number generate serious problems for treatment agencies, particularly for those which eschew chemo- therapeutic supports. Such individuals need to be returned to the court, which then gropes for other ways to deal with them.

The question of how to cope with this dilemma remains and has no easy answers. It appears that civil commitment might work better if provision were made for court expansion through the addition of more judges, prosecuting attorneys, other staff and "Special Parts," so that clogged court calendars could be cleared. These problems are, of course, not restricted to drug addiction but are representative of the entire criminal justice system today.

In weighing what route to take, careful review of the pros and cons suggests that court deferment would become a more viable methodology if, beyond the customary criminal justice processing functions, personnel for screening and referral of eligible candidates to treatment programs were made available to the court. In addition, if a state coordinating agency such as NACC, with a wide spectrum of services ranging from closed intramural to open community-based settings, were assigned authority via legislation to hold patients through all their vicissitudes, even firmer and more consistent procedures could be devised.

The question of civil rights and liberties has figured prominently in discussions about civil commitment as a device for compelling treatment. Psychiatrists and doctors such as Szasz (1963, 1970) and Weil (1970) and sociologists like Schur (1965) hold that society has no right to define and control private behavior and see drug use as a personal affair. The natural corollary of this position is that treatment may not be indicated at all; or, if it is, it must be voluntary and not imposed since it then becomes punitive and valueless. The approach suggested here acknowledges the validity of much of this thinking, and draws upon the concept that, if authority is to be used at all, it must be rational (Brill and Lieberman, 1969; Brill and Meiselas, 1973). We must differentiate the various kinds of users involved to ensure that we are not confusing the experimental, social-recreational, and "adaptive" users with those who are clearly dysfunctional and troubled, and are engaging in behavior that is detrimental to themselves and society (Brill, 1971a; Meiselas and Brill, 1972).

In effect, the problem looms quite large since we ordinarily think of the drug problem in terms of illegal drugs. It is clear, however, that many legal psychotropic drugs as well as our number one drug, alcohol, are freely available today. Large numbers of individuals cannot use these drugs without getting out of control and becoming dysfunctional in time, with serious threat to their stability and life as well as the safety of others. Such individuals present serious problems even though they are not criminally-oriented; and they too may require structured treatment settings to control their acting-out behavior. From a rational and legal standpoint, while we are always concerned about the individual and his rights, we must also think of other individuals who may be hurt by his behavior. To underline an obvious point, we need to maintain our perspective on the welfare of society as a whole. To accomplish this at times means setting limits for those individuals who are out of control and engage in seriously disruptive behavior.

Perhaps a final aspect to be mentioned relates to the fact that most treatment people have been oriented to a "permissive" approach, which entails accepting the patient where he is, with all his strengths and weaknesses, and allowing him considerable initiative in the treatment process so that he can begin to mobilize himself and achieve independent functioning. Very often this frame of reference is accompanied by a strong anti-authority viewpoint which fails to take cognizance of the many patients who cannot be treated on a voluntary, motivated basis and whose behavior poses serious problems for themselves and others. Psychiatrists and social agencies have traditionally dealt with selected patients and been free to select those who were better motivated, dismissing others who failed to meet their standards. It should be clear, however, that if dysfunctional drug use is to be addressed both comprehensively and therapeutically as a non-criminal matter, we shall need to draw upon authority as an essential component of treatment.

CONCLUSION

The authors have sought to define and clarify the role of civil commitment within a comprehensive, multimodality program. They have underlined the need to stop equating civil commitment with the institutional-aftercare model of treatment if further movement in the use of this technique is to be accomplished. It will rather be necessary to view civil commitment as representing a form of "rational authority," to be used as a lever for structuring treatment for those patients who ordinarily do not seek assistance on a voluntary basis. It is anticipated that with further experience and continued evaluation further refinement of a differentiated, multiform, non-punitive use or authority could be developed.

The authors have traced some of the errors in the past, such as our reliance on a uniform single approach for curing *all* addicts, and insistence on total immediate abstinence—a goal clearly beyond the reach of most drug dependent people. Also emphasized was the growing realization that there is no such universal as "the addict," but rather a wide variety of individuals for whom varied approaches, both voluntary and involuntary, need to be developed.

In addressing this subject, the authors have sought to provide the basis for overcoming stereotyped thinking on the subject of authority. Hopefully, this will help us find ways to extend its usefulness for the many troubled individuals who can "make it" only within the setting of structured treatment programs.

REFERENCES

AUSUBEL, D. P. (1970) Why Compulsory Closed-Ward Treatment for Narcotic Addicts? Albany: New York State Narcotic Addiction Control Commission.
BRILL, L. (1972) "Response to the paper 'New York's candy-coated jails'." Drug Forum 1 (January): 201-206.
——— (1971a) "Drug abuse problems—implications for treatment." Abstracts for Social Workers 7 (Fall): 3-8.
——— (1971b) "Drug addiction," pp. 24-38 in Encyclopedia of Social Work. New York: National Association of Social Workers.
——— (1971c) Some comments on the paper 'social control in therapeutic communities' by Dan Waldorf." International Journal of the Addictions 6 (March): 45-50.

BRILL, L. and L. LIEBERMAN [eds.] (1972) Major Modalities in the Treatment of Drug Abuse. New York: Behavioral Publications.

——— (1969) Authority and Addiction: Boston: Little, Brown.

BRILL, L. and H. MEISELAS (1973) "The treatment of drug abuse: experiences and issues," pp. 49-62 in L. Brill and E. Harms (eds.) Yearbook of Drug Abuse. New York: Behavioral Publications.

CARRICK, R. W. (1966) "Southmore House: use of a 'halfway' house and integrated community approaches in the posthospital/correctional institution rehabilitation of narcotic addicts," in Rehabilitation of the Narcotic Addict. Fort Worth, Texas: Institute on New Developments.

CHAMBERS, C. D. and L. BRILL (1973) Methadone: Experiences and Issues. New York: Behavioral Publications.

CONRAD, H. T. (1972) "NIMH Clinical Research Center, Lexington, Kentucky," pp. 23-42 in L. Brill and L. Lieberman (eds.) Major Modalities in the Treatment of Drug Abuse. New York: Behavioral Publications.

DISKIND, M. H. and G. KLONSKY (1964) "A second look at the New York State parole drug experiment." Federal Probation 28 (December).

DOLE, V. P. and M. E. NYSWANDER (1966) "Rehabilitation of heroin addicts after blockade with methadone." New York State Journal of Medicine 55: 201 ff.

DOLE, V. P., M. E. NYSWANDER and A. WARNER (1968) "Successful treatment of 750 criminal addicts." Journal of the American Medical Association 206 (12): 2708-2711.

ELDRIDGE, W. B. (1967) Narcotics and the Law. Chicago: University of Chicago.

GEIS, G. (1972) Not the Law's Business. Publication No. 72-9132. Rockville, Md.: NIMH Center for Studies of Crime and Delinquency.

HOGAN, F. S. (1972) "Report by New York City District Attorney," p. 77 in E. M. Brecher and the Editors of Consumer Reports, Licit and Illicit Drugs. Boston: Little, Brown.

JAFFE, J. H. (1972) "Alternatives to incarceration of drug offenders: problems and prospects." Paper presented at meeting of the American Bar Association (August 16), San Francisco.

KAY, D. C. (1973) "Civil commitment in the federal medicine program for opiate addicts," pp. 17-35 in L. Brill and E. Harms (eds.) Yearbook of Drug Abuse. New York: Behavioral Publications.

KIEFFER, S. N. (1966) "New developments at the Fort Worth Hospital," in Rehabilitation of the Narcotic Addict. Fort Worth, Texas: Institute of New Developments.

KRAMER, J. C. (1972) "The state versus the addict: uncivil commitment," in J. Susman (ed.) Drug Use and Social Policy. New York: AMS Press.

LINDESMITH, A. R. (1965) The Addict and the Law. Bloomington, Ind.: Indiana Univ. Press.

MAYER, M. J. (1972) Quarterly Reports of Court Referral Project. Mimeographed, privately circulated.

McGEE, R. A. (1965) "New approaches to the control and treatment of drug abusers in California," pp. 263-273 in D. M. Wilner and G. G. Kassebaum (eds.) Narcotics. New York: McGraw-Hill.

MEISELAS, H. (1971) "The New York State Narcotic Addiction Control Commission: its programs and activities," in N. Straus (ed.) Addicts and Drug Abusers: Current Approaches to the Problem. New York: Twayne Publishers.

——— (1965) "Narcotic addiction program of the New York State Department of Mental Hygiene," in D. M. Wilner and G. G. Kassebaum (eds.) Narcotics. New York: McGraw-Hill.

MEISELAS, H. and L. BRILL (1972) "Drug abuse in industry: issues and comments." Industrial Medicine 41 (August): 10-14.

National Advisory Commission on Criminal Justice, Standards and Goals (1973) Drug Abuse. Washington: Government Printing Office.

National Board, National Alliance for Safer Cities (1972) Statement of Drug Abuse and Crime. Adopted September 29.

PERITO, P. L. (1972) "Sentencing and dispositional alternatives in drug cases." Paper presented at meeting of the American Bar Association (September 30), New York.

President's Commission on Law Enforcement and the Administration of Justice (1967) Task Force Report: Narcotics and Drug Abuse. Washington: Government Printing Office.

RASOR, R. W. (1972) "The USPHS institutional treatment program for narcotic addicts at Lexington, Kentucky," in L. Brill and L. Lieberman (eds.) Major Modalities in the Treatment of Drug Abuse. New York: Behavioral Publications.

SCHUR, E. M. (1965) Crimes Without Victims. Englewood Cliffs, N.J.: Prentice-Hall.

Special Action Office for Drug Abuse Prevention (SAODAP) (1972a) Drug Abuse: A National Emergency. Washington: Executive Office of the President.

——— (1972b) Treatment Alternatives to Street Crime (TASC). Washington: Executive Office of the President.

SZASZ, T. S. (1970) "The right to drugs—a matter of freedom?" Long Island Newsday, October 21.

——— (1963) Law, Liberty and Psychiatry: An Inquiry into the Social Uses of Mental Health Practices. New York: Macmillan.

TERRY, C. E. and M. PELLENS (1969) The Opium Problem. Montclair, N.J.: Patterson-Smith.

VOSS, H. L. and R. C. STEPHENS (1973) "The relationship between drug abuse and crime." Drug Forum 2 (2).

WEIL, A. (1970) "Altered states of consciousness." Unpublished manuscript, September 8.

WOOD, R. W. (1966) "California rehabilitation center," in Rehabilitation of the Narcotic Addict. Fort Worth, Texas: Institute on New Developments.

YABLONSKY, L. (1965) The Tunnel Back: Synanon. New York: Macmillan.

Chapter 8

COMPOUNDING A FELONY: DRUG ABUSE AND THE AMERICAN LEGAL SYSTEM

STEVEN M. GREENBERG

FIRST DOWN—TWENTY FIVE TO GO

Imagine, if you will, that the drug abuse crisis in our country was the result of a conspiracy. A conspiracy so vast in its scope as to boggle the mind of a James Bond. The purpose of this conspiracy would be, of course, to so confound and confuse the United States of America that she consistently and mindlessly would pursue a course of absolute idiocy. That she would steadfastly perform acts that were antagonistic to her best interests—that would alienate her people, destroy her health, ruin her morale. Imagine the minds of her legislators befuddled, the souls of her judges and policemen hardened and twisted into hatred, the intellects of her educators confused, and her citizenry reduced to the level of a frenzied mob. Conjure up the picture of evil alien rulers rubbing together their hands in glee over the sight of the most powerful nation in the world destroying itself from within, like a scorpion dispatching itself with its own stinger.

And then ask yourself—if the truth is not too painful—whether any evil aliens or sinister plots could have succeeded in impairing our national welfare as totally as we have done through our frenzied efforts to react to a phenomenon that we never really attempted to understand. Try and recall the period in our history when people first began to realize that drugs were going to be a white middle-class problem in the United States, and consequently decided to do something about it. Look back on all the legislation, all the drug education programs, all the legal and illegal police activities, and yes, even all the National Football League public service announcements on drug abuse. Are we any closer now to what we wanted to accomplish back in 1964 in terms of keeping drug abuse within "acceptable" limits? If we could be magically transported back to those fateful years of the 1960s and be given a chance to do the whole thing over again, and then if we deliberately attempted to *create* the drug problem, could we, even with the benefit of hindsight, be more successful at throwing our country into crisis?

It is time to face the fact that after several frantic, heartbreaking years of reaction and overreaction to drug usage, we have accomplished virtually nothing—nothing except the exposure of our legal system as an inept, sometimes oppressive and corrupt instrument for the enforcement of public and private morality. We have not curbed drug abuse . . . we haven't even slowed it. What we have done is to further alienate an entire generation of our children, already alienated by the reality they perceive around them.

The reasons for this alienation are largely outside the scope of this chapter, except as they were created and enforced by our legal system. However, it is interesting to speculate on whether we would have reached the sorry position in which we find ourselves had we reacted differently to the multiplicity of issues which dominated the 1960s, and which originally led to the alienation of our young people.

For instance, had the Vietnam war ended in 1965 or 1966, would the "passive" 1950s have erupted into the massive disruptions and violence of the 1960s? If the nation had reacted to the shame of watching an overtly racist social system enforce its values by utilizing firehoses, clubs, guns, bayonets, and vicious dogs to subdue non-violent school children, and committed itself on a long-term basis to establishing real equality for blacks, would our children have turned away from their television sets in fear and disgust and taken to the streets? And finally, if we had reacted with acceptance, or even paternalistic amusement to long hair, bare feet, unorthodox dress, and the conception of a new type of brotherhood for our country, instead of with disgust, envy, hatred, fear and violence—if we had taken the flower that was offered instead of slapping the bearers' hands away—could we not have kept our children, instead of driving them away?

GAMES PEOPLE PLAY:
I KNOW YOU BELIEVE YOU UNDERSTAND
WHAT YOU THINK I SAID, BUT I AM NOT SURE YOU
REALIZE WHAT YOU HEARD IS NOT WHAT I MEANT

It is, of course, impossible to recreate the past. But we can strive to understand it so that we can avoid reliving it around another set of issues. We can only accomplish this if we remove the emotionalism that surrounds this entire era and admit simply that no two large social groups are going to perceive what has happened in the same way. It is not that they *will* not understand each other, but that they *can* not. They do not have the mutually shared background, culture, and experience that would enable them to take a vastly complex set of data, analyze it, and come to similar conclusions.

It seems logical that after several thousand years of philosophers asking the question, "What is reality?", and after an equally long period without an answer from the realists, someone would realize that, ultimately, reality is whatever we perceive it to be. Perhaps people who have the time and ability to contemplate such matters have long ago come to this conclusion. But most of us do not take the time to contemplate under even normal circumstances. And when we think that we are involved in a crisis, or faced with an emergency, we tend to be even less inclined to analyze, or think, or plan.

This is why intelligent men can see the nature of the drug problem as (1) a result of an oppressive capitalist-imperialist political system, or (2) a sociological problem caused by a multiplicity of social ills, or (3) a symptom of the decline in the moral fabric of our nation, or (4) a Mafia plot, or (5) a Communist plot, or (6) a C.I.A. plot, or (7) a government-big business plot, or (8) a purely medical-technical problem, or (9) as no problem at all.

Consider the different factors that go into the shaping of a middle-class freak, a ghetto-bred black militant, a career military man, an urban policeman, a rural judge, and a Supreme Court Justice. It seems incredible that anyone would expect these persons to even frame their questions in the same way. They certainly cannot be expected to come up with the same solutions.

A MODERN-DAY TRAGEDY

Whatever group a person owes allegiance to, and whatever his background, it seems manifest to all but a few persons (who form the drug-scene equivalent of the Flat-Earth Society), that there are significant differences between the use of marijuana and the use of other commonly abused drugs. Leaving aside for other places and times the arguments relating to the physical and psychological effects of marijuana usage, it is apparent that our legal system has recognized these distinctions implicitly, but not explicitly.

This has resulted in the creation of a dual-reality system which has made a mockery out of the criminal justice system of our country, and which has produced a setting in which the detection, apprehension, prosecution, and punishment of marijuana users has become a game. The predominant characteristic of this game is that most of the participants know the rules, but pretend not to.

As this analysis proceeds, two things should be borne in mind. First, this entire discussion is geared to the legal system in urban areas. It is not meant to be applied to Texas and other small rural areas where a first-time marijuana offender is treated with the same consideration as a black man accused of raping the white mayor's daughter.

Second, most first-time drug offenders arrested for possession of an illegal substance other than marijuana are treated the same as marijuana offenders. Consequently, the discussion which follows, particularly that which encompasses the operation of our courtrooms, is equally applicable to other types of drug abuse cases. Now, back to the game.

The first rule of the game, and the one which is enforced most diligently, is that the following statement must never be uttered by any person working within the criminal justice system:

EVERYBODY SMOKES DOPE!

This profound statement should not be taken to mean that every *person* in the country smokes marijuana. It merely means: Policemen smoke dope. Probation officers smoke dope. Narcotic agents smoke dope (and sell it). *Judges smoke dope.* Prosecutors smoke dope. Defense attorneys smoke dope. Plumbers, schoolteachers, principals, deans, carpenters, Disabled War Veterans, Republicans, doctors, perverts, and librarians smoke dope. Legislators smoke dope. Even writers of articles on drug abuse smoke dope.

EVERYBODY SMOKES DOPE!

Why is it illegal?

That's the game.

And now, in their order of appearance . . .

Our Cast

 (1) The Freak

 (2) The Probation Officer

 (3) The Parent

(4) The Legislator
(5) The Narcotics Officer (Narc)
(6) The Defense Attorney
(7) The Judge
(8) The Police Officer
(9) The Prosecutor (mentioned in passing)

The Bit Parts

Many of our characters, playing minor roles in the process, will be dealt with rather summarily in this article. This is not to imply that they are not critical to the process. It merely means that, in most cases, they either have little control over the operation of the system as it applies to them, or they have little understanding of their role and, consequently, cannot alter the system's effects.

For instance, Number 1, the freak, could easily avoid a huge percentage of his involuntary contacts with the police. That he fails to do so is usually an indication of carelessness, or stupidity, or worst of all, greed. It is quite conceivable that the careful freak could avoid detection for a lifetime if he took just minimal security precautions. His failure to do so insures his entry into the system as a pawn. From that time on, he has very few chances to affect the course of his movement through the process.

The probation officer, Number 2, is often in the same position of powerlessness vis-a-vis the system, but for quite different reasons. His problem is that, in many instances, he has minimal or no contact with the persons who are supposed to be placed in his care. Frequently, judges place convicted offenders on "non-reporting" probation, taking them out of the probation officer's hands. In other cases, the demands of the probation officer's caseload are such that he quite rationally neglects to keep close tabs on minor drug offenders so that he might deal more comprehensively with those under his care who merit more attention. Thus, the probation officer's relationship to the criminal justice system in most cases falls under heading of (please forgive the reference) "benign neglect."

The parent, alas, is also a bit player. Basically, this is because by the time a drug abuser is arrested, it is too late for the parent to do anything but offer moral and financial support. Many parents panic at this juncture and immediately begin searching for a drug program for their child. Whether the child has a drug problem or not is generally not considered or at issue. While the parent's role at this point is critical for the future welfare of his child, the part he plays is almost independent of the legal system.

The Stars

In a cast of characters dominated by villains, our legislators must stand out as among the arch-villains because they for the most part create the system under which the rest of the cast operates. Furthermore, they, in their lofty position, should be able to oversee the entire system. This should give them some perspective on the problem. Unfortunately, because of a number of factors based on the nature of the political process, they tend to act in times of crisis as if their motivations for action come directly from the lowest possible common denominator of their electorate.

Saul Alinsky theorized that the maximum effective life-span of any social organization was seven years. After this period the organization operated not to fulfill the function for which it was first established, but merely to perpetuate itself. Every legislature in this country is more than seven years old, and a large percentage of legislators serves for more than seven years.

If you examine the voting records of the members of any legislative body you will find two major factors which influence their votes. First, on a number of issues the lawmakers will be "bought for" long before they get into office. Being bought and paid for is commonly known as "soliciting campaign contributions." On these issues, the votes of a legislator will be very consistent. But this area of larceny does not concern us; issues which arouse the passions of the mob rarely fall into this category. (The exception to this rule is found in Congress, where the drug lobbyists have made considerable inroads into Congressional independence.)

The area which does concern us is that in which the astute lawmaker must "judge the temper of the electorate." This means descending into the masses and gauging the depth of their hysteria. Generally, this is not done to actually ascertain what voters are thinking—most legislators have competent leg men for that—but to obtain a later justification for changing course abruptly if necessary. This tactic is known in football parlance as "following your blocking." The underground has a better expression for it . . . they call it "copping out."

What the legislator really accomplishes through the use of this tactic is self-absolution from all responsibility for his decisions. The legislator doesn't lead the lynch mob, he merely furnishes the rope.

Nevertheless, the responsibility for much of what has occurred in our country over the last few years can be traced directly to the action or inaction of the men who author our laws. Although it is beyond the scope of this chapter to rehash the entire history of drug abuse legislation in this country, it would be useful to discuss the various trends which have occurred in the past few years.

State and national legislation relating to drug abuse generally falls into one of five different areas. They are, in the order of decreasing priority (determined on the basis of when significant efforts to control these areas were initiated):

(1) Laws governing private usage.

(2) Laws governing street sales.

(3) Laws governing import.

(4) Laws authorizing funding for local drug abuse rehabilitation agencies.

(5) Laws restricting the overproduction of harmful drugs by legitimate manufacturers.

Americans are a peculiar people. More than any other country in modern times they have avowed their dedication to the highest principles of freedom. They have written and enforced a constitution emulated the world over for its protection of the major freedoms of the common man from the government which he has set above him. On the other hand, Americans have tolerated almost without qualms, restrictions on their rights of personal privacy that other less democratic nations would not dare to enforce.

One explanation for this is that laws are generally passed to protect everyone else but the people who write them. For instance, in the area of pornography, we are constantly passing laws to insure that *other* people don't see or hear proscribed materials. No up-and-coming, dedicated young smut fighter seriously believes (or cares to admit) that he himself will become an uncontrollable sex deviate if he views pornography: It is always the other person whose passions will become inflamed. No one in our country views more smut than those who are sworn to fight against its distribution. Are they the weird characters who jump from behind buses and yell "Wheeeee!" as they expose their private parts? Probably not, although anything is possible.

Virtually all laws which attempt to influence private morality suffer from the same defect. Just as prohibition was initiated largely by non-drinkers, laws against the use of drugs were passed by those who hadn't the least idea of what drug usage was like. This is not to imply that the abuse of drugs is a good thing, but only to say that if it was, the persons who legislated its illegality would be the last ones to know it.

President Nixon's reaction to the official report of the National Commission on Marijuana and Drug Abuse is an indication of an attitude often found in matters of this type, and parallels the attitude shown by the same Administration to the report of the National Commission on Pornography. That is, that *many of the persons responsible for setting the moral and legal tone for our nation do not want to know the truth!* The truth is irrelevant to their reality.

What *is* relevant to their reality is that, for political considerations, they do not want to be on record as being a political leader who presided over the legalization of drug usage—not in this era of the ascendancy of the silent majority. And if we have to throw a few thousand of our children into jail to preserve the purity of our politicians' voting records . . . so be it.

This brings up a point which is conceded as fact by virtually every person in the freak world, and by many straights. It is clear to these people that the majority of the drug abuse efforts in the middle and late 1960s was politically inspired. By this I mean that the rationale behind the legislation was not the control of drug abuse, but the deliberate harassment and suppression of an emerging minority group felt to be politically dangerous and morally disruptive. No other rationale can explain the severity of the sentences mandated for crimes which were basically passive in nature and consensual on the part of the "victims." Nothing else can explain the failure on the part of lawmakers to distinguish between users and pushers, between addicts and those who could control their usage. And finally, no theory other than political suppression can account for the concentration of emphasis on the small-time user and pusher and the massive disinterest in pursuing the major illegal suppliers of narcotics and other dangerous substances.

Three factors finally combined, however, to clear the eyes of the legislators so that they could see their way clear to enter into the second phase of legislation. First, the number and intensity of massive confrontations between the establishment forces and the anti-war activists began to decline after 1968, as Nixon "de-escalated" the War and the Draft. Second, more reasoned voices began to be heard throughout the nation pointing out the inescapable fact that the prior policy of controlling drug usage at the street level was a total failure. And third, it became increasingly dangerous for police officers to make drug arrests at any large gathering of persons without provoking the very types of massive confrontations which the establishment was trying to avoid.

Three things had been accomplished during this period: the thousandfold increase of drug usage in this country; the division of the country into armed camps—young against old; the recognition on the part of the establishment that a policy change was in order.

Consequently, in the late 1960s and early 1970s legislatures began to reduce the penalties for simple possession of drugs (particularly marijuana), and increase the penalties for sale, and for possession of amounts great enough to be considered presumptively to be held for the purpose of sale. (It is fascinating to note the wide disparity from state to state in the amounts of marijuana, for instance, needed to raise this presumption.)

This policy, while a bit more reasoned, still suffered from a basic flaw. For the most part, it affected the same people as had the prior policy, i.e., the people on the streets. Legislators could not seem to grasp the fact that they were dealing with persons who not only used drugs, but who freely distributed them to their friends and associates at cost, for a small profit, or many times for free. One could almost intuitively sense the visual images which passed through lawmakers' heads as they pondered these measures. They were still concerned by the shadowy figure of the middle-aged pusher hanging around the school yard who periodically approached Johnny (later to be called John when old enough to be "victimized" by a prostitute) and uttered the time-honored line, "Hey kid! Wanna have a reefer?", thus starting Johnny down the path to marijuana "addiction," crime, and ultimately, THE BIG "H." It is not surprising that these efforts failed. Most of our legislative marksmen had no conception of what their target looked like.

Furthermore, and most tragically, legislators actually believe, in many instances, that stiffer penalties deter the commission of crimes. At worst, this is patently untrue. At best, it is clearly unproven. (See, for example, the study made by the California State Assembly Committee on Criminal Procedure, "Crime and Penalties in California," which found no evidence that severe penalties effectively deter crime.)

In no area is this more apparent than in criminal drug-abuse legislation. Whatever the harshness or permissiveness of the laws in a particular state, no legislature can honestly state that the laws it passed have had any effect whatsoever on drug usage. Ironically, many observers have come to the conclusion that the vigorous enforcement of laws relating to drug abuse have actually led to an increase in drug-related crimes. This is because an increase in the harassment of pushers drives the price of drugs up. Consequently, the addict, who must steal from five to ten dollars of merchandise for every one dollar of drugs he needs, is forced to turn a greater number of tricks in order to acquire an ample supply.

The rules of the game in relation to the passing of legislation relating to the imposition of penalties for drug abuse during these two periods have been relatively simple . . . and simplistic: First, act quickly, before there is time to study the situation. Second, don't let scientific evidence corrupt your point of view . . . rely on your gut reaction and the inflamed passions of your constituency. Third, don't hesitate to sacrifice someone else's child for the cause (you can always use your influence to get your own child off). And finally, start from the bottom—you offend less important people by doing so.

While the law enforcement system has not yet realized or admitted the failure of its efforts to curb drug abuse, it has been forced to explore other alternatives in its efforts to dry up the supply of drugs on the street level. And so, while continuing its street-level activities, it has initiated efforts to curb the traffic before it filters down to the grass roots.

This leads us into the third level of legislative endeavor, the recent efforts to halt the import of proscripted substances. Actually, this is not strictly a legislative effort. We have had laws on the books for years which mandated the Federal Customs Service to halt the import of these materials. What really occurred was not a change in our laws in this area, but an executive mandate (accompanied by an appropriate increase in funds) to utilize all the weapons at the disposal of the Justice Department and the Customs Bureau.

While it is not yet known whether this effort is as yet stemming the tide of importation, certainly the quantities of substances seized are impressive. Furthermore, the seizure of large quantities of drugs excites the public imagination and makes great publicity for the Administration. It may well be asked, however, whether the dramatization of the seizures, and the publishing of the street value of the drugs (often inflated beyond the wildest dreams of the importer), doesn't incite and encourage other potential importers to try and make the one big kill that will set them up for life.

And, as in every other drug abuse effort, there is a large measure of doubt as to whether even these stepped-up efforts are having any effect. Early in December 1971, Myles J. Ambrose of the Customs Bureau announced that substantial progress was being made in the fight against importation. Mr. Ambrose went on to say that "our efforts here and along the Mexican border are paying off."

However, on November 30 *The New York Times,* quoting Federal Customs sources, stated: "Along the sparsely settled frontier that divides the United States and Mexico, airborne drug-runners are doing a booming business, and Federal agents say that they do not know how to stop them." Again, on December 5 the *Times* reported: "Federal officials in Florida and along the Mexican border . . . reported a dramatic increase in the activity of aerial drug-runners. More and more heroin is being flown into this country from Mexico and the French Caribbean Islands."

If nothing else, the Customs Bureau should develop a system which will allow its right hand to know what its left hand is doing. Tracing the history of federal bureaucracy, however, this may in the long run prove more difficult than curbing drug abuse.

As dramatic as these efforts have been in terms of publicity, they do not deal with at least one crucial area of the drug abuse crisis. That is, what do we do with our children? Specifically, what do we do with the persons who have become dependent on drugs, and how do we develop means independently of the legal system to deter persons from starting out on a path that will eventually lead to drug dependence or addiction?

For many years, this area was the stepchild of legislative action. And while efforts in this area have increased significantly in recent years, they still lag far behind the demonstrated needs for rehabilitative, educational, and research needs. While it is outside the scope of this chapter to deal with the specific amounts of monies needed or expended in efforts which fall outside of blatant propaganda or "scare" education, and law enforcement, it is significant to note that the following deficiencies exist:

(1) To this date, the nation has yet to come to grips with its largest substance abuse problem: alcohol.

(2) Most rehabilitation programs are understaffed and underfunded.

(3) The sum total of all rehabilitative-program efforts do not touch even a small minority of those needing assistance.

(4) Few rehabilitative programs can boast of over a 15 percent "cure rate."

(5) There is no competant evidence available to indicate that drug abuse has been slowed or brought under control.

(6) There is no widespread agreement on whether *any* type of drug abuse education is effective, *any* treatment method valid, or even as to what constitutes a "cured" drug abuser.

Finally, the legislature has the power and the duty to act in one other area of control, but has been extremely loath to do so. It is perhaps in this area that the record has been most shameful. For our Congress, under the influence of an extremely strong lobby, has, at the cost of many hundreds of lives, refused steadfastly to control the greatest purveyors of medicinal death in our country, the legitimate drug manufacturing companies. For most of the duration of our current drug crisis, those who control the destiny of our country have refused to face the fact that the largest percentage of drug-related deaths have been the result of chemicals legally produced and sold at incredible profits by legitimate drug concerns.

While it is indisputable that overpermissive doctors and over-cooperative pharmacists play their role in this continuing tragedy, the greatest responsibility and culpability still lies with the manufacturers who, with full knowledge of the outcome of their actions, produce billions of excess dosages of medicines, and then deliberately withhold and suppress information about the harmful effects of their products.

At the very least, the culpability of the drug manufacturers embraces their failure to adequately research the effects of the products they peddle. But the guilt of these companies extends well beyond the area of sloppy research. In his syndicated column, Jack Anderson (November 19, 1972) reported the results of a secret report issued by Claude Pepper's House Crime Committee which strongly indicted the drug industry for their lack of responsible behavior. The report revealed that "90 percent of the drugs in the illicit market are manufactured by legitimate pharmaceutical companies." The report went on to say:

> This Committee discovered that there were more than three billion amphetamines being produced each year. The only desirable medical uses for amphetamines are for the treatment of narcolepsy and hyporkinesis in children. One million doses of amphetamine . . . would have been more than adequate to supply the medical need for treating those diseases.

Although a bill finally passed both Houses which cut production of amphetamines by 82 percent, the Committee estimated that the drug industry lobbyists successfully delayed its passage by as much as two years. Perhaps the American people will some day hold these companies and their profit-oriented directors responsible for their actions. To the great shame of Congress, it has not. Congress only addresses itself to monopoly, not to murder. America may ultimately overdose on free enterprise.

The next character to be discussed is the narcotic agent. While I consider the narcotic agent (narc) to be one of the vital persons in the criminal justice system, I am going to treat him in rather a cursory fashion. This is done partially because of space limitations, and partially because I feel that the narc should be covered in great detail in some other work.

There is a great disparity of opinion as to whether a narc should be classified as a law officer or as a criminal. This is because the narc consistently utilizes methods which tend to produce crime, rather than to discourage it. Even the most honest of the genre tend, because of the nature of their work, to use methods which border on illegality. For example, when a narc infiltrates a group suspected of trafficking in narcotics, he will routinely engage in the same sort of activities for which group members will later be arrested—in order to attain the group's trust. This means in many cases that he will not only use drugs, but will ofttimes *procure* them so that he might share his dope, like any other member of the group.

The less honest narcs generally will do anything to get their man . . . even if he is innocent. This includes, but is by no means limited to, the following "techniques":

(1) Entrapment—becoming the motivating force behind the crime.

(2) Blackmail—threatening to "make it tough" on an offender if he does not turn in or "set up" someone else.

(3) Sexual relations with group members—in order to fit in.

(4) Perjury.

(5) Planting—actually placing narcotics on a person or onto their property so that they might be arrested.

(6) Selling drugs on the side to supplement their income—also utilized for "fitting in" purposes.

(7) Fraudulent charges—the so-called "grudge arrest" used to settle scores with uncooperative persons.

Perhaps the most charitable thing I can say about narcotics agents is that they are a necessary part of a failing system. They are a reflection of the depths to which we will sink in our efforts to control men's lives and morals. Their activities are designed to control drug usage and sales on the street—where it has been demonstrably proven that activities such as theirs will be futile in effecting a solution.

In most cases our next character, the defense attorney, has a minimal role to play. For all practical purposes, if the police have effected a search which conforms to constitutional requirements, and the search has disclosed a substance in the possession and control of the defendant which laboratory analysis establishes to be narcotics, and the prosecution doesn't mishandle its own case, the defense attorney is limited to collecting his fee and attempting to make some sort of deal.

In possession cases, the attorney's main function is to conceal the fact that the worst his client is likely to face is probation. The more his client is allowed to worry, the higher the fee he can justify. Of course, if the client has a prior record, or if the charges are more serious, the attorney's job becomes more difficult. Furthermore, the adept attorney is familiar with all the various facts that the prosecution must prove in order to establish its case, and can often prevent a conviction which would have been effected had the lawyer not been present. (Many judges will not protect the rights of a defendant who insists on defending himself—especially in cases involving minor violations.) Whether this has anything to do with justice remains to be seen.

In difficult cases, the defense attorney will attempt to swing some sort of deal. Generally, in first offenses involving simple possession, the prosecution and the judge will be willing to accept a six-month to one-year period of probation coupled with a withholding of adjudication. In more difficult cases, however, the asking price gets stiffer. Where the offense involves a sale of drugs, or where the defendant has a prior record, the defense lawyer's most common tactic is to place the defendant into a rehabilitation program. This allows the state to feel that it has achieved a beneficial result ... even if the defendant had no prior history of drug usage or dependancy.

As a last result, bribes have been known to change hands. In these cases the defendant is either released outright, given a small sentence, or if publicity on the case is too great, sentenced normally. Later, when publicity has subsided, the attorney returns to the courtroom on a "Plea for Mitigation" and the sentence is appropriately reduced.

As long as we have entered into the shadowy area of judicial behavior, we might as well deal directly with judges.

One of the most incredible follies indulged in by the American people is the election of judges. It too often constitutes the election of the incompetent by the uninformed. This is not to imply that some capable jurists are not chosen to sit on the bench by this method. But their ascendancy is neither contemplated nor caused by the system. It is an accidental by-product. This is because of a number of factors, some of which I will list:

(1) Many jurisdictions have no requirements for positions on the bench except membership in the state bar association.

(2) Potential jurists rarely have records on which to campaign that have any relevance to the office that they are seeking, and often distort their past accomplishments (a firmly entrenched political tradition).

(3) Most candidates are virtually unknown to the general public. This tends to allow the best campaigner, rather than the best jurist, to win.

(4) Judicial races, especially in the past few years, have generally been decided on a narrow range of highly emotional issues rather than on issues of competency.

One of the most dangerous results of the turbulant years of the 1960s was the politicizing of our judicial system. Ordinarily, races for judicial office attracted about the same amount of enthusiastic attention normally associated with the celebration of Groundhog Day. In the last few years, however, a number of issues have focused attention on the judicial elections.

For instance, in the late 1960s the American public discovered crime. No one was sure where crime had come from, but everyone recognized that it was among us. Even the nicest people were becoming victims. This sad state of affairs was generally attributed to two factors—lenient judges, and drugs.

Now, campaigning, which had once been a dreary and difficult job, became much more stimulating. Aspiring judges who had, during the fifties and early sixties, been forced to run campaigns based on strong commitments to civil rights and personal liberties, now found that their stands were outmoded and politically dangerous. Besides, it had become increasingly difficult in these harried times to continue looking benevolent, tolerant, and wise. Now the public furnished them with a positive mandate to take a more simplistic approach to issues. Many of them jumped at the chance.

It wasn't long before the first timid cry of "law and order" turned into a stampede against liberalism. Suddenly the best asset an aspiring judge could possess was a 90-percent conviction rate as a prosecutor. (He neglected to mention that this included a large majority of cases that never even went to trial, i.e., that were disposed of on a plea.) His best campaign promise was that drug users and pushers, and other criminals, would be "nailed" when they came before him. Lurking in the background of all this rhetoric was the implicit assumption that any person coming before him would be considered guilty until proven innocent.

This is the reality structure in which many judges decide their cases. Once elected, or faced with the necessity of campaigning against another law-and-order candidate, the judge must weigh every decision for its political implications, lest his opponent rise up and smite him with a mighty wind. The situation is comparable to the political situation in the South prior to the 1960s, when it was considered mandatory to "out-nigger" the opposition in order to win an election.

Of course, when a judge runs on a platform which states that he will clear the streets of criminals, he knows that he is lying. In the first place, the judge is but one figure in the judicial process and has many decisions taken out of his hands. Two examples of this are pre-trial intervention programs, which remove a potential defendant from the legal system before ever coming before a judge, and plea bargaining, which is an absolute necessity in many jurisdictions to avoid overcrowding of the courts. In the second place, if the judge sentenced every drug defendant coming before him to a jail term (disregarding for the moment the entire spectrum of other criminals who pass before him), our jails and penitentiaries would be hopelessly swamped, and our penal system virtually destroyed under the strain.

Society and the policeman share an almost classic sado-masochistic relationship. Often, however, it is difficult to determine which party is the sadist, and which the masochist.

On the one hand, the police department is the dumping ground for every conceivable social problem. The policeman bears the brunt of social forces he cannot control. He is denied adequate compensation for his work, restrained by court decisions he does not understand, maligned and distrusted by a large portion of society, and constantly asked to control the uncontrollable—enforce the unenforceable.

On the other hand, a significant minority of police officers consistently, deliberately, and ruthlessly violate the rights of the citizens with which they deal, and violate the Constitution and laws they are sworn to uphold. Police, acting in the line of duty, may be responsible for more violations of the law per capita than any other group.

Probably in no other area is the police officer as abusive of his authority as in the area of drug arrests. Because of the nature of society's response to the drug abuse crisis, the controls that would ordinarily be placed upon the policeman have been removed or ignored by his superiors and by the general public.

This is partially the result of the fact, mentioned above, that drug abuse has been treated as a political crime. It is part of the reality structure of many policemen that "hippie-type" persons carry drugs. Since these persons were considered to be revolutionaries or anarchists, it was felt that they had no right to be afforded the safeguards of the American Constitution.

This encouraged policemen to harass and search any persons who looked as if they "should" be carrying drugs. Since, in most instances, these searches were illegal, policemen were forced to develop techniques and patterns of testimony which would enable them to successfully admit the evidence at a court hearing. These techniques will be discussed below.

Many of us have formed our impressions of the judicial process from old Perry Mason television programs. Our image is that of the wise, compassionate jurist, secure in his knowledge of the law, dutifully listening to every argument of counsel and every statement of witnesses, and skillfully balancing and evaluating the evidence to achieve a just verdict.

We enter with the belief that liars will be punished for perjury, that policemen will tell the truth, that prosecutors will perform their dual duty to convict the guilty and exonerate the innocent. And lastly, tragically, we enter with the belief that all who come before the bar of justice will be treated with dignity, as equals, that the word of a black man balances that of a white, that the word of a citizen is as good as that of a policeman, and that justice does not depend on the color of your skin, or the size of your wallet, or your age, or hair style, or mode of dress. It takes but a few moments to disabuse the average citizen of all these misconceptions.

The first thing he will notice is that when the testifying police officer fails to appear, the case will often be continued (postponed) until a later date. If the defendant fails to appear, however, a bench warrant is issued for his arrest. This is the first clue that, as Orwell said, some are more equal than others.

The next clue is much more subtle, and much more critical. The observer, if he is especially perceptive, will notice a strange and quite horrifying fact. *In the large majority of cases in which a police officer testifies, he has absolutely no recollection whatsoever of either the identity of the defendant or the facts surrounding the case.* Some enterprising defense attorneys have attempted to take advantage of this by refusing to allow their clients to stand up in open court until identified by the police officer. Often this tactic meets with vehement reactions from judges, who often fail to see the significance behind the maneuver. They are more concerned with the defense attorney's failure to play the game than they are with the fact that the only witness against a person cannot identify him.

This brings us into the critical area of police testimony. In cases where the policeman cannot remember the essential facts of a case, he has but two alternatives (other than admitting his lack of knowledge, which would be a violation of the rules): first, he can consult his little notebook in order to refresh his memory, or second, he can offer perjured testimony.

The problem with the first alternative is that his book facts are often insufficient. This forces him to "flesh out" his case with certain stock phrases and facts which, he has learned, appear over and over again in actual situations. This is done so often that in some kinds of cases such as public drunkenness, it actually is unnecessary to have either the policeman or the prosecutor show up in court . . . tape recordings of their voices would suffice. Police officers are studiously taught to testify in a pattern delivery which will insure the greatest number of convictions. Truth is irrelevant and, in some types of cases, embarrassing to the policeman.

This is particularly true in drug-related cases. The typical police view on drug arrests is this: Many people of a particular type habitually engage in illegal drug usage. These are the same people who riot on campuses, flaunt immoral behavior and vile language, refuse to perform their patriotic duty when called upon, and disrupt society. They are criminals whose removal from the streets will be a benefit to society. Consequently, anything done to remove them is morally justifiable.

Unfortunately for the policeman, courts have often refused to abide by this rationale. Most judges refuse to railroad a defendant in open court on the basis of flagrantly illegal searches and arrests. So the police officer soon learns to say exactly what is necessary to obtain a conviction, even if this constitutes a gross misrepresentation of fact. Many judges and prosecutors are quite aware of this perjured testimony, but trials are conducted as if none of this is going on. It is rare that an attorney or defendant can break through this conspiracy of silence, since this too is considered a violation of the rules. Only the defendant, helpless in his rage and frustration, is unaware that everyone involved in the trial knows that the policeman is lying.

The most common reason for perjured police testimony, other than the paucity of their remembrances, is the deliberate attempt to cover up their own illegal activity on the street. Probably 90 percent of the contraband seized in small quantities by the police is found in places where police ordinarily would not be allowed to search. To validate these illegal searches, the police resort to one of two techniques.

The first technique is known as "dropsy." Dropsy is claimed by the police in situations where they have searched a suspect without probable cause or consent and found contraband. To insure the admission of the illegally seized evidence, the police will "improvise" a story similar to the following: As I drove past ——— School, I noticed two or three suspicious-looking suspects standing in the schoolyard, who glanced apprehensively at me as I passed. I drove on down the street, parked my vehicle, and walked toward them. As I approached, one of the suspects reached into his pocket and dropped a clear plastic bag at his feet. I bent down to pick it up and noticed that it contained a substance which resembled marijuana.

This is really extraordinary clumsiness, since both the officer and the suspect know that the officer has no right to make a search under circumstances like these. The only two rational explanations for this behavior are either that the majority of drug users suffers from an allergy which causes them to drop things in the presence of policemen, or that policemen lie.

The second technique employed by enterprising policemen is based on a legal doctrine, established by a line of Supreme Court decisions, which states that a police officer is not required to ignore contraband which is in plain view merely because he did not have the authority to search for that contraband. This is a most logical and necessary guide for police conduct.

Unfortunately, the doctrine is ofttimes abused. In all too many cases, police will conduct an illegal search of a premises or automobile, and then justify their actions under the plain-view doctrine. This results in illegal arrests, and the abridgment of the rights of many innocent persons whose possessions are ransacked without constitutional safeguards being afforded or common decency respected.

There are, of course, other techniques used by the police which should offend public sensibilities. Police all too frequently engage in personal invective, grudge arrests, physical abuse, and other activities which may ultimately affect the outcome of a case. But these are rarely evidenced at trial. What is evidenced is a callous disregard for the truth that cheapens the entire judicial process.

For the most part, the men we have discussed in the chapter are not evil. They have families, friends, loved ones. They participate in the whole range of activities outside of their employment which establishes their places as normal American citizens . . . not as storm troopers or monsters. Why then, when they assume their role as legislators, or police, or judges, do they comport themselves so poorly? What is there in American social development that bleeds compassion and understanding out of our political system? How long can we follow this path of self-righteousness before we destroy what so many have strived to create?

These are questions which must be, shall be, answered by the future. For the present, however, one thing is certain. This whole process culminates in the punishment of our society for its inability to deal with its own problems. For it is, in the long run, our society which has suffered. We have alienated and criminalized a whole generation of the best of our young people. We have bent the mandates of our Constitution and laws, corrupted our political and legal systems, squandered our efforts and wasted our money. We have become, all of us, less free.

Chapter 9

DRUGS, DRUG-TAKING AND DRUG-SEEKING: NOTATIONS ON THE DYNAMICS OF MYTH, CHANGE, AND REALITY

JAMES A. INCIARDI

The persistent spirit of mythic fervor is perhaps the most potent factor in the conversion and motivation of people to action. And this phenomenal curiosity endures despite any rational analyses and invalidations offered by members of the scientific community. Myth implies collective fantasy, drawing its fabulous plots from a sanctuary of notions based more on traditions and convenience than on fact. Myth is a body of lore regarded as "roughly true" on some plane of universalized experience; it serves as an instrument, a functioning device and controlling image that tenders philosophical meaning to the data of subjective realities; it guides conduct by orienting, sustaining, weakening, or suppressing sets of given action patterns. And myth has no limitations in the spectrum of time or place; nor is it restricted to the ancient or modern kaleidoscope of themes descriptive of supernatural and preternatural events, actors and capacities, or to the psychic world. The cosmopolitan nature of myth can extend to the unpretentious, offering significance and meaning to discrete levels of individual or social endeavor.

* * * *

The chronicle of *technological man,* from its earliest pages, reflects a notable dependence on myth in the perception and understanding of any use of drugs for enhancing either pleasure or performance. And this cognitive phenomenon has endured in spite of more explicit agents of coherence made manifest by the balanced lenses of science and logic. For indeed, the treasuries of evidence descriptive of drugs, drug users, and drug-taking available throughout recent decades in the fields of pharmacology, toxicology, medicine, sociology, and psychology are typically ignored in favor of the prevailing mythical systems. It is generally believed, for example:

- that all drug users are degenerate and dependent individuals, despite current data which suggest that perhaps fewer than 10 percent of these users become dysfunctional as a result of their drug-taking;

- that heroin addiction represents the primary drug problem in the United States, despite the recent findings which highlight more widespread levels of involvement with the legally manufactured and distributed drugs;

- that drug addicts are primarily products of the urban ghettos, despite the efforts of contemporary empirical research which have isolated and described numerous and alternative populations of addicts and other users at a multitude of positions in the social complex;

- that all drug-dependent persons are essentially similar, when realistically there are probably as many types of addicts and users as there are kinds of drugs;

- that the drug addict is most commonly a "heroin only" user, when, by contrast, the contemporary addict is a "poly-drug" user with significant numbers having concurrent addictions;

- that all "dope fiends" are criminally involved, in spite of baseline data which indicate that significant proportions of contemporary drug users are economically independent and not necessarily prone toward predatory acts;

- that addict criminality is impersonal and focused on non-violent property crime, when, by contrast, current addict criminality typically circumscribes a wide variety of both property *and* personal offenses.

Similarly, contemporary *drug mythology* has tended to support the favored, although misguided, notions that:

- there is an "addiction-prone personality";
- the use of marijuana leads to heroin addiction;
- severe punishment of drug users will prevent others from using drugs;
- "scare tactics" in educational programs will prevent drug use;
- life sentences for drug pushers will curtail drug selling;
- more effective law-enforcement techniques will serve to curtail the parameters of the drug problem;
- implementation of the "British system" will eliminate street crime by addicts;
- methadone effects a total "blockade" of the effect of heroin;
- drug users are responsible for as much as 80 percent of all urban property crime;
- drug-taking is a phenomenon limited to the adolescent and young adult cohorts and is directly related to the radical character of the "new" generation.

These discursive listings reflect but a sampling of the mythical images that intersect the continuity of contemporary drug awareness. Yet even these few ideational curiosities have functionally galvanized the perceptions and responses of many populations. And the actional dispositions which flow from such contorted belief systems tend to engender inappropriate alternatives and mechanisms for the study, understanding, treatment, and rational control of drug use and drug-related behaviors. Within this context, this essay reflects upon some common mythical notions which circumscribe contemporary drug awareness, and contrasts these with the more enlightened orientations suggested by the graphic diction of rigorous empirical inquiry. More specifically, the characteristic structure of the "drug problem"—the drugs, the users, and the related antisocial and criminal behaviors—is examined within the framework of myth and changing societal conditions and realities.[1]

THE GENESIS OF THE DRUG MYTHS

Myth descends from a process, a progression—a series of actions, statuses, responses, changes, and functions. It passes directly and characteristically from the coexistence of both literary and folk traditions as they are grounded in associative ways of thinking. The art form of myth is drama, with plot, arrangement of characters, and dialogue; the attendant performance displays a collection of personages, themes, and events, and their interpretation invariably becomes a deceptive reflection of phenomenal reality. And there is reason for this! Misinterpretations of the drama naturally flow from the relative and variable limitations of human understanding; they flow from capricious direction, from the malevolent and baleful design of some self-seeking benefactor; or they flow from the contaminating influences of undisciplined inquiry and unsystematic analysis. The resultant conceptions of the unfolding drama tend to emerge, often necessarily, beset with deviations of fact or approximations to fact. And this spirit of mythmaking—apparent, for example, in the religious alchemy of the generations of Christian writers or the ahistorical sensationalism of the nineteenth-century American "dime novelists"—involves the complex interaction of generalized social processes with events and circumstances indeed peculiar to a given set of phenomena.

Drug myths descended from a polygamous order of reciprocal actions directed by the political, social, economic, legislative, intellectual, scientific, religious, and moral postures of alternative segments of an acquisitive and competitive society. They emerged, in part:

- from the more rural creeds of nineteenth-century Methodism, Baptism, Presbyterianism, and Congregationalism which emphasized individual human toil and self-sufficiency while designating the use of intoxicating substances as an unwholesome surrender to the evils of an urban morality;

- from the medical literature of the late 1800s which arbitrarily designated the use of morphine and opium as a vice, a habit, an appetite, and a disease;

- from the early association of opium smoking with the Chinese—a cultural and racial group which had been legally defined as alien until 1943 and even today is perceived of as odd and mysterious;

- from the direct effects of American narcotics legislation which served to define all addicts as criminal offenders;

- from nineteenth- and twentieth-century police literature which stressed the involvement of professional and habitual criminals with the use of drugs;

- from the initiative of moral entrepreneurs and moral crusaders who defined drug use as evil, and hence influenced and directed the perceptions of both local and national opinion makers and rule creators;

- from the publicized findings of misguided research efforts, those contaminated by the use of limited and biased samples, impressionistic data, methodological imbalances, and inexperienced practitioners;

- from the sacred repository of intellectual and cultural lag—the gap which persists between the generation and publication of new data and the ultimate dismissal of earlier proclamations;

- from the suppression of controversial or disquieting knowledge by the cohorts of private, public, and corporate bodies whose internal interest structures are more effectively supported by alternative and distorted conceptions of reality.

And too, the construction of drug mythology descends from the intrusions of mass media—from the auditory arrests of psychosocial motion and the static abstractions from live processes—which are given credence through the electromagic of cinematography, video, and radiotelegraphy. Here, sentimentalized melodramas—*The Man with the Golden Arm, Monkey on My Back, Valley of the Dolls, Superfly*—offer uninitiated or complacent audiences with misshapen portraits of the worlds of drug use. In an almost masturbatory ethos, the creativity of production supports the existing collective *images* and *interests* by a filtering and purging of truths which tend to contrive a negative sculpture of the moral fabric of the spectatorship at large. All drug use emerges and endures in some monolithic construct of *hard-core addiction,* and the active participants in the phenomenon are generally limited to personages far removed from the ideal typical citizen of "conventional America." Yet drug use circumscribes many constructs and personages, and numerous levels in the socio-cultural system of hierarchies.

ALTERNATIVE WORLDS OF DRUG-TAKING

A focused analysis of the history of drug-taking in the United States reflects a complex of phenomena characterized by the emergence, growth, and alteration or decline of numerous and distinct *patterns* of use and addiction. Each pattern represents differential involvement on the part of various social groupings and population segments. Patterns of both narcotic and non-narcotic drug use co-exist within larger non-using populations, with significant variations in spacial and temporal perspectives, and in concomitant individual and social problems. Patterns descriptive of the alternative processes in drug use and addiction represent a confluence of activities, including approaches for the initiation and maintenance of the drug-using career and variations in the nature and extent of drug-taking, drug-seeking, and criminal behaviors.

Unique patterns of drug use can be readily described. The literature focusing on the social organization, occupational structure, and way of life of the *professional thief,* for example, suggests a pattern of narcotic drug use that was characteristically peculiar to safe burglars, sneak thieves, confidence swindlers, shoplifters, and pickpockets. Drug-taking typically involved the use of heroin or morphine by needle, or the smoking of opium. Spree use of the drugs was common for the purpose of reducing the boredom of incarcerations, or as part of occasional, yet intensive and short, periods of pleasure-seeking behavior. Addiction to narcotics was not generally widespread among professional thieves, with the exception of pickpockets. These offenders used narcotic drugs as a response to the tensions incident to their mode of larceny, or for a "loss of nerve" or a failing of manual dexterity.[2] Ball (1965) described an alternative pattern of narcotic drug use that was exhibited by the middle-aged white Southerner of the 1930s. His addiction typically focused on morphine or paragoric, and the drugs were obtained from physicians through legal or quasi-legal means. His initiation into drug-taking occurred in a medical context, during the treatment for some real or imagined illness. This addict was rarely a member of any deviant subculture and had little contact with other users and addicts. Other patterns of narcotic drug use involving more specialized "groups" have also been described by Winick (1960, 1961), Sutter (1966), and Finestone (1957a). *Yet in counterpoint, contemporary mythical fervor has fostered only a monotheistic conception of drug use—heroin/street addiction.*

The *heroin/street addiction* pattern of drug involvement represents a stereotyped reductionist construct composed of elements drawn from the data of empirical inquiry, as well as from the pantechnicon of myth, journalistic sensationalism, armchair scientism, academic postulation, and clinical conjecture.[3] The "pattern" reflects upon the socially and economically deprived levels of the urban population. The participating exhibitors typically began their experimentation with drugs as adolescents for the sake of excitement or thrills, to conform with peer group activities and expectations, or to strike back at the authority structures which they formidably opposed. Marijuana was generally the first illicit drug, and subsequent drug use focused primarily on heroin. The status of "addiction" emerged as a result of a physiological dependence on the drug combined with the user's *addiction-prone personality*—a personality type described as involving strong dependency needs and pronounced feelings of inadequacy. As the careers of the street addicts endured, the "heroin-only" character of their drug intake remained constant. (The concurrent use of sedatives, however, did appear among members of this population and significant numbers of black addicts used cocaine in conjunction with heroin.) The drugs were usually purchased with funds obtained illegally. Offense behaviors were *non-violent* and *impersonal,* including drug sales, confidence games, burglary, and a range of alternative property crimes of a direct acquisitive nature. (Female addicts, if criminally involved, were either drug sellers or prostitutes.) Finally, the life cycle of the heroin/street addict brought him into some rehabilitative setting during his mid-twenties, followed by a repeating pattern of "cure" and relapse. He ultimately ended his career in addiction through long-term incarceration, through death from drug overdose, or through a mysterious "maturing-out" process during his mid-thirties.

This pattern of heroin/street addiction, although generalized from a combination of that which was real, hypothetical, conjectured, and manufactured, has nevertheless served as a descriptive reflection of *one* world of drug use on the urban street scene. Yet the highly visible character of the actional complex it engagingly made manifest created a tendency on the part of professional and lay observers to envision most forms of drug use within the same singular frame of reference. As such, it emerged as a conceptual port of call for any attempt to explain drug-taking behaviors, as well as for the myriad of legal, social, medical, and therapeutic efforts to manage the full spectrum of drug-using and drug-seeking activities. And while this stereotyped obstructionist conceptualization of drug use *continues* to endure, resting in a hardened edifice of accepted doctrine, its utility for comprehending even the highly visible street addict has all but disappeared! The heroin/street addiction pattern has been undergoing rapid transformation since the mid-1960s. The transient product of this evolutionary process of change and modification is a *poly-drug pattern of addiction,* representing a new and significantly alternative complex of drug-taking and drug-seeking phenomena.

THE STRUCTURE OF POLY-DRUG USE

Poly-drug use, in a more collective sense, refers to the simultaneous usage of numerous varieties of both legal and illicit drugs, including narcotic analgesics, sedative-hypnotics, tranquilizers, antihistamines, antidepressants, amphetamines and other stimulants, psychotogens, and organic solvents and inhalants. And this character of drug-taking emerged in its dynamic proportions following the abrupt changes in the technology of drugs which began some two decades ago.

- Since 1950, technological innovations introduced and enthusiastically promoted a new array of *non-barbiturate sedatives* into medical practice. They have been alternatively categorized as "tranquilizers," "sedatives," "relaxants," or "psychotropic agents," and indeed served as primary initiators of the mid-century drug revolution. The most popular preparations have included:

meprobamate	(Miltown®–Wallace)
	(Equanil®–Wyeth)
	(Meprospan®–Wallace)
	(Meprotabs®–Wallace)
glutethimide	(Doriden®–Ciba)
ethinamate	(Valmid®–Lilly)
ethchlorvynol	(Placidyl®–Abbott)
methyprylon	(Noludar®–Roche)
chlordiazepoxide	(Librium®–Roche)
methaqualone	(Quaalude®–Rorer)
	(Sopor®–Arner-Stone)
	(Somnafac®–Smith, Miller & Patch).

● There are the *phenothiazines,* first synthesized during the 1880s yet dramatically expanded during the 1950s and '60s for the treatment of psychomotor excitement and manic states:

chlorpromazine	(Thorazine®–Smith, Kline & French)
prochlorperazine	(Compazine®–Smith, Kline & French)
trifluoperzine	(Stelazine®–Smith, Kline & French)
thioridazine	(Mellaril®–Sandoz).

● There are the newer amphetamine drugs which have significantly expanded the scope of stimulant preparations:

amphetamine	
w/methamphetamine	(Obetrol®–Obetrol)
	(Amphaplex®–Palmedico)
amphetamine	
w/sedative	(Bamadex®–Lederle)
	(Biphetamine-T®–Strasenburgh)
	(Appetrol®–Wallace)
	(Quadamine®–Tutag)
	(Eskatrol®–Smith, Kline & French)
levo-amphetamine	
succinate	(Pedestrol®–Len-Tag)
	(Amodril®–North American)
	(Cydril®–Tutag)
methamphetamine	
w/sedative	(Adipex®–Lemmon)
	(Fetamin®–Mission)
	(Desbutal®–Abbott).

- There are *non-amphetamine stimulants* which engender effects similar to the amphetamines:

phenmetrazine	(Preludin®—Geigy)
methylphenidate	(Ritalin®—Ciba)
diethylpropion	(Tenuate®—Merrell).

- There are *analgesic preparations* which have been the subjects of both national and international promotional campaigns:

propoxyphene	(Darvon®—Lilly)
pentazocine	(Talwin®—Winthrop).

- There has been the synthesis of numerous hallucenogenic drugs which can be readily produced in the illicit laboratory setting:

LSD	(d-lysergic acid diethylamide)
DMT	(N, N-dimethyltryptamine)
DET	(N, N-diethyltryptamine)
PCP	(phencyclidine hydrochloride)
DOM	(4-methyl-2, 5-dimethoxy-α-methylphenethylamine)
MDA	(3, 4-methylenedioxyamphetamine)
TMA	(3, 4, 5-trimethoxyphenyl-β-aminopropane).

The widespread use of both legal and illicit substances fostered by the changes in the technology of drugs can be readily illustrated. Data descriptive of the incidence and prevalence of drug use within the general population of New York state, for example, indicate that of 13,800,000 persons ages 14 years and above:

- 982,000 (7.1%) are users of barbiturates;
- 531,000 (3.8%) are users of non-barbiturate sedatives;
- 1,411,000 (10.2%) are users of relaxants/minor tranquilizers;
- 161,000 (1.2%) are users of major tranquilizers;
- 167,000 (1.2%) are users of antidepressants;
- 543,000 (3.9%) are users of diet pills;
- 375,000 (2.7%) are users of pep pills;
- 470,000 (3.4%) are users of other prescription stimulants;
- 1,364,000 (9.9%) are users of non-controlled narcotics/non-narcotic analgesics;
- 175,000 (1.3%) are users of legal opiates;

- 1,032,000 (7.5%) are users of marijuana/hashish;

- 203,000 (1.5%) are users of LSD;

- 152,000 (1.1%) are users of other psychotogens;

- 111,000 (0.8%) are users of methedrine;

- 64,000 (0.5%) are users of heroin;

- 101,000 (0.7%) are users of cocaine; and

- 35,000 (0.3%) are users of solvents/inhalants. [4]

Within this same statewide population, the *general* character of poly-drug use can be observed. For example: of the 1,411,000 users of relaxants/minor tranquilizers, 37 percent (N=525,000) use such drugs on a regular basis (six or more times per month). Of these 525,000 regular users of relaxants/minor tranquilizers, a significant proportion also use numerous other categories of both legal and illicit drugs on a regular basis (see Table 1). Similarly, among the 1,032,000 users of marijuana/hashish, 47 percent (N=487,000) engage in such drug-taking on a regular basis; these regular users, furthermore, also use numerous additional varieties of drugs on a regular basis (see Table 2). And this

Table 1.   INCIDENCE OF THE REGULAR USE OF OTHER DRUGS AMONG 525,000
REGULAR USERS OF RELAXANTS/MINOR TRANQUILIZERS

Total regular users	*525,000*	*100%*
I. *Legal drugs*		
Barbiturates	90,000	17.1
Non-barbiturates sedative-hypnotics	61,000	11.6
Pep pills	30,000	5.7
Antidepressants	28,000	5.3
Non-controlled narcotics & prescription non-narcotic analgesics	28,000	5.3
Major tranquilizers	24,000	4.6
Diet pills	19,000	3.6
Other stimulants	8,000	1.5
II. *Illegal drugs*		
Marijuana or hashish	42,000	8.0
LSD	6,000	1.1
Solvents or inhalents	6,000	1.1
Methedrine	3,000	.6
Cocaine	1,000	.2

SOURCE: Chambers (1971: 44), Chambers and Inciardi (1971: 40).

Table 2.   INCIDENCE OF THE REGULAR USE OF OTHER DRUGS AMONG 487,000
REGULAR USERS OF MARIJUANA/HASHISH

Total regular users	487,000	100%
I. *Legal drugs*		
Pep pills	67,000	13.8
Barbiturates	61,000	12.5
Relaxants/minor tranquilizers	42,000	8.6
Diet pills	35,000	7.2
Non-barbiturate sedative-hypnotics	20,000	4.1
Non-controlled narcotics & prescription non-narcotic analgesics	20,000	4.1
Stimulants other than amphetamines & cocaine	19,000	3.9
Major tranquilizers	10,000	2.1
Antidepressants	10,000	2.1
Controlled narcotics (non-heroin)	4,000	.8
II. *Illegal drugs*		
LSD	45,000	9.2
Methedrine	32,000	6.6
Psychotogens other than LSD	19,000	3.9
Heroin	17,000	3.5
Cocaine	6,000	1.2
Solvents/inhalants	3,000	.6

SOURCE: Chambers (1971: 102), Chambers and Inciardi (1971: 88).

phenomenon of multiple drug use is seemingly characteristic of the regular users of other categories of drugs.

The specific patterns of poly-drug use can also be noted within numerous and alternative population sub-groups. A pilot analysis of remnant "Beats" from New York City's Greenwich Village, for example, isolated a drug-taking pattern which included high-frequency, long-duration marijuana and hashish use (Inciardi, 1972). At stages within the evolution of these drug careers, sporadic or sometimes even regular use of LSD was introduced. This was typically combined with intermittent experimentation with other hallucinogenic drugs as they became available on the Village illicit drug market. This primary pattern of use was frequently supplemented with the simultaneous use of a variety of other drugs, mostly amphetamines and inhalants. The addiction to narcotic drugs was less common. When evident, it was usually a part of an early stage of the user's drug career. While widespread experimentation with and concurrent use of other drugs tended to be persistent, the long-term career patterns could be typified as stabilized around a variety of psychotomimetic compounds.

Poly-drug use, when combined with the addiction to narcotic drugs, reflects a pattern of drug-taking and drug-seeking significantly different from the more traditional frame of *heroin/street addiction*. And further, the *poly-drug/street addiction* pattern presents an alternative spectrum of problems and considerations relative to the management and control of the pattern participants.

POLY-DRUG USE AND STREET ADDICTION

The poly-drug character of contemporary street addiction can be appropriately illustrated through a selection of brief analyses of the demographic attributes and the drug-taking and drug-seeking behavior patterns of patients admitted to alternative narcotic treatment facilities in various parts of the nation since the turn of the current decade.

Initially, extensive data were collected in this behalf relative to a defined universe of 200 urban street addicts. These subjects represented the total population of a residential treatment facility operated by the New York State Narcotic Addiction Control Commission, and case records as well as interview materials were gathered during the latter part of 1970. Briefly described, all of the patients were males, with the majority (78 percent) receiving compulsory treatment as "criminal commitment" cases in this state-operated civil commitment program. This patient population was relatively young, reflecting a median age at admission of 20 years; 49 percent (N=98) were black, 21 percent (N=42) were white/non-Spanish-speaking; 29 percent (N=58) were Puerto Rican, and 1 percent (N=2) were Chinese. Drug use was typically initiated with alcohol at a median age of 13 years. Drug involvement began at a median age of 14 years, and as indicated in Table 3, a host of different substances appeared in this onset situation. Marijuana, for example, represented the first illicit drug for two-thirds of the group, and a variety of legally manufactured and distributed substances defined the character of drug onset for all but six of the remaining cases.

Table 3.   DISTRIBUTION OF ONSET DRUGS AMONG 200 NEW YORK ADDICT-PATIENTS

Onset Drugs	Addict-Patients	
	No.	%
Total Cases	200	100%
Marijuana	137	68.5
Solvents/inhalants	52	26.0
Heroin	6	3.0
Codeine cough syrup	3	1.5
Other legal drugs	2	1.0

Table 4. DISTRIBUTION OF ONSET DRUGS BY CURRENT AGE AMONG 200 NEW
YORK ADDICT-PATIENTS

	Current Age					
	Under 21 yrs.		21-25 yrs.		Over 25 yrs.	
Onset Drugs	No.	%	No.	%	No.	%
Total Cases	99	100.0%	55	100.0%	46	100.0%
Marijuana	56	56.6	39	70.9	42	91.3
Solvents/inhalants	38	38.4	12	21.9	2	4.3
Heroin	3	3.0	2	3.6	1	2.2
Codeine cough syrup	1	1.0	2	3.6	1	2.2
Other legal drugs	1	1.0	–	–	–	–

It might be noted here that the appearance of marijuana as an onset drug
(other than alcohol) in as many as 68.5 percent of the case histories does not
necessarily represent a reflection of the older onset pattern typically characteristic of the stereotyped "heroin-only" addict. By contrast, a tangible
relationship between age and *type of onset drug* is clearly suggested in Table 4.
While 91.3 percent of the older addicts began with marijuana, only 70.9 percent
of the middle cohort and 56.6 percent of the youngest cohort were initiated
with this drug. And this was inversely proportioned to an age-related increase in
the use of organic solvents and inhalants in the onset situation.

The prevalence of poly-drug-taking within this population of civilly and
criminally committed addicts is readily emphasized in Table 5. Of the 200
patients, all had been users of a median of three types of narcotic analgesics. In
addition, 99 percent had long histories of marijuana use, three-fourths had
regularly used numerous varieties of sedatives and stimulants, and the incidence
and prevalence of other drug use were also significant. And finally, a median of

Table 5. POLY-DRUG USE AMONG 200 NEW YORK ADDICT-PATIENTS

Drug Categories	Total Users		Median Types Used Within Category
	No.	%	
Total Cases	200	100%	–
Narcotic analgesics	200	100	3
Sedatives	157	79	3
Tranquilizers	22	11	2
Stimulants	145	73	2
Marijuana	197	99	1
Psychotogens	55	28	2
Solvents/inhalants	93	47	2
Speedballs	136	68	2

12 different drugs with a range of 2-44 further reflected the polygamous character of their drug-taking.

A somewhat comparable set of West Coast data can also serve in highlighting the emergence of a poly-drug pattern of street addiction. Of 773 heroin addicts who were seeking outpatient detoxification in San Francisco from November 1969 through September 1970, the majority were poly-drug users (see Sheppard and associates, 1972). Initially, 25 percent (N=191) of the 773 cases were defined as "old style junkies," and were typical of the street addicts of years past. They were generally ghetto-bred, long-term heavy users of heroin, and their involvement with any additional varieties of drugs was appreciably low. *All of these vintage street addicts, furthermore, had become fully meshed into their own peculiar drug-taking subculture prior to January 1964.*

A second cohort, accounting for 19 percent (N-149) of the population, were defined as "transition junkies." This group had been initiated into the regular use of heroin during the period January 1964-January 1967. They had little in common with the earlier "street junkies," yet, by contrast, they represented the beginning phase of the poly-drug pattern. The final segment, designated as "new junkies" and involving 56 percent (N=433) of the total patient population, had not become legitimate and formalized members of the community of street addicts until a time after January 1967. They were typically poly-drug users, manifesting extensive experiences with heroin, marijuana, LSD, amphetamines, sedatives, and alcohol, and their careers in illicit drug-taking began at significantly early stages in their lives. Furthermore, with a mean age of 23.5 years, they were predominantly from white middle class backgrounds, and a total of 33 percent (N=143) were females.

Comparative poly-drug-taking phenomena can also be drawn from a block of data descriptive of addict cohorts in a southeasterly sector of urban America. Specifically, case file and/or personal interview materials were compiled during the latter part of 1972 regarding 88 street addicts sampled from five treatment populations within the Metropolitan Dade County (Florida) Comprehensive Drug Program.[5] Of this group of patients 49 percent (N=43) were black, 49 percent were white, and the final 2 percent were Indian; and the median age of the composite sample was 18 years. Their careers in drug-taking began at a median age of 13 years. Marijuana represented the onset drug for 48 percent (N=42) of the group, solvents and inhalants for 17 percent (N=15), codeine cough syrup for 17 percent (N=15), sedatives for 6 percent (N=5), heroin for 6 percent (N=5), and the other drugs or alcohol for the remainder. The use of multiple varieties of drugs is dramatically indicated in Table 6. Poly-drug use was not only widespread, but in addition it was the typical pattern for all but three patients.

These data, drawn from treatment populations located in three opposing parts of the nation, illustrate the changing character of the street addict. For in contrast with previous observations and conceptions, contemporary street addicts are poly-drug users, they become involved with drugs during or prior to puberty, they seek treatment at a younger age, and they reflect increased involvement on the part of females and members of non-ghetto populations. And of equal importance is the observation that these addicts are not only *poly-drug users,* but they are also *poly-criminals.*

The phenomenon of poly-criminality can be illustrated through an overview of the self-reported criminal activities of a sub-sample of 38 addict-offenders drawn from the New York civil/criminal commitment population described previously.[6] This investigation indicated not only that the addicts were extensively involved in criminal activities, but furthermore, they were rarely apprehended for the offenses committed. Of 6,766 alleged offenses committed during a median period of four years, less than one percent were cleared by arrest, with a ratio of one arrest for every 120 crimes perpetrated.

Analysis of the relevant data in tabular (see Chapter 5, Table 7) and other interview materials suggest a *situational* nature in the poly-drug users' criminal involvement. Less stress was placed upon burglary by these users in contrast with addicts previously studied.[7] The wide range of offense categories and the lack of specialization on the part of the subjects would suggest that the selection of an offense type was based on circumstances. The subjects repeatedly indicated that such choices were dictated by chance and situational content. Furthermore, while *personal* crime represented only 7 percent of the total, as much as 60 percent of the addicts engaged in such activities.

The descriptions offered here which reflect upon the poly-drug use pattern of drug-taking and drug-seeking must not be viewed in a thoroughly dogmatic

Table 6. POLY-DRUG USE AMONG SAMPLED ADDICT-PATIENTS, METROPOLITAN DADE COUNTY, FLORIDA COMPREHENSIVE DRUG PROGRAM

| | Total Users | | Median Types Used |
Drug Categories	No.	%	Within Category
Total Cases	88	100%	—
Narcotic analgesics	88	100	7
Sedatives	83	94	7
Tranquilizers	48	55	3
Stimulants	84	95	8
Marijuana	86	98	1
Psychotogens	61	69	4
Solvents/inhalants	59	67	2

context. Additional research efforts must be directed toward a more comprehensive assessment of the structure and process of this phenomenon. Nevertheless, these preliminary insights tend to firmly establish that drug use can no longer be viewed within the single frame of reference of *heroin/street addiction.* This re-emphasizes, furthermore, that many of the contemporary theoretical perspectives and pragmatic approaches for the treatment and control of drug-dependent persons indeed fall within a reductionist stereotypical model, and are, at best, inappropriate.

* * * *

In retrospect, the history of drug-taking and drug-seeking behaviors in the United States reflects more than a century of modifications in the more portent aspects of these phenomena—the drugs, the characteristic populations of users, and the representative patterns of use. Yet concomitantly, history can also testify to a static dependence on *myth* by members of the wider society in their typical perceptions of, and responses to, drug phenomena. And there is reason to believe that this tendency will persist as society grows more mature. Currently, the drug myths continue to support the drama of the heroin/street addict and contribute to the diminution of the poly-drug complex through diversions of clinical attention. Immediate reversals in this respect mandate concerted efforts on the part of researchers, clinicians, and educators in the rapid acquisition and dissemination of comprehensive data descriptive of the structure and management of all drug-using behaviors.

NOTES

1. A number of the more popular and enduring myths descriptive of heroin addicts traditionally focus on the alleged "maddening" effects of the drugs and the "degenerate" character of the users. These "dope fiend myths" have been discussed at length in Lindesmith (1940), Michelson (1940), and Eldridge (1962), and will only be briefly referenced here.

2. For a complete description of the criminal career of the professional thief and the nature and scope of his pattern of drug involvement, see Inciardi (1974).

3. The configuration of real and imagined characteristics descriptive of heroin/street addiction and its participants appear in Ray (1961), Chein and associates (1964), Winick (1962), Lindesmith (1961, 1965), Finestone (1957b), Ball (1965), Ball and Chambers (1970), Schur (1962), Maurer and Vogel (1967), Wakefield (1963), Hulburd (1952), Kolb (1962), Anslinger and Tompkins (1953), Meyer (1952).

4. These data, fully reported in Chambers (1971a/b) and Chambers and Inciardi (1971), are based on a general population survey involving some 7,500 personal interviews administered during August 1970.

5. The five selected treatment settings included an outpatient detoxification unit, a methadone clinic, and a jailhouse therapeutic community operated by the Comprehensive Drug Program, as well as a residential therapeutic community and a crisis intervention center affiliated with this same Comprehensive Drug Program. The 88 cases were selected on a non-random basis due to such limitations as the incompleteness of files, and varying patient availability, cooperation, and reliability.

6. These data have been described at length elsewhere. See Inciardi and Chambers (1972).

7. There are virtually dozens of studies which highlight the notion that addict criminality is focused in the areas of drug law violations and acquisitive property crimes. See, for example, Kavaler (1968) and Meyer (1952: 82-91).

REFERENCES

ANSLINGER, H. J. and W. F. TOMPKINS (1953) The Traffic in Narcotics. New York: Funk & Wagnalls.

BALL, J. C. (1965) "Two patterns of narcotic addiction in the United States." Journal of Criminal Law, Criminology and Police Science 56 (June): 203-211.

BALL, J. C. and C. D. CHAMBERS [eds.] (1970) The Epidemiology of Opiate Addiction in the United States. Springfield: Charles C Thomas.

CHAMBERS, C. D. (1971a) An Assessment of Drug Use in the General Population: Special Report No. 1, Drug Use in New York State. Miami: Division of Addiction Sciences, University of Miami School of Medicine.

——— (1971b) Differential Drug Use Within the New York State Labor Force. Miami: Division of Addiction Sciences, University of Miami School of Medicine.

CHAMBERS, C. D. and J. A. INCIARDI (1971) An Assessment of Drug Use in the General Population: Special Report No. 2, Drug Use in New York State, Drug Use in New York City, Drug Use in Selected Geographical Regions of New York State. Albany: New York State Narcotic Addiction Control Commission.

CHEIN, I., D. L. GERARD, R. S. LEE and E. ROSENFELD (1964) The Road to H. New York: Basic Books.

ELDRIDGE, W. B. (1962) Narcotics and the Law. Chicago: American Bar Foundation.

FINESTONE, H. (1957a) "Cats, kicks, and color." Social Problems 5 (July): 3-13.

——— (1957b) "Narcotics and criminality." Law and Contemporary Problems 22 (Winter): 60-85.

HULBURD, D. (1952) H is for Heroin. Garden City: Doubleday.

INCIARDI, J. A. (1974) Careers in Crime. Chicago: Rand-McNally.

——— (1972) "Patterns of drug use among Village 'Beats'." International Journal of the Addictions 7 (December): 649-653.

INCIARDI, J. A. and C. D. CHAMBERS (1972) "Unreported criminal involvement of narcotic addicts." Journal of Drug Issues 2 (Spring): 57-64.

KAVALER, F. (1968) "A commentary and annotated bibliography on the relationship between narcotics addiction and criminality." Municipal Reference Library, Notes XLII (April): 45-63.

KOLB, L. (1962) Drug Addiction: A Medical Problem. Springfield: Charles C Thomas.

LINDESMITH, A. R. (1965) The Addict and the Law. Bloomington: Indiana Univ. Press.

——— [ed.] (1961) Drug Addiction: Crime or Disease? Bloomington: Indiana Univ. Press.

——— (1940) " 'Dope Fiend' Mythology." Journal of Criminal Law and Criminology 31 (July-August): 199-208.

MAURER, D. W. and V. H. VOGEL (1967) Narcotics and Narcotic Addiction. Springfield: Charles C Thomas.

MEYER, A. S. (1952) Social and Psychological Factors in Opiate Addiction. New York: Columbia University Bureau of Applied Social Research.

MICHELSON, T. (1940) "Lindesmith's Mythology." Journal of Criminal Law and Criminology 31 (Nov.-Dec.): 375-400.

RAY, M. B. (1961) "The cycle of abstinence and relapse among heroin addicts." Social Problems 9 (Fall): 132-140.

SCHUR, E. M. (1962) Narcotic Addiction in Britain and America. Bloomington: Indiana Univ. Press.

SHEPPARD, C. W., D. E. SMITH and G. R. GAY (1972) "The changing face of heroin addiction in the Haight-Ashbury." International Journal of the Addictions 7 (Spring): 109-122.

SUTTER, A. G. (1966) "The world of the righteous dope fiend." Issues in Criminology 2 (Fall): 177-222.

WAKEFIELD, D. [ed.] (1963) The Addict. Greenwich, Conn.: Fawcett.

WINICK, C. (1962) "Maturing out of narcotic addiction." Bulletin on Narcotics 14: 1-7.

——— (1961) "Physician narcotic addicts." Social Problems 9 (Fall): 174-186.

——— (1960) "The use of drugs by jazz musicians." Social Problems 7 (Winter): 240-253.

Chapter 10

FORECASTS FOR THE FUTURE:
WHERE WE ARE AND WHERE WE ARE GOING

CARL D. CHAMBERS and
JAMES A. INCIARDI

... No single law enforcement problem has occupied more time,
effort and money in the past four years than that of drug abuse and
drug addiction. We have regarded drugs as "public enemy number one,"
destroying the most precious resource we have—our young people—and
breeding lawlessness, violence and death.

> —*Richard Nixon*
> The White House
> March 14, 1973

Without question, the President was expressing both our national frustration surrounding this specific social problem as well as our national commitment to control if not solve the problem.

Our frustrations accurately reflect our apparent inabilities to prevent the young from becoming so involved with drugs that they become dysfunctional casualties *and* our inabilities to effectively treat and rehabilitate them once these services become necessary.

Our national commitments are best viewed within the contexts of how we allocate our monies and other resources. Spending for federal drug abuse prevention and law enforcement programs alone have increased from $150,000,000 to $719,000,000 since 1971, a fivefold increase in three years (Budget of the United States Government, 1974):

ESTIMATED FEDERAL EXPENDITURES FOR DRUG ABUSE
PREVENTION AND LAW ENFORCEMENT PROGRAMS

Fiscal	Millions of Dollars
1971	150.2
1972	413.2
1973	654.8
1974	719.0

The current federal effort was redesigned by executive order in 1971 and promulgated into law in 1972. This effort is best viewed as a coordinated two-foci approach to the problem—supply-restricting (enforcement) and demand-restricting (prevention).

The *supply-restricting* or Drug Law Enforcement Programs were designed to reduce the availability of illicit narcotics and dangerous drugs. Federal obligations for such programs have risen from $36,000,000 in 1969 to $257,000,000 in 1974. The primary foci for these programs are international law-enforcement cooperation and cooperative federal-state-local law-enforcement efforts to identify and arrest street-level pushers.

A recent Office of Management and Budget (1973) analysis of the Drug Law Enforcement Programs reported in the 1974 Budget of the United States included the following "accomplishments" of these programs:

- Substantial increases in funding and manpower for both the Bureau of Narcotics and Dangerous Drugs (BNDD) and the Bureau of Customs. These funds support concentrated attacks on smuggling and increased domestic and international investigation of major drug traffickers. In 1972 the Departments of Justice and Treasury removed from the U.S. market or seized overseas:

    5,613 pounds of heroin,
    887 pounds of cocaine,
    451,800 pounds of marijuana, and
    220 million dosage units of dangerous drugs.

- Initiation of a coordinated attack on drug trafficking in over 40 target cities by teams of narcotics agents from federal, state, and local law enforcement agencies. The Office of Drug Abuse Law Enforcement was responsible for 4,245 arrests since the spring of 1972.

- An intensified investigation of the income tax returns of middle- and upper-level narcotics traffickers aimed at reducing the amount of working capital available for illegal drug operations by assessing and collecting taxes and penalties on unreported income.

- Development of a national narcotics intelligence system to assure proper analysis and distribution of trafficking intelligence information.

- Activation in 1972 of the ban on cultivation of the opium poppy in Turkey and formulation of narcotics control action plans in 59 foreign countries to secure international cooperation in the global war on heroin.

- Preparation and release in 1972 of the World Opium Survey, presenting a comprehensive picture of the location and quantity of opium poppy cultivation.

- Establishment of special narcotics courts in New York City with federal assistance to assure rapid prosecution of narcotics offenders.

The *demand-restricting* or Drug Abuse Prevention Programs were designed to reduce the demand for illicit narcotics and dangerous drugs. Federal obligations for such programs have risen from $46,000,000 in 1969 to $528,000,000 in 1974. *Demand-restricting activities account for some 67 percent of the total federal funds for drug abuse programs in 1974.* The activities funded include treatment programs for addicts, prevention and education programs, research, and training.

The U.S. Office of Management and Budget (1973) analysis prepared for the 1974 federal budget included the following "accomplishments" of these programs:

- An expansion of federally funded treatment facilities, providing the capacity to treat over 100,000 addicts annually. Funds will be available to expand the capacity for addict treatment to over 250,000 addicts by mid-1974, if necessary. More federally funded treatment facilities were created in 1972 than in the previous fifty years.

- A nationwide review of all methadone maintenance programs. As a result of that review, new methadone regulations were issued on December 15, 1972, designed to assure high-quality treatment for addicts and to prevent illicit diversion of this synthetic narcotic substance.

- A worldwide treatment and rehabilitation program for military service-men, including a large-scale screening and early intervention program to identify and treat drug abusers before they become dependent. From June 17, 1971 to September 30, 1972, 250 drug treatment and rehabilitation facilities were activated. During this period, an average of 8,500 servicemen were receiving treatment.

- A newly developed Veterans Administration treatment system that offered care to more than 20,000 veterans in 1972.

The design for these supply-demand restricting programs includes a close linking of the two. The linkage is based upon the following assumptions:

Law enforcement efforts that reduce the supply of drugs also serve to lower drug potency and drive up the price of drugs, thus reducing experimental usage. Together, higher prices combined with lower potency and scarcity can motivate abusers to seek treatment (Office of Management and Budget, 1973).

The major federal effort to link the criminal justice system to the treatment service system has been the Treatment Alternatives to Street Crime program (TASC) which is operational in a number of major cities. The TASC program involves identifying the heroin-dependent person shortly after arrest and offering special opportunities to enter a variety of programs. The overall goals of TASC are to decrease the incidence of drug-related crimes with its attendant cost to the community, to interrupt the drug-driven cycle of street-crime-to-jail-to-street-crime, by providing the possibility of treatment for drug-addicted arrestees and to decrease the problems in detention facilities resulting from arrestees who are addicted and manifesting acute problems such as withdrawal.

Intervening in the ordinary process of the criminal justice system, by placing addicts in treatment, is a challenge because of its potential benefits and obvious logistical difficulties. It is an opportunity to help both the individual and the community because it focuses on individuals who under present conditions are released into the community immediately after an arrest, untreated, and with little hope that their behavior will change.

Given the primary focus of this book upon the relationship between drug taking, crime, and criminal processing, an elaboration of the major components of *supply-restricting law enforcement* activities are provided below (see Budget of the United States Government, 1974).

The *Office for Drug Abuse Law Enforcement* (DALE) in the Department of Justice conducts operations against street pushers with criminal investigators from BNDD and Customs and with special U.S. attorneys. These groups serve on task forces with state and local enforcement personnel in over 40 target cities. Special grand juries expedite consideration of cases. In its first eight months of operation, DALE arrested 4,245 alleged heroin pushers and convicted 470.

The *Office of National Narcotics Intelligence* (ONNI) in the Department of Justice was created to bring together all information regarding production, smugglers, trafficking, and sale of drugs. ONNI brings together intelligence information, coordinates and analyzes the information, and disseminates combined reports to federal and state and local enforcement agencies for their use.

The *Bureau of Narcotics and Dangerous Drugs* in the Justice Department increased its agents and compliance officers in the United States and overseas from 808 in 1969 to 1,652 in 1973. Its principal activities include the investigation of major drug traffickers; enforcement of federal antidrug laws; the conduct of research and specialized drug training programs for foreign law-enforcement agents; and the provision of technical assistance of federal, state, and local personnel. BNDD supported foreign governments in seizing 4,342 pounds of hard drugs and 115,000 pounds of marijuana from illicit foreign markets in 1972 compared to 3,173 pounds of hard drugs and 40,000 pounds of marijuana in 1971.

The *Law Enforcement Assistance Administration* (LEAA) in the Department of Justice provides financial support for state and local drug law-enforcement efforts.

The *Bureau of Customs* in the Department of the Treasury is responsible for the interdiction of illicit drugs at U.S. borders. Over the past four years, Customs has increased its personnel in order to expand its efforts to monitor traffic at points of entry, police borders, and conduct research into drug-detection techniques. The Bureau seized 1,077 pounds of hard narcotics and 218,500 pounds of marijuana in 1972.

The *Internal Revenue Service* (IRS), also within the Treasury Department, attacks mid-level and top-ranking traffickers through intensive investigations of incomes and tax returns. As estimated $10,100,000 has been spent on IRS activities in 1972. In 17 months, IRS has assessed $82,500,000 in taxes, collected $15,800,000 in currency and property, and obtained 44 indictments and 20 convictions.

The *Department of State* is responsible for mobilizing the efforts of foreign governments against the overseas production and distribution of narcotics and dangerous drugs, and for coordinating the narcotics programs of all federal agencies abroad. The *Agency for International Development* (AID) in the Department of State assists other countries in stopping the illicit production,

Table 1. DRUG ABUSE MONIES BUDGETED FOR 1974

A. Drug Law Enforcement Programs

Agency	Millions for Fiscal 1974
Justice:	
LEAA	$ 44.1
BNDD	74.1
Other	6.7
State:	1.5
AID	42.7
Treasury:	
IRS	19.7
Customs	66.2
Agriculture	1.8
Transportation	.1
Total	$256.9

B. Drug Abuse Prevention Programs

Agency	Millions for Fiscal 1974
Treatment and rehabilitation:	
Special Action Office	$ 40.0
Health, Education, and Welfare:	
National Institute of Mental Health	159.4
Social and Rehabilitation Service	.6
Veterans Administration	23.8
Defense	46.0
Justice:	
Bureau of Prisons	4.2
Law Enforcement Assistance Administration	—
Subtotal	$274.0
Education and information:	
Health, Education, and Welfare:	
National Institute of Mental Health	$ 9.3
Office of Education	—
Social and Rehabilitation Service	—
Defense	11.1
Justice:	
Law Enforcement Assistance Administration	—
Bureau of Narcotics and Dangerous Drugs	1.1
Subtotal	$ 21.5

Table 1 (Continued)

Training:	
Health, Education, and Welfare:	
National Institute of Mental Health	$ 15.4
Office of Education	3.0
Social and Rehabilitation Service	—
Veterans Administration	.4
Defense	3.4
Justice:	
Law Enforcement Assistance Administration	1.0
Subtotal	$ 23.2
Research:	
Special Action Office	$ 19.5
Health, Education, and Welfare:	
National Institute of Mental Health	34.6
Social and Rehabilitation Service	1.3
Veterans Administration	1.0
Defense	5.7
Justice:	
Law Enforcement Assistance Administration	.2
Bureau of Narcotics and Dangerous Drugs	1.5
Subtotal	$ 63.8
Evaluation:	
Special Action Office	$ 1.0
Health, Education, and Welfare:	
National Institute of Mental Health	4.4
Defense	2.0
Justice:	
Bureau of Prisons	.1
Law Enforcement Assistance Administration	.1
Subtotal	$ 7.6
Planning, direction, and support:	
Special Action Office	$ 6.7
Health, Education, and Welfare:	
National Institute of Mental Health	19.8
Office of Education	—
Social and Rehabilitation Service	.1
Veterans Administration	.3
Defense	1.9
Justice:	
Bureau of Prisons	.2
Subtotal	$ 29.0
Total	$419.1

processing, and traffic in narcotics. AID provides equipment, training in narcotics control techniques, and assistance for development of alternative crops or other income-producing activities.

The *Department of Agriculture* supports research projects to develop means of eradicating the opium poppy and develop suitable substitute crops.

The *Department of Transportation* enforces narcotics laws through the *Federal Aviation Administration* (FAA) and the *Coast Guard.* FAA supports federal, state, and local authorities in their efforts to combat use of commercial planes in smuggling, and the Coast Guard polices coastal waterways and ports.

Some 33 percent of the total monies available for 1974 in drug abuse are budgeted for these Drug Law Enforcement Programs. These monies, some $260,000,000 are budgeted for distribution as shown in Table 1, Part A.

The reader is directed to Chapter 4 for state and local references to "costs" associated with addressing this social problem.

As indicated earlier, *the remaining 67 percent of the total monies available for 1974 in drug abuse are budgeted for Drug Abuse Prevention Programs.* These monies, some $419,000,000, are budgeted for distribution as listed in Table 1, Part B.

This, then, represents an overview of our *current* effort at addressing the drug problem. What, in turn, are our forecasts for the future? We believe the following will be significant issues which will require careful planning and refocusing of our prevention and intervention efforts:

- At the present, a significant focus for reducing crime is to increase the number of addicts in treatment. Not everyone who is addicted *wants* to be treated, or once in treatment is motivated to remain. What happens when we reach saturation in this pool? We believe "outreach recruiting" and "criminal justice diversion" projects will become the primary means of bringing addicts into the treatment system.

- At the present, most "control" efforts addressing this social problem function as if drug use and drug-related crime were operating independently of the other major social problems in our urban settings. We believe the long-term reduction of addict crime will come about only after society addresses the correlate problems of poor housing, unemployment, etc.

- At the present time, most of society in general and law-enforcement people in specific react to all drug *use* as if it were the most dangerous dysfunctional abuse. We believe some drug experimentation and some social/recreational use of drugs will become "normal" behavior.

Prevention and intervention efforts will become focused upon the persons so involved with drugs that this use becomes a significant role in their lives and they cease adequate functioning in their other roles. What tasks enforcement and treatment are to play in this new "order" of things is yet to be determined! The pursuit of apprehension and punishment of those involved in *victimless crime* must change if our criminal justice system is to endure and to be effective.

- Finally, criminal justice policies and programing are founded upon the issue of "crime in the streets." However, only minimal comprehensive data are available relative to the issue of the *drug/crime* relationship. Appropriate planning in the areas of treatment and control depend upon a concerted research effort in this area, and must be directed at answering the following questions:

  a) What is the nature and full extent of the different types of crimes committed by different typs of drug users?

  b) How much drug-related crime remains unrecorded in official statistics?

  c) How many crimes do drug users commit in order to maintain their desired level of drug experience?

  d) What is the economic cost to the nation for each drug-using career, in terms of stolen property and expenditures for law-enforcement activities, prevention and education, treatment, and rehabilitation?

  e) How is stolen property recycled back into the economy?

  f) What is the social and economic organization of drug selling at the street level?

  g) How organized is drug-related crime?

  h) Does criminal behavior change as type of drug involvement changes?

  i) To what extent does criminal behavior exist concurrently with drug rehabilitation, and similarly, to what extent do drug use and drug-seeking behavior exist simultaneously with the latter two phenomena?

  j) To what extent do the various types of drug rehabilitation programs alter one's criminal behavior?

  k) What is the impact of new or different enforcement or control programs on the availability of various illicit drugs?

l) What are the relative involvements of organized crime, professional criminals, and "amateurs" in the various drug traffics?

m) What effects have drug-related crimes on their "victims," in terms of economic losses, changes in attitudes towards addicts, and law-enforcement personnel?

REFERENCES

Budget of the United States Government (1974) Washington: Government Printing Office.
Office of Management and Budget (1973) Federal Programs for the Control of Drug Abuse. Washington: Office of Management and Budget.

ABOUT THE AUTHORS

ABOUT THE AUTHORS

LEON BRILL has been Director of Program Planning for the New York State Drug Abuse Control Commission since 1970. His prior experience includes conducting a series of NIMH follow-up studies and demonstration programs in New York City and establishing a New Jersey State program in drug abuse. He also served as Co-Director for drug abuse programs in the Bronx for the Albert Einstein College of Medicine and collaborated with Dr. Jaffe at the AECOM in operating the first cyclazocine program and one of the earliest methadone programs. He is a certified psychologist in New York State, with a certificate in Applied Psychoanalysis from the William Alanson White Institute of Psychiatry in New York. He has been active as a therapist, in both individual and group therapy, working with problems of drug-dependency and others.

CARL D. CHAMBERS is currently an Associate Professor in the Department of Psychiatry—University of Miami School of Medicine, and Senior Vice President of Resource Planning Corporation. He received his Ph.D. in Medical Sociology at the University of Colorado, followed by a post-doctorate fellowship in drug research at the NIMH Clinical Research Center at Lexington, Kentucky. His twelve years of experience in the fields of substance abuse and deviant behavior includes a position with the Center for Educational and Psychological Research at Baghdad University in Iraq. He has also been Research Director for the Narcotic Addiction Rehabilitation Program in West Philadelphia, the New York State Narcotic Addiction Control Commission and the Metropolitan Dade Country Comprehensive Drug Program.

DANIEL GLASER has been Professor of Sociology at the University of Southern California since 1970. Prior to that he was Associate Commissioner for Research of the New York State Narcotic Addiction Control Commission, and also on the faculties at Rutgers University, the University of Illinois, and the University of Chicago. He is the author of *The Effectiveness of a Prison and Parole System* (rev. 1969), *Social Deviance* (1971), and *Adult Crime and Social*

Policy (1972). He is the past chairman of the Criminology Section of the American Sociological Association, past president of the Illinois Academy of Criminology, and also serves as editor of *Sociology and Social Research.*

LEROY C. GOULD is currently Research Associate at the Department of Psychiatry (Sociology), Yale University School of Medicine. Prior to that he was Director of Epidemiology and Evaluation at the Connecticut Mental Health Center, Drug Dependence Unit, and also served as consultant to the Vera Institute of Justice (an experimental heroin maintenance clinic), the Addiction Research Treatment Corporation in New York City, and the Governor's Special Committee on Criminal Offenders for the State of New York. He received his Ph.D. in Sociology from the University of Washington, and has also served on the faculties at the University of Washington and Yale University. He is author of *Connections: Notes from the Heroin World* and numerous articles in professional journals.

STEVEN M. GREENBERG, partner in the Miami law offices of Pertnoy, Spaet and Greenberg, received his J.D. degree from Ohio State University in 1968. His former affiliations include the presidency of Switchboard of Miami, Inc. (a drug hotline), and serving as a member of the Metropolitan Dade County Youth Relations Board and the Dade County Agency Committee of the Health Planning Council Drug Abuse Task Force. In addition to serving as Counsel for the Dade County Comprehensive Drug Program, he is also an instructor in the NIMH Regional Drug Training Program, and a group leader on Hotline Services—Governor's Council on Criminal Justice, Drug Abuse Program.

JAMES A. INCIARDI is currently a faculty member in the Department of Psychiatry—University of Miami School of Medicine, and a senior associate with Resource Planning Corporation He received his Ph.D. in Sociology at New York University and has more than twelve years experience in the clinical and research aspects of substance abuse and criminal justice. He has worked directly with criminal offenders and drug users with the New York State Division of Parole and served in a research capacity with the New York State Narcotic Addiction Control Commission. Most recently he was Associate Director of Research for the Metropolitan Dade County Comprehensive Drug Program and the Division of Addiction Sciences at the University of Miami School of Medicine.

RUFUS KING graduated from Princeton with a B.A. in Political Science, and then received his J.D. from the Yale Law School in 1943. He served as Attorney for the Air Transport Association toward the end of World War II, and in the early 1950s served as Counsel for the Senate Crime Committee, Senate District Committee, Senate Interstate and Foreign Commerce Committee, and House Judiciary Committee. He has been in private law practice in the District of Columbia since 1953, and has served on many professional commissions, including the American Bar Association Commission on Organized Crime, the ABA-AMA Joint Committee on Narcotic Drugs, and the ABA Section of Criminal Law. In 1972 he authored *The Drug Hang-Up,* soon to be released in paperback.

WILLIAM H. McGLOTHLIN, Professor in Residence in the Department of Psychology at the University of California at Los Angeles, received his Ph.D. degree in 1954 from the University of Southern California. In the last few years he has been principal investigator on a variety of NIMH grants pertaining to drug use, including research on the long-lasting effects of LSD, a survey of hallucinogenic drug use, and a systems analysis of drug control approaches. He currently is conducting an evaluation of the California Civil Addict Program; is a consultant with the World Health Organization; and is serving on the NIMH Narcotics Addiction and Drug Abuse Review Committee and the Scientific Advisory Board of the National Coordinating Council on Drug Education.

HAROLD MEISELAS, a psychiatrist, is Vice-Chairman of the New York State Narcotic Addiction Control Commission. Prior to this appointment in 1970 he had served both as Deputy Commissioner and Associate Commissioner. Before joining NYS NACC he was Director of the State Department of Mental Hygiene's division of narcotics and chief of that agency's narcotic research unit. In these capacities he has played a key role in both the development of services for drug addicts and the organization of research activities. He received his medical degree from New York Medical College. His training in psychiatry includes work performed at the Mt. Siani Hospital and Psychiatric Institute of New York City, the Manhattan State Hospital, and the Medical Field Service School of the Brooke Army Medical Center in San Antonio, Texas.

DAVID M. PETERSEN is Associate Professor of Sociology and Director of the NIMH Drug Research and Treatment Traineeship Program at Georgia State University in Atlanta. He received his M.A. from the University of Georgia, and his Ph.D. was granted in 1968 by the University of Kentucky. He taught at Ohio State University and the University of Miami School of Medicine (Division of Addiction Sciences) before moving to Georgia State in 1973. He is a senior associate with Resource Planning Corporation and a member of the American Social Health Associations' Eastern Task Force on Drug Abuse. He has co-edited several books dealing with crime and delinquency, and is currently working on two additional manuscripts: *Corrections: Problems and Prospects* (edited with C. W. Thomas) and *The Female Addict* (authored with Carl Chambers).

VICTOR TABBUSH, Associate Professor of Economics at the University of Arizona, received his Ph.D. in 1973 from the University of California at Los Angeles. While studying for his doctorate he was Research Associate to William McGlothlin on a study of the economics of illegal drugs which resulted in a report to the U.S. Department of Justice, Bureau of Narcotics and Dangerous Drugs, entitled "Alternative Approaches to Opiate Addiction: Costs, Benefits, and Potential." He also contributed an appendix to that report entitled, "The Social Costs of Narcotic Addiction." His primary fields of interest include micro theory, macro theory, labor, industrial organization, economic development, and the economics of crime.

INDICES

AUTHOR INDEX

A

Abbott, W., 41, 47, 56
Adams, M. E., 146, 155, 158
Adams, S., 155, 158, 166
Anslinger, H. J., 23, 25, 35, 145, 218, 219
Ausubel, D. P., 176, 180

B

Babst, D. V., 86, 120
Baganz, P. C., 120
Bailey, W. C., 153, 165
Ball, J. C., 39, 40, 42, 47, 55, 56, 128, 141, 208, 218, 219
Ball, M. J., 141
Barker, N., 74
Barr, N. I., 167
Bassin, A., 165, 166
Bates, W. M., 129, 141
Beccaria, C., 71, 74
Becker, H. S., 51, 55
Bejerot, N., 120
Bellassai, J. P., 162, 166
Bentham J., 71, 74
Bergner, L., 82, 107, 123
Bewley, T. H., 99, 120
Bihari, B., 82, 83, 88, 123

Bloch, H. I., 82, 117, 123, 163
Bloom, W. A., 88, 116, 120
Brecher, E. M., 18, 34, 35
Brill, H., 99, 120, 141
Brill, L., 109, 121, 123, 124, 126, 140, 142, 152, 153, 156, 162, 164, 172, 173, 174, 175, 176, 178, 179, 181, 182
Brown, B. S., 168
Bynder, H., 162, 169

C

Caine, E., 166
Carey, J. T., 45, 55
Carrick, R. W., 152, 165, 166, 181
Chambers, C. D., 45, 55, 86, 107, 121, 122, 123, 124, 126, 127, 128, 130, 131, 132, 133, 137, 138, 139, 140, 141, 142, 172, 176, 181, 212, 213, 218, 219
Chatham, L. R., 110, 111, 120, 121
Chein, I., 41, 55, 58, 66, 74, 218, 219
Clark, J. E., 82, 107, 123
Clark, R., 145, 166
Clark, W. H., 147, 168
Collier, W. V., 138, 141
Collis, M., 35

SUBJECT INDEX

A

addict registry, 58, 59, 80

addiction-prone personality, 205, 208

addicts, estimates of population, 18, 22, 25, 28, 31, 33, 41, 58, 62-63, 80-81, 86

aftercare, 53, 156-59

alcohol, 18, 43, 48, 52, 55

Alcoholics Anonymous, 55

Alinsky, Saul, 188

Ambrose, Myles J., 192

American Bar Association, 26, 17, 34

American Medical Association, 19, 26-27, 34

amphetamines, 27, 29, 59, 209

analgesics, 209

Anderson, Jack, 194

Anslinger, Harry J., 23, 24, 28, 35

antabuse, 55

antagonist programs, 81

antidepressants, 209

antihistamines, 209

"Army disease", 18

B

barbiturates, 27, 29, 34, 39, 54, 59

Bay of Pigs, 30

Benzedrine, 39

Bernstein Institute, 82

blackmarket, 64, 65

British East India Company, 19

British system, 35, 42, 62-63, 97-102, 205

Brown, Edmund (Pat), 28, 29, 35

Boggs Act (1951), 26

Bureau of Customs, 225

Bureau of Narcotics, 23, 25, 26, 31, 42, 59, 63, 66-67, 77, 80, 143, 222

C

caffein, 39

California Rehabilitation Center, 109-111

Chinese, 18, 19, 22, 206

chlordiazepoxide, 210

chlorpromazine, 210